OVERSIZE

ACPL ITEM
DISCARDED

S0-BWX-632

THE
Vegetarian
Connection

THE
Vegetarian
Connection

Joel Rose

Facts On File Publications
New York, New York • Oxford, England

THE VEGETARIAN CONNECTION

Copyright © 1985 by Joel Rose

Library of Congress Cataloging in Publication Data

Rose, Joel.
  The vegetarian connection.

  1. Vegetarianism.   2. Vegetarian cookery.   I. Title.
TX392.R7 1984   613.2′62   83-11523
ISBN 0-8160-1003-X
0-8160-1200-8 (pb)

Printed in U.S.A.

10 9 8 7 6 5 4 3 2 1

Composition by Monotype Composition
Printed by Maple Press

THIS BOOK IS DEDICATED TO MY
MOTHER AND FATHER

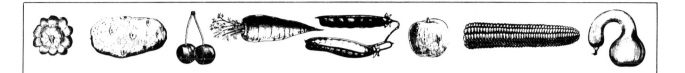

Contents

Introduction

One night I was sitting around the dinner table with a group of men, when the conversation turned casually to diet. Remarkably, everyone at the table but me had had open-heart by-pass surgery. I had only recently finished the first draft of this book, and decided that none of my friends knew what they were talking about! Here were four men with four separate diets. One said, "Lay off red meat." The next, "Lay off salt." Another said, "Eat plenty of meat." He swore his doctor told him to eat all he can. "That's to get back your strength," the fourth agrees, "but my doctor said, . . ." and he went on to explain the bizarre dairy-rich regimen his heart specialist swore would keep him in peak health.

I asked them if they knew exactly what had happened to them; if they understood that their blood vessels had become clogged with cholesterol and that the surgeon had only clipped out some of the worst blockage, near the heart.

Sure, they all understood that.

Then I asked them if they also understood that without changing their eating habits, it would not be a long time before they were in trouble again?

Well?

We all looked at each other. Four men, all suffering from the same ailments. Four different doctors, four prescriptions for success, and I had this sick feeling that none of their doctors was even close to the right advice.

I am not a doctor or a health expert. I'm not a dietitian or a neo-nutritionist. When I was growing up my father was a waiter at a famous New York delicatessen. Our refrigerator was full of pastrami and corned beef. My parents have not changed their eating habits since, but after a brush with macrobiotics, my interest in nutrition has evolved to eating as well and healthfully as I can. Now I have a child of my own, and because of this I became interested in doing this book. I became involved also because more and more of my friends and those I respected were changing their eating habits, cutting back on meat, adjusting to a fact that was becoming increasingly evident: the American diet must change.

I unraveled many strands to make this book. I talked to ordinary people who had been vegetarians their whole lives or for only a few months or a year or five years. They led me in various directions, and I for the most part followed, recording what I discovered, giving access to it. I read magazines, saw movies, watched "health" TV. I answered advertising, sent out hundreds of letters, and made phone calls. What I've come up with is a more thorough reference than I had initially anticipated, and there is still much I didn't include. *The Vegetarian Connection* is meant as an access directory. I began the project as a neophyte, and so I draw attention to what the beginner might need to survive, to continue on a healthful, rational, vegetarian, "right-eating" way of diet. But I also try to open doors for people who are perhaps much more expert than I. This book is meant as a reference, a starting place. The vegetarian network is vast. Use it.

Joel Rose

P.S.: A network is a living, growing thing. I am perfectly aware that by the time this book gets into print, some organizations, stores, restaurants, newsletters, and products will be no more. New people, new ideas, and new energy will have taken their places. Included in this book is a card, so that you can keep this book current, useful, and important. Send me your ideas, your information, your guidance. Send me the information you think will make the next edition useful and alive for you. Also, beware. Most people and organizations have your interest at heart, but there are also rip-off artists out there, who use the lure of good health and well-being to separate people from their money. Try to know who you're doing business with. Remember inclusion in this volume in no way indicates an endorsement on my part; so be smart!

1

What Is Vegetarianism?

The official definition of a vegetarian, according to the North American Vegetarian Society and the International Vegetarian Union, is "anyone who lives on the products of the vegetable kingdom with or without the use of eggs and dairy products to the entire exclusion of the flesh of all animals (flesh, fish, meat and fowl) for food." In 1978 a Roper poll estimated the number of vegetarians in the United States to be 10 million. Today the United States Department of Agriculture makes that estimate 12 million. Of these 90% are lacto-ovos, that is, people eating dairy products, such as milk, butter, yogurt, and eggs. Remarkably, 80% of the U.S. population, according to the same Roper poll, believes that such a diet is beneficial to health. Approximately 40 to 50 million Americans limit their meat consumption in some way.

Most people think the word vegetarian is derived from the Latin for vegetable, but this is not true. Vegetarian comes from the Latin word *vegetus,* which means "full of life."

The historical record of vegetarianism began in the sixth century B.C. Generally given credit for its inception is Pythagoras, who praised its hygienic nature and the kinship it fostered between man and animals. A secondary aspect of the diet was as a protest against the excesses of ancient Rome.

Vegetarian philosophy was preserved through the Renaissance by the Catholic church. St. Francis of Assisi was an early adherent to the vegetarian way of life. During the Renaissance some of the world's greatest thinkers eschewed meat, Leonardo da Vinci and Sir Isaac Newton among them.

Modern vegetarianism is generally considered to have begun in 1809 with the Bible Christian church of Manchester, England. A separate vegetarian society was formed in the 1840s, and found its way to the United States under the leadership of William Metcalfe in Philadelphia. Forty-one members comprised this group.

Early Americans who became ardent members of the nineteenth century natural food and vegetarian movement were Sylvester Graham (Graham crackers), Dr. John Harvey Kellogg (Kellogg's cornflakes), and C.W. Post (Post Toasties). Reknowned author Upton Sinclair was an outspoken meat industry reformer and ethical vegetarian.

Today vegetarianism includes among its adherents well-known people from all walks of life and in all professions: basketball player Bill Walton, actresses Cloris Leachman, Susan St. James, Brigit Bardot and Raquel Welch, as well as actor Clint Eastwood, and Nobel Prize–winning author Isaac Bashevis Singer.

INTRODUCTORY BOOKS

The following volumes offer an overview and a cursory knowledge of vegetarianism.

Are You Confused? by Paavo Airola. Health Plus Publications, PO Box 22001, Phoenix, AZ; $5.95. A clear, broad-based introductory volume, offering answers to many of the most commonly asked questions about vegetarianism.

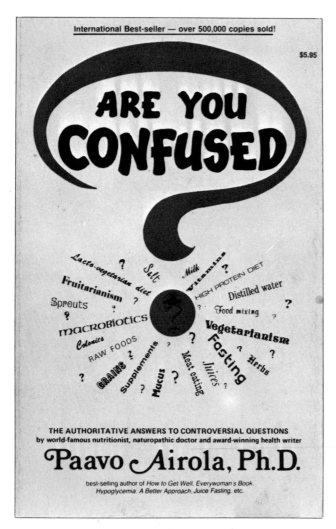

Diet for a Small Planet by Frances Moore Lappé. Ballantine Books, 201 E 50 St, New York, NY 10022, 1982; $3.50. A revolutionary book advocating the conservation of our food resources through the dietary replacement of vegetables, fruits, and grains for meat and other animal foods.

Eating for the Eighties: A Complete Guide to Vegetarian Nutrition by Janine Coulter Hartbarger and Neil J. Hartbarger. Saunders Press, West Washington Sq, Philadelphia, PA 19105, 1981; $6.95. An up-to-date, informative guide to nutrition, with an emphasis on maintaining a balanced diet without meat consumption. Helpful chapters on pregnancy, babies and athletes.

The International Vegetarian Handbook, published by the Vegetarian Society of the United Kingdom Ltd, Parkdale, Dunham Road, Altrincham, Cheshire, England. Available from the American Vegan Society, Malaga, NJ 08328, 1984; $5.00. The 1983/84 version is the fourteenth edition of this exhaustive guidebook. Information on vegetarian hotels, restaurants, health food stores, wholesalers, societies, homes, travel hints and more. The handbook concentrates on the United Kingdom, but cursorily covers the United States, Europe and the rest of the world.

Judaism and Vegetarianism by Richard H. Schwartz. Exposition Press, 325 Rabro Dr, PO Box 2120, Smithtown, NY 11787, 1982; $10.00 hardcover, $6.00 paperback. An incisive study of the role of traditional Jewish laws in vegetarian nutrition. Includes recipes.

The New Vegetarian by Gary Null. Delta, New York, NY, 1978; $5.95. A young nutritional expert who understands the politics of our national food production system, Null makes a case for adopting a more healthful diet in the face of today's culture. In this volume Null, one of the nutritionists who has damned meat as a "chemical feast," offers the vegetarian and the meat-eater an alternative to the average American diet. Although there are many reasons for people to choose vegetarianism as a way of life (moral, ethical, religious) it seems better health and well-being through diet is the most prevalent, and Null concentrates on building one's health through natural eating.

The Vegetarian Alternative: A Guide to a Healthful and Humane Diet by Vic Sussman. Rodale Press, 33 E Minor St, Emmaus, PA 18049, 1978; $6.95. An easy-to-read introduction for the person who wants to cut down or eliminate meat from his or her diet.

The Vegetarian Handbook: A Guide to Vegetarian Nutrition by Roger Doyle. Crown Publishers, One

Park Ave., New York, NY 10016, 1979; $6.95. An accessible guide to scientific findings and research on vegetarianism. A reference volume for those seeking better health who want to avoid common stumbling blocks and pitfalls.

A Vegetarian Sourcebook by Keith Akers. G.P. Putnam and Sons, 200 Madison Ave, New York, NY 10016, 1983; $15.95. Discusses the nutritional, ethical, and environmental arguments for vegetarianism.

Vegetarianism: An Annotated Bibliography by Judith C. Dyer. The Scarecrow Press, 52 Liberty St, PO Box 656, Metuchen, NJ 08840, 1982; $16.00. A thorough bibliography with 1,400 annotated entries covering books, periodicals, pamphlets, government documents, cookbooks, newspaper articles, editorials, and even letters to the editor. The book has a section on audio-visuals, and includes pre–twentieth century writings for those interested in the history of the vegetarian movement.

Vegetarianism: A Way of Life by Dudley Giehl. Harper and Row, 10 E 53 St, New York, NY 10022, 1979; $10.95. With an introduction by Isaac Bashevis Singer. A well-documented, far-reaching study of vegetarianism including ethical, religious, historical, and aesthetic considerations. Discusses the impact of vegetariansim on individual and national heath, the environment, and the economy.

VEGETARIAN ORGANIZATIONS

Today, the vegetarian network is a supportive, instructive, helpful subculture, making its way into the mainstream more and more each day. And as vegetarianism becomes less a fad and more a rational, concerned movement, vegetarians are beginning to form an important political and social web. Our concern for health and fitness as well as rising meat prices make vegetarianism an attractive, intelligent alternative in these times. The following sources will supply support, companionship, instruction, and education to the neophyte as well as the expert.

The Center for Science in the Public Interest, 1755 S St, NW, Washington, D.C. 20009; (301) 332-9110. The voice of consumers in Washington, CSPI works to protect the public from misrepresented and/or dangerous products that enter the nation's food supply. Membership is $20.00 per year ($12.00 to senior citizens and full-time students), including a subscription to *Nutrition Action,* an excellent publication that keeps members in contact with the center's work.

International Vegetarian Union, c/o Mr. Maxwell G. Lee, Honorary General Secretary, International Vegetarian Union, 10 King's Dr, Marple, Stockport, Cheshire, SK6 6NQ, England. The International Vegetarian Union is a nonprofit organization with membership open to any vegetarian society whose executive authority is vested exclusively in vegetarians. Associate membership is open to any organization that is in sympathy with animal welfare, humanitarian, health, or similar relevant objectives. The major aim of the IVU is to further vegetarianism worldwide by promoting knowledge of vegetarianism as a means of advancing the spiritual, moral, mental, physical, and economic well-being of humanity.

To this end the IVU:

· Promotes both world and regional congresses to publicize and develop interest in the vegetarian cause, and to give opportunities for vegetarians to meet together.

· Encourages the formation of vegetarian organizations and cooperation between them.

· Promotes research into all aspects of vegetarianism. The scientific council of the International Vegetarian Union acts in this capacity on behalf of the IVU.

· Aims to publish and encourage the publication of material on all aspects of vegetarianism.

· Represents the vegetarian cause on appropriate international bodies.

· Acts as a contact organization for inquiries about all aspects of vegetarianism from any part of the world.

North American Vegetarian Society, PO Box 72, Dolgeville, New York, NY 13329; (518) 568-7970. Created in 1974 to host the 1975 World Vegetarian

Congress in Orono, Maine, NAVS's primary function is to organize the annual North American Vegetarian Conference. Yearly conferences feature carefully selected speakers, panel discussions, films, cooking demonstrations, recreation, and entertainment. Membership is $12 per calendar year (or $18 for a family), which includes a subscription to *Vegetarian Voice,* an information-packed newspaper. There are two types of membership: Regular membership is for vegetarians fully and consistently abstaining from all flesh, fish, and fowl; associate membership is for nonvegetarians.

NAVS serves as an umbrella for many local vegetarian societies. If contacted, they will help establish vegetarian groups and act as an adviser to other organizations. NAVS is an information center, a publisher and distributor of books and literature, and the representative of the International Vegetarian Union in North America.

Society for Nutrition Education, 1736 Franklin St, Oakland, CA 94612; (415) 444-7133. Promotes nutritional well-being not only for vegetarians, but for all people. Its 5,000 members include nutritionists, dietitians, community and public health practitioners, college and university faculty, nutritional researchers, nutrition and food scientists, home economists, consumer affairs specialists, school foodservice administrators, daycare and preschool specialists, and nutrition and health science students. SNE publishes the *Journal of Nutrition Education,* a quarterly of ideas, information, and research on nutrition education. They have a library of educational films and publications, as well as a mail-order bookstore. An annual conference is designed to meet the educational needs of professionals and students of nutrition education. SNE has a public policy advisory council, in conjunction with a Washington D.C. lobbyist, which monitors and recommends legislative action. A legislative committee of nearly 1,000 members works to affect nutritional policy. Members can attend the annual meeting and are eligible to submit papers and audiovisuals for presentation. A one-year membership is $45.00.

NOTE: The society is not able to provide dietary information to the public.

Vegetarian Association of America, PO Box 68, Maplewood, NJ 07040; (201) 731-4902. A clearinghouse for information about the vegetarian way of life. Through their newspaper, *Vegetarian Living,* one can keep up with what's happening in the local, national, and world vegetarian movement, learn about the fight against world hunger, correspond with other vegetarians in the "Friendship" column, read book reviews, interviews, restaurant reviews, and discover retreats and vegetarian resorts. *Vegetarian Living* is $6.00 for four issues. Ten dollars includes a subscription plus a one-year membership in the association, a subscription to the newspaper, and to the *Vegetarian Post,* a members-only supplement, which includes details of vegetarian conventions, a how-to guide to establishing local vegetarian groups, a recipe exchange, a members' friendship section, and letters to the editor.

The Vegetarian Information Service, PO Box 5888, Bethesda, MD 20814; (301) 530-1737. Founded in 1976 by activists in Washington D.C., the aim of the VIS is to enlighten the U.S. public and government officials on the merits of vegetarianism. The group collects and organizes available information, eventually disseminating it to the media, governmental offices, and commercial institutions. In addition, the VIS organizes conferences and symposia.

Action for Life, an offshoot of the VIS sharing the same address, was formed in 1980 to help unify and activate the vegetarian and animal rights movements. Its objectives are to train and mobilize concerned individuals for vegetarian and animal rights through conferences and related task force activities.

Funding for these groups is tax-free and is provided entirely through the donations of individuals. Contributors of $20 or more receive periodic mailings and help support VIS programs.

VEGETARIAN INFORMATION /ERVICE, INC.
P.O. BOX 5888   BETHESDA, MD 20814

LOCAL VEGETARIAN GROUPS

Local organizations offer the opportunity for one to meet people who share similar interests and concerns. Most groups feature monthly meetings, potluck dinners, conversation, companionship, and exchange. They also often feature speakers, sponsor group outings, and offer accessible libraries. Many groups have newsletters which they will send you. Please include a stamped, self-addressed envelope.

ARIZONA

Tucson Vegetarian Society, c/o Carmine Cardamone, 1415 North Third Ave, Tucson, AZ 85705.

CALIFORNIA

Contra Costa Vegetarian Society, c/o Leonard Keith, 627 W 13 St, Antioch, CA 94509.

East Bay Vegetarians, 3959 Fruitvale Ave, Oakland, CA 94602.

Imperial Valley Vegetarian Society, c/o Ken Patterson, 1239 Rippey, El Cajon, CA 92020.

Jewish Vegetarian Society, PO Box 38281, Los Angeles, CA 90038.

Marine Vegetarians, 85 Yosemite Rd, San Rafael, CA 94903.

San Francisco Vegetarian Society, 1450 Broadway, #4, San Francisco, CA 94109.

Tutmonda Esperantista Vegetarana Asocio, c/o Scott Smith, 2455 Calle Roble, Thousand Oaks, CA 91360. International organization of vegetarians who use the international Esperanto language.

Vegetarian Inclined People (VIP), c/o Dorothy Gardner, president, 383 Walnut St, Arroyo Grande, CA 93420.

Vegetarian Society, PO Box 4303, Palm Springs, CA 92263.

Vegetarian Society, Inc, PO Box 5688, Santa Monica, CA 90405.

COLORADO

Vegetarian Society of Colorado, c/o Jim Milligan, secretary, 901 Sherman, #909, Denver, CO 80203.

CONNECTICUT

New Haven Vegetarian Society, 73 Orchard Heights Dr, Hamden, CT 06514.

DISTRICT OF COLUMBIA

The Vegetarian Society of D.C., PO Box 4921, Washington, D.C. 20008.

FLORIDA

American Jewish Vegetarian Society, PO Box 403591, Miami Beach, FL 33140.

Better Health and Nutrition Society of Palm Beach, c/o Stanley A. Kroll, 707 Chillingworth Dr, West Palm Beach, FL 33409.

Central Florida Vegetarian Society, PO Box 31, Umatilla, FL 32784.

Indian River Vegetarian Society, c/o Muriel Collura Golde, 288 Tecca Dr, Oliver Estates, New Smyrna Beach, FL 32069.

Life Balancing Center, Inc, c/o Peter Reuter, 1950 Sandra Dr, Clearwater, FL 33516.

Shangri La Natural Hygiene Institute, Bonita Springs, FL 33923.

Vegetarian Gourmet Society, PO Box 8060, Hollywood, FL 33084.

Vegetarian Inclined People, c/o Mrs. Janet Miller, 452 North Saxon Blvd, Deltona, FL 32725.

Vegetarian Society of Miami, 131 NE 175 St, North Miami Beach, FL 33162.

GEORGIA

Society for Better Living, c/o LaRamon Durham, RR No 1, Box 102-B, Union Point, GA 30669.

ILLINOIS

Chicago Vegetarian Society, PO Box 14269, Chicago, IL 60614.

International Non-Violence and Vegetarian Society, 4039 Enfield Ave, Skokie, IL 60076.

Jewish Vegetarian Society, c/o Stewart Doblin, 1265 Westmoor Rd, Winnetka, IL 60093.

INDIANA

South Suburban Vegetarian Community, c/o Ted Zagar, 4216 Tod Ave, East Chicago, IN 46312.

LOUISIANA

Vegetarian Society of Louisiana, c/o Bruce Klapper, 217 Morelan Dr, Lafayette, LA 70507.

MAINE

Maine Vegetarian Society, c/o Skip Howard, PO Box 934, Bangor, ME 04106.

Society for the Advancement of Vegetarian Ethics (SAVE), c/o Ann Renner, 52 Mayflowerhill Dr, Waterville, ME 04901.

MARYLAND

American Vegetarians, 7202 Trescott Ave, Takoma Park, MD 20912.

Baltimore Vegetarians, PO Box 1463, Baltimore, MD 21233.

Jewish Vegetarian Society of Maryland, c/o Izak Luchinsky, PO Box 5722, Baltimore, MD 21208.

MASSACHUSETTS

Vegetarians in New Energy Sources, c/o Maynard S. Clark, 155 Westminster Ave, Arlington, MA 02174.

MICHIGAN

Michigan Vegetarian Society, c/o Robert Zuraw, president, 6563 Devereaux, Detroit, MI 48210.

MINNESOTA

Jewish Vegetarian Society, c/o Gretchen Pellegrini, 72 South St, Waltham, MN 02154.

Vegetarian Network Service, c/o Tom H. Roan, president, PO Box 941, Minneapolis, MN 55440.

NEW JERSEY

American Vegan Society, 501 Old Harding Highway, Malaga, NJ 08328.

Animals Need Your Kindness Corps, Inc., PO Box 65, West New York, NJ 07093.

Beaver Defenders, Unexpected Wildlife Refuge, Newfield, NJ 08344.

Jewish Vegetarian Society, c/o Rabbi Noach Valley, Adat Yisrael, Dover Jewish Center, 18 Thompson Ave, Dover, NJ 07801.

Universal Symbol Committee, c/o Martin Samelson, 14 Peter Ave, Kendall Park, NJ 08824. Also at the same address: Vegetarian Cycling and Athletic Club.

Vegetarian Society of Mercer County, c/o John and Diane Roberts, 1530 Elizabeth Ave, Trenton, NJ 08629.

NEW YORK

Adirondack Foothills Vegetarian Society, c/o Tim and Peggy Spencer, Behrendt, Shawangunk Swamp, Cold Brook, NY 23324.

African-American Vegetarian Network, 163–38 145 Rd, Jamaica, NY 11434.

Afro-American Vegetarian Society, PO Box 46, Colonial Park Sta, New York, NY 10039.

Foundation for Nutritional Research, c/o Anna Mae Massy, 722 E 102 St, Brooklyn, NY 11236.

The Herbert Vegetarian Society, c/o Nancy Crosby, 115 Old Lyme Rd, #1, Williamsville, NY 14221.

Jewish Vegetarian Society, c/o Judah Grosberg, PO Box 144, Hurleyville, NY 12747.

Jewish Vegetarian Society, c/o Rose Nankin, RR3, Box 260, Addison, NY 14801.

Jewish Vegetarian Society, c/o Richard Schwartz, CUNY, Sunnyside Campus, 715 Ocean Terr, Staten Island, NY 10301.

Jewish Vegetarian Sprout, Jewish Vegetarian Society, c/o Jonathan Wolf, 210 Riverside Dr, Apt 1E, New York, NY 10025.

Queens Jewish Vegetarian Society, c/o F. Mitrani, 54–18 Kissena Blvd, Flushing, NY 11355.

Society for Natural Living, c/o Edythe Schecter, 711 Brightwater Ct, Brooklyn, NY 11236.

Sunshine Health Center, c/o David Settles, 938 E. 212 St, Bronx, NY 10469.

Sympathetic People for Animal Rights on Earth, 9 Pinebrook Rd, South Monsey, NY 10952.

Vegetarian Activist Collective, c/o Connie Salamone, 616 6 St, Apt 2, Brooklyn, NY 11215.

Vegetarian Society of New York, c/o Murray Mickenberg, secretary, 277 Broadway, New York, NY 10007.

Whole Life Center, c/o Leonard Burg, 665 E 181 St, #7A, Bronx, NY 10457.

OHIO

Elyria–Lorain Vegetarians, 1288 East Ave, Elyria, OH 44035.

Summit Vegetarian Society, c/o Paul A. Hayden, 807 Washington Ave, Cuyahoga Falls, OH 44221.

Ultimatist Vegetarian Society, c/o Church of the Ultimate Reality, Rev James Phillips, PO Box 06251, Columbus, OH 43206.

Vegetarian Educational Growth Society, PO Box 10110, Cleveland, OH 44110.

OKLAHOMA

Tulsa Vegetarians, c/o Sharon Campbell, PO Box 1202, Broken Arrow, OK 74013.

Oklahoma State Vegetarian Union, 11118 E 17 St, Tulsa, OK 74128.

OREGON

Portland Vegetarian Society, c/o Hans McCormack, director, Box 1555, Beaverton, OR 97206.

PENNSYLVANIA

Berks County Vegetarian Society, c/o William and Linda Bey, RD #1, Box 53A, Barto, PA 19504.

Jewish Vegetarian Society, c/o Toni Levi, 1611 Fox Chase Rd, Philadelphia, PA 19152.

Philadelphia Vegetarians, Box 175, Philadelphia, PA 19105.

Vegetarians of Delaware Valley, 613 Convent Rd, Ashton, PA 19014.

RHODE ISLAND

Vegetarian Society of Rhode Island, c/o Cheryl Bellamy, 454 Ten Rod Rd, North Kingstown, RI 02852.

TENNESSEE

East Tennessee Vegetarian Society, PO Box 1974, Knoxville, TN 37901.

League of Vegetarian Eaters (LOVE), c/o Lige H. Weill, Jr., PO Box 854, Knoxville, TN 37901.

TEXAS

Metroplex Vegetarian Society, PO Box 33061, Fort Worth, TX 76133.

VERMONT

Middlebury Vegetarian and Nutritional Awareness Society, c/o Grier Weeks, Box C-3550, Middlebury, VT 05753.

WASHINGTON

People for Compassion in Fashion, PO Box 268, Bothell, WA 98041.

Seattle Vegetarian Society, PO Box 5431, Seattle, WA 98105.

WISCONSIN

Jewish Vegetarian Society, c/o Debbie Friedman, 18 Chippewa Ct, Madison, WI 53711.

Vegetarian Society of Milwaukee, c/o Dr. Bernard Sharp, 7201 West Burleigh St, Milwaukee, WI 53210.

INTERNATIONAL VEGETARIAN GROUPS

British Natural Hygiene Society, "Shalimar," First Ave, Frinton-on-Sea, Essex, England CO13 9E7.

International Biogenic Society, Apartado 372, Cartago, Costa Rica.

Jewish Vegetarian Society, Bet Teva, 855 Finchley Rd, London, England NW11 8LX.

The Vegan Society, 47 Highland Road, Leatherhead, Surrey, England.

The Vegetarian Society of the United Kingdom Limited, Parkdale, Dunham Rd, Altrincham, Cheshire, England WA14 4QG

Vegetarijansko Drustvo, Preradoviceva 33, 41000 Zagreb, Yugoslavia.

Vegfam, c/o The Sanctuary, Nr. Lyford, Okehampton, Devon, England EX20 4AL.

CANADA

Calgary Vegetarians, c/o Pamela Gill, 117 7 St, NW, Calgary, Alberta T2N 1S1 Canada.

Toronto Vegetarian Association, 28 Walker Ave, Toronto, Ontario M4V 1G2 Canada.

Vancouver Island Vegetarian Association, c/o Pat Bastone, 9675 Fifth St, Sidney, British Columbia V8L 2W9 Canada.

Vegetarians of Windsor, Vegetarian Information Center, PO Box 83, Ruthven, Ontario N0P 2G0 Canada

RADIO

Dr. Carlton Fredericks. Check local radio listings.

Dr. Fredericks discusses and offers his views on nutrition and well-being.

Infinity. Saturday nights at 11:30 and Sunday nights at 10:30 on KCBS in San Francisco, 740 on the AM dial. A spectrum of subjects including New Age topics.

Natural Living. Nationally syndicated weekly, in some areas daily, radio show moderated by nutritionalist Gary Null. Monday to Friday, 12 noon to 1 P.M. on WBAI, 99.5 FM in New York. Check listings in your area, Null interviews and makes investigative forages into the health industry and its satellites. Advice on mind, body, and spirit.

Spark of Life. Ken Anderson, nutritionist. Daily live radio call-in talk show on nutrition. Monday to Friday, 7:00 P.M., KXEG in Phoenix, 1010 on the AM dial.

TELEVISION

Alive and Well: USA Cable Network. Monday to Friday 8–10 p.m. Fitness and health format. Not exclusively vegetarian, but some solid information.

Better Health. A nationally syndicated, weekly, half-hour show that focuses on modern health issues. Check local television listings.

Cable Health Network. Twenty-four hours, presently reaching into 11 million households. Covering a wide variety of subjects and concerns, including nutrition, exercise, illness and disease.

Human Potential Television. HPTV is a 30-minute magazine format program aired on cable television. The show deals with a wide variety of subjects, including aging, the New Age media, alternative health care, environmental health, yoga and herbalism. *HPTV Digest,* a newsletter and guide to programming, is available from: Human Potential Television, 45 W 81 St, Ste 206, New York, NY 10024.

World Good News Network (WGNN). Still in its embryonic stage, WGNN hopes to provide an alternative to establishment media. Planning to transmit around the globe via 24-hour television,

radio, and print media, WGNN is still in need of financing, but is starting within budget and hoping to expand. The network publishes a newsletter to keep contributors and interested parties abreast of progress. Contact: WGNN, Television Center, Xavier University, Cincinnati, OH 45207. Local representatives: Bill Donovan, Albany, New York; (518) 392-3923. Claire Gilbert, New York City; (212) 633-6812. Naomi Klapper, Washington, D.C.; (301) 652-8203. David Smith, Cincinnatti, OH; (513) 745-3461. Linda Joyce, Los Angeles, CA; (213) 318-3782. Ellen Brauss, Santa Barbara, CA; (805) 968-1863. Michael Toms, San Francisco, CA; (415) 864-0700.

CINEMA

Vegetarian World. Directed by Jonathan Kay. Kay Film Productions Ltd., 186 Sorauren Avenue, Toronto, Ontario, Canada M6R 2E8 Format: 16mm film (28.5m, color) ¾″, VHS, Betamax tape. Price: purchase, $550; rental, $75. Narrated by actor William Shatner. A fascinating, entertaining 30-minute film tracing the roots of vegetarianism. It shows the deep cultural and historical significance of vegetarianism in 10 countries worldwide. Director Kay says, "I'm confident that the film will prove to be very useful in educating people about vegetarian culture and philosophy."

Diet for a Small Planet. Bullfrog Films, 1973; 28 minutes; 16mm film. Institute for Food and Development Policy, 2588 Mission, San Francisco, CA. 94110

VEGETARIAN MAGAZINES

Vegetarian Times. 41 E 42 St, New York, NY 10017. $1.95 at the newsstand. One-year subscription (12 issues), $19.95. An excellent, professionally produced monthly, offering information on a wide range of topics. Helpful, interesting, and encouraging reader interaction.

Whole Life Times. 18 Shepard St, Brighton, MA 02135. $1.25 an issue at newsstands; subscription rate is $11.95 for 10 issues. A journal dedicated to making America healthy. Advertisements interspersed with helpful, enthusiastic articles. Also a useful local directory included in each issue. Note well: This can be especially beneficial to travelers, because for two dollars *Whole Life Times* will forward you a copy of a local directory for Los Angeles, Boston, or New York.
  Whole Life Times L.A. PO Box 3579, Santa Monica, CA 90403.
  Whole Life Times New England. 18 Shepard St, Brighton, MA 02135.
  Whole Life Times New York. 89 Fifth Ave, 6th Floor, New York, NY 10003.

INTERNATIONAL VEGETARIAN MAGAZINES AND PUBLICATIONS

AUSTRALIA

Australian Vegetarian. Box 46, Rundle St PO, Adelaide 5000, Australia.

Health and Vision. 723 Glenhuntly Rd, South Caulfield 3162, Victoria, Australia.

BELGIUM

Nieuw Leven. Schepersweg 112, 3600 Genk, Belgium.

COSTA RICA

The Essene Way of Biogenic Living. International Biogenic Society, Apartado 372, Cartago, Costa Rica.

DENMARK

Vegetarisk Forum. Paul Peterson, editor. Bondemarken 14, 2800 Bagsvaerd, Denmark.

ENGLAND

The Hygienist. British Natural Hygiene Society, "Shalimar," First Ave, Frinton-on-Sea, Essex, England CO13 9E7.

The Vegetarian. Parkdale, Dunham Road, Altrincham, Cheshire WA 14 4QG, England. The official journal of the Vegetarian Society of the United Kingdom, this magazine has been published continuously since 1848. An excellent publication to keep tabs on the large, active British vegetarian community. It is full of information and source material not only for active political and social issues, but also for restaurants, spas, bookshops, vegetarian homes for both the elderly and the young, products, movements, and much more. Published bimonthly.

FRANCE

Revue Mazdaznan. 3 Square du Tarn, 75017 Paris, France.

La Vie Claire. 4 Place du General de Gaulle, 94520 Mandres Les Roses, France.

Vivre en Harmonie. 5 rue Emile-Level, 75011 Paris, France.

La Voix Des Vegetariens. 140 Boulevard Voltaire, 75011 Paris, France.

GERMANY

Der Vegetarier. Prof. W. Brockhaus, Editor. Blucherstrasse 6, 5600 Wuppertal, Federal Republic of Germany.

HOLLAND

Kiemkracht. Marterrevier 33, Cuyk (N. Br.), Holland.

De Kleine Aarde. Postbus 151, 5200 AD, Boxtel, Holland.

Leven en Laten Leven. Duinweg 14, 9479 TM Noordlaren, Holland.

IRELAND

Esperantista Vegetarano. c/o Christopher Fettes, St. Columbia's College, Rathfarnham, Dublin 16, Éire.

ITALY

Eubiotica. Via Fossano 2, Torino, Italy.

L'idea Vegetariana. Sede Nazionale, Via dei Piatti, 3, 20123 Milano, Italy.

JAPAN

Health and Love. 718 Daisen, PO Nirayama, Shizuoka, Japan.

NIGERIA

Soul Message–Vegview. Harmony Place, 142 St. Michael's Rd/East St, PO Box 1343, Aba, Imo State, Nigeria.

PORTUGAL

Helios. Rua do Salitre 136, 1°, Lisbon 2, Portugal.

Natura. Rua Antero de Quental, 35.1°-D, 110 Lisbon, Portugal.

SWEDEN

Halsonytt-Vegetarianen. Radmansgaten 88, 112 29 Stockholm, Sweden.

SWITZERLAND

Regeneration. Schwarzenbachweg 16, CH-8049, Zürich, Switzerland.

POSTERS

Meateaters' Nightmare posters. Concocted by vegetarian artist W.J. Cole, *Meateaters' Nightmare* is a series of 12 humorous works of art depicting people against meat. They are available for $5.00 a piece from The Works Gallery, 7 Lum Lane, Newark, NJ 07105.

2
What Are The Different Types Of Vegetarianism?

Vegetarians come in many varieties. There are lacto-ovos and vegans, fruitarians and natural hygienists, monodietists and breatharians. Most make sense once you understand the diet and its particular implications, but some (breatharians for example) stretch the imagination in their claims for good health, and, frankly, common sense warns you they are impossible, and may be dangerous. Ask your physician before you decide to drastically change your eating habits; not all vegetarian diets may be right for you.

LACTO-OVO VEGETARIANS

Statistically, most vegetarians are lacto-ovos. That is, many vegetarians supplement their diet of grains, legumes, vegetables, fruits, nuts, and seeds with animal protein such as milk, eggs, cheese, and so forth. It is only recently that scientists and nutritionists have come to realize that it is possible to get the necessary protein exclusively from vegetable sources.

LACTO VEGETARIANS

Lacto vegetarians will drink milk and use milk products, but will not touch an egg. This may be a wise decision, considering the atrocities of the henhouse: overcrowding, artificial insemination,

antibiotics, hormones and "growth factors" in feed, and 24-hour artificial light to induce laying. Free-ranging eggs, those laid by hens who are allowed outside to peck and grub, are best for those who indulge.

VEGANS

Veganism means living on plant products exclusively. Vegans (pronounced vee-gans) will not touch meat or any meat product. They won't wear leather, fur, wool, or silk. A vegan diet excludes all flesh, fish, fowl, animal milk, all dairy products, and any other food of animal origin, such as cheese, butter, yogurt, eggs, honey, or gelatin. Vegans generally make efforts to avoid less-than-obvious animal by-products, such as oils and secretions, used in toiletries, cosmetics, household goods and other commodities. Veganism encourages alternatives for all such materials.

For reasons of spirituality, ethics, ecology, health, and economics, vegans are enthusiastic about their diet. Numerous studies agree. One is an unpublished longitudinal study being conducted at California's Loma Linda University by Drs. Roland Phillips and David Snowdon, who have been monitoring the health of 25,000 Seventh-Day Adventists. This 20-year study supports the claims of the vegan diet. Veganism is most likely the best diet choice to maintain a healthy heart and circulatory system (no food in the plant world contains cholesterol), while keeping the body free from toxicity and cancer. The National Academy of Science does stress, however, that vegans supplement their diet with vitamin B_{12} and use a variety of plant foods such as legumes, rice, and other whole grains.

American Vegan Society, 501 Old Harding Highway, Malaga, NJ 08328. The society educates people regarding the benefits of the vegan way of life. They maintain facilities at their headquarters, SunCrest, in Malaga, New Jersey. These facilities are open during scheduled times of the year for live-in cooking classes, discussion, and other educational purposes. A convention is held each year. The society publishes the newspaper *AHIMSA.* AHIMSA stands for the compassionate way: abstinence from animal products; harmlessness with reverence for life; integrity of thought, word, and deed; mastery over oneself; service to mankind, nature, and creation; and advancement of understanding and truth. AVS membership is $8.00 per calendar year, and includes a subscription to *AHIMSA.*

The Vegan Society, Dept. J, 47 Highlands Rd, Leatherhead, Surrey, England. There are a number of vegan groups in England. Get in touch through this Vegan Society.

ETHICAL VEGETARIANS

Ethical vegetarians oppose the needless death of any living thing. They refuse to eat meat because they abhor the slaughter of animals. According to the International Development Research Center in Ottawa, Canada, meat production in Western countries is cheating the rest of the world of much-needed food. This is because so much food is fed to animals, with poor return. One-third of the world's grain supply goes to fatten animals with more protein going into the animals in the form of legumes, grain, and fish meal than comes out in the form of meat. One must also mention the way the animals are treated, and how we in turn are treating ourselves by eating this tainted meat.

BOOKS

Animal Factories by Jim Mason and Peter Singer.

Crown Publishing, One Park Ave., New York, NY 10016, 1980, 174 pp; $10.95 list or $10.00 postpaid from Farm Animal Reform Movement (address below). The big business of animal production in America has gone berserk. Specialized meat-producing farms crowd animals in miserable cages and stalls for the purpose of increasing production while limiting labor input. Such procedures increase animal stress, promote germ transference, and make the air filthy. In order to cope with these terrible conditions farmers feed their animals antibiotics and sulfa drugs, use disinfectant and pesticides, and liberally spread chemicals through the animal habitation areas. (One such chemical designed to kill flies buzzing around henhouses is fed to the chicken and comes out in the feces. The fly lights on the chicken excrement and dies. No one seems to acknowledge the fact that the poison will also come out in the eggs that we, the consumers, are supposed to eat.) *Animal Factories* does not blame the farmer alone for the horrors of the industry. The factory farmer is at the mercy of agribusiness. These companies feed a market, and that market is you and I.

ANIMAL RIGHTS AND ENVIRONMENTAL GROUPS

AGAPE. c/o Ginnie Bee, 2913 Woodstock Ave, Silver Springs, MD 20910. An organization started by a small group of people concerned with the need to educate and motivate religious groups to work for rights of animals. AGAPE requests $5.00 per information kit; this money will supply needed financing as they progress.

American Fund for Alternatives to Animal Research (AFAAR). 175 West 12 St, 16G, New York, NY 10011. AFAAR tries to salvage thousands of animals from painful research tests, provides opportunities for concerned investigators to develop new alternatives, and exerts pressure on government agencies to allocate a greater proportion of funds for developing non-animal research.

Animal Defence League of Canada. PO Box 3880, Station C, Ottawa, Ontario, Canada K1Y 4M5.

Animal Rights Network, Inc. PO Box 5234, Westport, CT 06881. The main effort of the Animal

Rights Network is producing their magazine, *Agenda,* which contains discussion space for animal rights issues, and presents news items, reviews, and the activities of other concerned groups. Animal Rights also produced a 20-minute slide presentation designed for use in high school classes, and religious and social groups. A teacher's guide accompanies the filmstrip (with music and narration). The cost is $25.00. A year's subscription to *Agenda* is $15.00.

Animal Rights Network of Berks County. PO Box 8547, Reading, PA 19603. Concerned about the exploitation and abuse of animals, they publish *The Unicorn* (subscription rate is $8.00), a monthly newpaper featuring investigative reports, international news on animal rights, vegetarian information, personal experience articles and more. Devoted to educating the public.

Attorneys for Animals Rights (AFAR). 333 Market St, Suite 2300, San Francisco, CA 94105.

"They seemed to be almost like little folk from some other planet, whose language we could not yet quite understand."
—Grey Owl

Beauty Without Cruelty. 175 12 St #16G, New York, NY 10011. Works to inform the public about the massive suffering of all kinds of animals in the fashion and cosmetics industries, while providing information about substitute fashions that have not involved death, confinement, or suffering of any animal.

Beaver Defenders. Unexpected Wildlife Refuge, Newfield, NJ 08344. "Beavers are the world's best vegetarians," according to Hope Sawyer Buyukmihci, the founder of the group and the preserver of the wildlife refuge. Interesting books are available from the group regarding beaver life. All proceeds go to the refuge. Membership, which includes a newsletter, is $5.00 per year.

The Committee to Abolish Sport Hunting. 453 E 84 St, New York, NY 10028.

Defenders of Wildlife. 1244 19 St NW, Washington, D.C. 20036.

Farm Animals Concerns Trust (FACT), PO Box 14599, Chicago, IL 60614. Information sheet about the abuses of factory farming. One-year subscription, $15.00.

Farm Animal Reform Movement (FARM), PO Box 70123, Washington, D.C. 20088. The purpose of FARM is to promote reverence for life and to eliminate abuses of farm animals and alleviate other adverse impacts of animal agriculture on human health, world hunger, and natural resources. FARM was formed in 1981 as the Farm Animal Task Force by a group of consumer, environmental, and animal rights advocates. Membership, which includes a newsletter, is $15.

FARM ANIMAL REFORM MOVEMENT
P.O. BOX 70123: WASHINGTON, DC 20088

Friends of the Earth, 1045 Sansome St, San Francisco, CA 94111; and 530 7 St SE, Washington, D.C. 20003. An activist environmental lobbying organization. One of the earliest opponents of the nuclear power industry, supporters of solar energy and other clean, renewable energy sources. Preservers of wilderness areas, and defenders of breathable air and endangered species. Publishes the newsmagazine, *Not Man Apart*. Regular membership is $25 per year.

· 4649 Sunnyside Avenue North, Seattle, WA 98103
· 19 Niolopa Place, Honolulu, HI 96817

Greenpeace U.S.A., 2007 R St NW, Washington, DC 20009. Committed group dedicated to environmental issues such as saving whales and baby harp seals.

Regional offices:

· 386 Congress St, Boston, MA 02210
· 2619 South Main St, Ann Arbor, MI 48104
· 2029 E 13 Ave, Denver, CO 80206
· Fort Mason, Building E, San Francisco, CA 94123

Lifeforce, Box 3117, Main Post Office, Vancouver, British Columbia, Canada V6B 3X6.

Mobilization for Animals, PO Box 1679, Columbus, OH 43216.

Mobilization for Animals (Canada), PO Box 244, Station P, Toronto, Ontario M5S 2S8 Canada. Mobilization for Animals is an all-volunteer international coalition of individuals and groups in 23 countries, dedicated to bringing an end to animal suffering. They work to raise public awareness and bring about change through rallies, distributing information, grassroots organizing, speaking in communities and on campuses, and trying to seek alternatives to the use of animals in scientific experimentation.

People for the Ethical Treatment of Animals (PETA), Box 56272, Washington, D.C. 20011.

Society for Animal Protective Legislation (SAPL), PO Box 3719, Georgetown Sta, Washington, D.C. 20007.

Society for Animal Rights, 421 South St, Clarks Summit, PA 18411.

Wee Care, 1744 West Devon Ave, Ste 7, Chicago, IL 60660. Yearly membership with newsletter, $15; with extra mailings, $20. If you're corresponding with WEE CARE please enclose an SASE, a good practice in all instances.

FILMS

Film to Liberate Laboratory Animals, Inc, 725 Lisbon St, San Francisco, CA 94112. This film, completed in 1983, has been produced to expose the realities of the use of animals in the research field. It is being sold for $510, but can also be rented. Rental fees are as follows: $85 plus $15 round-trip UPS shipping charges; if admission is being charged for viewing, there is an additional charge of 50% of the gate.

HEALTH VEGETARIANS

Health vegetarians choose not to eat meat simply because they view it as unhealthy. It is not uncommon in the commercial meat industry to put antibiotics in animals' feed to keep them healthy. Unfortunately, microbes can become resistant to antibiotics, so that when one of us eats meat tainted with antibiotics he or she is actually inhibiting the way antibiotics will work

on disease in his or her own body.

National Resources Defense Council, 122 E 42 St, New York, NY 10017. A nonprofit environmental group with an interest in, among other things, the correlation between meat production, consumption, and health.

NATURAL HYGIENISTS AND NATURAL FOOD EATERS

These vegetarians consume only raw fruit, vegetables, nuts, sprouted seeds and grains. The food should be fresh and pure. Natural hygienists call for plenty of rest, sunshine, and clean air and water. They are raw food vegans. Very often the diet of a natural hygienist is more than a way of eating, it is a philosophy of life that tries to recapture an age of innocence when the earth's food, air, and water were all pure and unspoiled, and life was simpler.

American Natural Hygiene Society, Inc, 698 Brooklawn Ave, Bridgeport, CT 06604. Publishes *Health Science* magazine. Membership, including a subscription, is $20 annually. The society has a

referral service for licensed doctors who are members of the International Association of Professional Natural Hygienists. The society offers vaccination counseling, holds an annual national convention, overviews a network of chartered local chapters, publishes through the Natural Hygiene Press, and produces video cassettes and a hygienic pamphlet series.

Hygienic Community Network, 1231A Oxford St, Berkeley, CA 94709. The network's aim is to serve as a link between people who subscribe to a natural hygiene diet by aiding in the formation of natural hygienic communities and providing information on existing or proposed communities. The Hygienic Community Network prints a directory once a year listing all members of the network and giving their interests, their type of diet, and their community desires. HCN membership includes personal correspondence networking, a free listing in the *HCN Directory,* and a subscription to HCN. Membership is $5.00 per year.

The following are addresses for local natural hygiene societies:

ARIZONA

Dr. Alan M. Immerman, 5109 East Thomas Road, Phoenix, AZ 35018.

CALIFORNIA

Sophie Holzgeen, 701 South St. Andrews Place, Los Angeles, CA 90005.

David Orner, 1539 22nd Ave, San Francisco, CA 94122.

CONNECTICUT

Jo Willard, 63 Longmeadow, Huntington, CT 06484.

FLORIDA

Mike Calhoun, 1177 Kane Concourse, Bay Harbor Islands, Miami Beach, FL 33154.

Esther S. Frankel, 190 Keeler Ave NW, Port Charlotte, FL 33954.

Frieda Kabelac, Route 7, Box MLC-46, Tallahassee, FL 32308.

Sid Kleiner, 3701 25th Ave SW, Naples, FL 33999.

Carol Phillips, 196 Carib Drive, Ormond Beach, FL 32074.

Ruth Schoenfeld, 1619 Pennsylvnaia Ave, Miami Beach, FL 33139.

HAWAII

Lee Bauer, PO Box 7, Kailua, HI 96734.

MICHIGAN

Corrine Goldstein, PO Box 37261, Oak Park, MI 48237.

Virginia Weitlauf, 16816 Monica, Detroit, MI 48221.

MISSOURI

James R. Dyer, 6127 Kingbury Ave, St. Louis, MO 63112.

NEW JERSEY

Robert F. Lucia, PO Box 57, Passaic, NJ 07055.

NEW YORK

Louise Braumueller, 127 Burdick Ave, Syracuse, NY 13208.

Christobel B. Morgan, 1027 Highland Ave, Rochester, NY 14620.

Mr. and Mrs. Samuel Rice, 139-19 34th Rd, Flushing, NY 11354.

OHIO

Mrs. Harry J. Kaplan, 3126 Ramona #4, Cincinnati, OH 45211.

PENNSYLVANIA

Dorothy Kelly, 453 Decatur Avenue, Forest Hills, PA 15221.

WASHINGTON

John D. Duff III, 14308 Duryea Lane South, Tacoma, WA 98444.

WISCONSIN

Dr. Bernard Sharp, 4232 West Highland Blvd #301, Milwaukee, WI 53208.

CANADA

Joe Aaron, 14 Lynhaven Rd, Toronto, Ontario, Canada M6A 2KB; (416) 781-0359.

Don Chricton, 97 Lakeshore Rd, Pointe Claire, Quebec, Canada H9S 4H7; (514) 695-3311.

John Draser, 604 Guelph St, Kitchener, Ontario, Canada N2H 5Y6; (519) 579-2033.

BOOKS

The Original Diet by Karen Cross Whyte. Troubador Press, 385 Fremont, San Francisco, CA 94105; $3.95. A history of diet from earliest humans to present, then pros and cons of a 100% raw foods vegetarian diet.

FRUITARIANS

Fruitarians eat raw fruits, vegetables, nuts, sprouted legumes, and grains. Ethical fruitarians, that is, those concerned about plant consciousness, will eat nothing that destroys the entire plant through harvest, for example, turnips, potatoes, carrots or beets. Ethical fruitarians will eat tomatoes, oranges, apples, beans, and watermelon. The fruitarian diet is an excellent cleansing diet, but it does not contain enough protein to sustain life over an extended period. It is a better tool than a permanent life choice, and many people use a fruitarian juice diet over a period of days or weeks as a means to scour their digestive system.

Fruitarian Network, 7202 Trescott Ave, Takoma Park, MD 20912. An organization that links fruitarians and provides information and literature to interested individuals and groups.

The Fruition Project, Box 872, Santa Cruz, CA 95061. An organization encouraging a fruitarian diet and the planting of fruit and nut trees.

MACROBIOTICS

The term macrobiotics comes from two Greek words. *Macro* means large or great, and *bios* refers to life. In ancient Greece the study of macrobiotics was the study of health and long life achieved by living in harmony with the environment. It was George Ohsawa who reemployed the term, teaching that with proper sensitivity and knowledge of diet we could reach accord with the cosmos. This balance is known as *yin/yang,* and the objective of the diet is to achieve this balance in ourselves through what we eat. Brown rice is the centerpiece of macrobiotics because it is considered by adherents to be the food that is closest to the composition of human blood. Macrobiotics are not necessarily vegetarians, and sometimes to achieve a balance of yin/yang a macrobiotic might eat a little meat or fish. The macrobiotic diet not only prevents illness but has curative effects as well.

The uninitiated might want to find a guide or teacher to introduce him or her to the macrobiotic philosophy. The following books and any of the East–West centers would be a perfect place to start.

BOOKS

All books listed below are available by mail from the *East–West Journal,* Dept G, 17 Station St, PO Box 1200, Brookline Village, MA 02147.

The Book of Macrobiotics by Michio Kushi. $11.95. An outline of the thinking of Michio Kushi, one of the foremost macrobiotic teachers. Practical advice for the use of macrobiotics in everyday life.

Zen Macrobiotics by George Ohsawa. 128 pp., $1.25. The book that launched the macrobiotic movement in the United States. Stimulating, enlightening, practical, full of common sense.

Macrobiotics: Experience the Miracle of Life by Michio Kushi. 26 pp., $2.95. This book contains all the basics of macrobiotic principles.

You Are All Sanpaku by William Duffy and George Ohsawa. University Press, $4.95. *Sanpaku* refers to a state of unhealth. The means of telling if one is sanpaku is to look at the eyes. If white shows under the iris it may be a sign of unwellness. This book is both fascinating and convincing, and, while it was one of the first books in the West on macrobiotics, it remains readable and helpful.

EAST–WEST CENTERS

There are East–West macrobiotic centers nationwide. Most offer a variety of activities including: study opportunities, public meals, cooking classes, lectures, macrobiotic counseling, seminars, bookshops, and supplies.

East–West Foundation. PO Box 850, Brookline Village, MA 02147. The East–West Foundation has put together a special introduction to macrobiotics. The package includes the macrobiotic approach to cancer, macrobiotic dietary recommendations, the *East–West Journal*'s natural food shopper's guide and activity calendar, and the *Directory of Macrobiotic Teachers and Counselors*. The package is $25.

Kushi Foundation, PO Box 1100, Brookline, MA 02147. The foundation is the parent organization of the Kushi Institute, the East–West Foundation, and the *East–West Journal*. They also publish the *Worldwide Macrobiotic Directory*. The directory links macrobiotic individuals with centers, foodstores, restaurants, and study houses. Listings are $10 for businesses/organizations or services; $5 for individuals. The directory itself is $3.95.

LOCAL EAST–WEST CENTERS

ARIZONA

Tucson East–West Center, Box 1048, Tucson, AZ 85702.

CALIFORNIA

East–West Center for Macrobiotic Studies, 3504 Ray St, San Diego, CA 92104.

East–West Center for Macrobiotic Studies, 708 North Grove, Los Angeles, CA 90046.

East–West Center, 1864 Pandora Ave, West Los Angeles, CA 90025. Cecile Levin, director.

East–West Center, 708 North Orange Grove, Hollywood, CA 90046. Roy Stevensz, director.

East–West Center for Natural Health Education, Three Creeks Country Center, 1122 M St, Eureka, CA 95501.

East–West Center at Harbin Springs, Box 782, Middletown, CA 95461.

East–West Center, 435 16th Ave, San Francisco, CA 94118.

COLORADO

East–West Community Center, 1931 Mapleton Ave, Boulder, CO 80302.

CONNECTICUT

East–West Center, 184 Main St, Middletown, CT 06457. Bill Spear, director.

FLORIDA

The Macrobiotic Foundation of Florida, 3291 Franklin Ave, Coconut Grove, FL 33133.

HAWAII

East–West Center, Honolulu, HI.

ILLINOIS

East–West Center, 1574 Asbury Ave, Evanston IL 60201. Keith Block, director.

KANSAS

East–West Center, 1423 Kentucky, Lawrence, KS 66044.

MARYLAND

East–West Foundation, 4803 Yellowwood Rd, Baltimore, MD 21209. Murray Snyder, director.

MASSACHUSETTS

East Templeton East–West Center, Box 18, High St, East Templeton, MA 01438.

MICHIGAN

Macrobiotic Association of Metropolitan Detroit, 15004 Mack Ave, Grosse Pointe Park, MI 48230.

MINNESOTA

Center for Macrobiotics, 673 Lincoln Ave, St. Paul, MN 55105.

Turtle Island Holistic Health Community (East–

West Center), 569 Selby Ave, St. Paul, MN 55102.

NEW JERSEY

Macrobiotic Health Information Center, 15 Old Farm Rd, North Caldwell, NJ 07006.

Monmouth Macrobiotic Center, 12 Matawan Terrace, Matawan, NJ 07747.

NEW YORK

The Albany East West Macrobiotic Center 40 Glenwood St #4, Albany, NY 12208

East–West Center for Holistic Studies, 141 Fifth Ave, New York, NY 10011.

PENNSYLVANIA

East–West Center, 108 East Maple Ave, Langhorne, PA 19047.

East–West Center, 606 South Ninth St, Philadelphia, PA 19147.

TEXAS

East–West Center of Dallas, 14369 Haymeadow Circle, Dallas, TX 75240.

East–West Center, 506 Avondale, Houston, TX 77006.

INTERNATIONAL CENTERS

ENGLAND

Kushi Institute of Great Britain, 188 Old St, London EC1, England.

GREECE

Macrobiotic Club of Rhodes, 3 Valaoritou St, PO Box 239, Rhodes, Greece. A wide selection of macrobiotic foods. Serves "medicinal" macrobiotic meals.

ITALY

Centro Est–Ouest, Via Ricasoli 55R, 50122 Florence, Italy. The director, Ferro Ledvinka, is qualified to teach and counsel macrobiotics by the Kushi Institute.

Sondazione Est–Ouest (East–West Foundation), Via de'Serragli, 4, 50123 Florence, Italy.

MEXICO

Asociacion Macrobiotica, Moctezuma 399, Ensen-ada, BCN Mexico. Ignacio and Loretta Beamonte.

TRINIDAD

Rex Lasalle, 417 Tragarete Rd, Woodbrook, Port of Spain, Trinidad.

MACROBIOTIC MAGAZINES

East–West Journal, PO Box 970, Farmingdale, NY 11737. Subscription rate; $18.00. Informative magazine for the macrobiotic community, great networking. Articles deal with nutrition, health and healing, consumerism, practical advice, cooking, gardening, and the arts.

Macromuse, PO Box 40012, Washington, D.C. 20016. A bimonthly macrobiotic forum, featuring articles, tips on getting started, questions and answers, book and movie reviews, readers exchange, topics for advanced study and interviews. Yearly subscription rate; $15.

News from the River, 2215 Blake St, Berkeley, CA 94704. Quoting Pelagius ("Since Perfection is possible, it is obligatory"), "News From the River" is a no-nonsense forum for macrobiotics. More scholarly than others, no advertising. Yearly subscription, $10.00 for individuals, $20.00 for an institution.

MACROBIOTIC TEACHERS AND COUNSELORS

ARKANSAS

Bill Tims, Rob Allanson, 45 Hartman, Fayetteville, AR 72701.

CALIFORNIA

Herman Aihara, Vega Institute, PO Box 426, Oroville, CA 95965. According to the *East–West Journal,* the leading teacher of macrobiotics on the West Coast.

Jacques and Yvette DeLangre, 160 Wycliff Way, Magalia, CA 95954.

Noboru Muramoto and Lino Stanchich, PO Box 2546, Escondido, CA 92025.

MARYLAND

Michael Rossoff, 11119 Rockville Pike, Ste 321,

Rockville, MD 20852.

NEW YORK

Michael Morales, 150-07 78th Ave, Kew Garden Hills, NY 11367.

TEXAS

Carl Ferre, 40 Hill St, Denton, TX 76201.

WASHINGTON

Blake Rankin, Granum, PO Box 14075, Seattle, WA 98114.

CANADA

Kolin Lymworth, 3505 W 31 St, Vancouver, British Columbia, Canada V6F 1X8.

MACROBIOTIC ARCHIVES

George Ohsawa introduced macrobiotics in Europe in the 1930s. Twenty years later his teaching and writing reached America. During these early years, however, a great deal of writing was lost or unavailable to the serious student. The Kushi Institute, with the help of Dr. Marc Van Cauwenberghe, who has the most complete collection of early Ohsawa work, is now transcribing, indexing, and reprinting much of this work. Volume 1 is 350 pages and costs $50.00. Order from The Macrobiotic Archives, c/o The Kushi Institute, PO Box 1100, Bookline, MA 02147.

Macroindex, 5329 Broadwater, Clarksville, Maryland 21029; $6.95. Comprehensive index to over 4000 major pieces of macrobiotic literature.

VIDEOTAPES

Michio Kushi, one of the foremost macrobiotic teachers, on tape. Tapes cost $100.00, plus $2.50 for shipping. Subjects include: Ancient Civilization; Creating Family Unity; Creating World Unity; Diagnosing One's Destiny; Karma and Reincarnation; Principles of the Order of the Universe; Relationship Between Thinking, Dreaming, Breathing and Activity; Self-Reflection/Problems of Open Marriages; and Understanding Meridians. Available from the Kushi Foundation, PO Box 568, Brookline Village, MA 02147.

MONODIETISTS

Monodietists choose to live eating only one thing, as for example, grapefruit. This diet is a poor long-term vegetarian choice, but could be used for a short time as a cleansing tool or a way to isolate food sensitivities. Always check with your physician or health expert before adopting this type of diet.

BREATHARIANS

Breatharians are cultists who believe they can exist on nothing but the nutrients and vitamins contained in the air, sunlight and fresh water. Although in theory this may be an interesting concept, in practice it may have dangerous health consequences.

The Breatharian Institute of America, 624 Six Flags Dr, Ste 200, Arlington, TX 76011. Wiley Brooks, the founder of the Breatharian Institute of America, claims that he not only breathes air, but eats it. He says he has been doing this for 18 years. He runs one-day intensive study groups ($100) and 7-day intensives ($500). Brooks claims you too can merely breathe and live forever, existing not on food, but on cosmic energy derived through the air. Believing the human body was constructed to live for 100,000 years, breatharians believe food and drink lowers the vibratory frequency of the body, causing (due to the high density of food) it to plunge to a point where it can no longer self-perpetuate. Death of the body, of course, is the result. Be warned, however, without proper instruction and transition, without knowing how to stop eating, *you will die*! As the breatharians say, "abrupt cessation of eating and drinking leads not to Breatharianism, but to an early grave." There are free presentations at the Institute every Friday at 7:30 p.m.

NOTE WELL: Before you spend your money, although true breatharianism is an interesting idea, Brooks has been labeled by some critics as a charlatan. It has been alleged he visits Seven-Eleven stores on the sly, and after a recent interview with a journalist he was seen to have filched some breath mints, toward what end we know not.

The Secret of Life by Dr. George Lakhosky. Order from: Survival Foundation, Omangod Press, PO Box 64, Route 171, Woodstock Valley, CT 06282; $6.00. A book strongly influential for breatharians.

Diet, Health and Living on Air by Morris Krok. $3.50. An analysis of living on air in accordance with yoga. Also from the Survival Foundation.

VITARIANS

Vitarians refuse to eat seeds, nuts, and grains, believing such food is unfit for human consumption, disrupting the human reproductive process and stimulating the lower passions. The chief proponent of the vitarian way of life is Dr. Johnny Lovewisdom, the Hermit Saint of the Andes, who lived at least part of his life in a 13,000-foot extinct volcano near Vilcabamba in the Loja Valley of Ecuador. The people of Vilcabamba grow to be very old, many claiming to be well over 100. Vilcabamba is also known to miraculously cure the ill, wretched, and impotent. Some claim it is the food grown there, others the uranium in the earth, but most scientists agree if there is anything that affects the age of these people, it is more than likely the isolated gene pool of the valley.

There is a 74-page book, *Spiritualizing Dietetics—Vitarianism,* that Dr. Johnny wrote. It may be difficult to track down, but a good place to try is through the Survival Institute, PO Box 64, Route 171, Woodstock Valley, CT 06282.

Love Wisdom Connection, Box 237, Loja, Ecuador. When Dr. Johnny Lovewisdom went to the Andes he was crippled and deathly ill. In Vilcabamba he not only recuperated, but flourished. This newsletter will keep you posted on the state of his thoughts, and how his little group of vitarians is doing.

SPROUTARIANS (LIVE-FOOD EATERS)

Sproutarians center their lives and diets around live foods, that is, sprouts. They grow their sprouts at home, thus controlling all aspects of their diet. This may be a workable philosophy. Sproutarians are people of the land even if they never leave their city apartment. They grow their own sprouts and eat them when they are young, most vital and full of vitamins, minerals, and enzymes. Sproutarians eat more than just sprouts, they eat fresh fruit and vegetables as well, but sprouts form the cornerstone of their diet.

The Sprout House, 210 Riverside Dr, New York, NY 10025. Steve Meyerwitz calls himself the "Sprout Man," and he enthusiastically gives information about his favorite subject. Also classes and sprouting paraphernalia.

The Sprout Letter, PO Box 62, Ashland, OR 97520. Jeff Breaky is the editor of this praiseworthy newsletter. It is full of useful information, and Breaky's concentration on spreading the word of his sproutarian philosophy is exemplary.

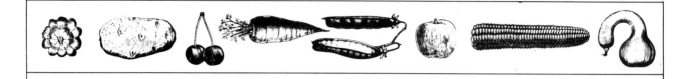

3

Who Are the Leading Authorities?

From its beginning, vegetarianism has had its famous followers. This is what some of them have said about their diets.

George Bernard Shaw, the Irish playwright, lived 94 years as a dedicated vegetarian. He said, "Mankind will never have peace until we stop killing and eating animals."

Once Shaw was very ill and his doctors warned him that unless he began to eat eggs and drink broth made with a meat base, he would die. Rather than heed the doctors' advice, Shaw called for his private secretary. In the doctors' presence Shaw dictated his final instructions: "I solemnly declare that it is my last wish that when I am no longer a captive of this physical body, that my coffin when carried to the graveyard be accompanied by mourners of the following categories: first, birds; second, sheep, lambs, cows, and other animals of the kind; third, live fish in an aquarium. Each of these mourners should carry a placard bearing the inscription: 'O Lord, be gracious to our benefactor George Bernard Shaw who gave his life for saving ours!' "

Also by Shaw: "Animals are my friends . . . and I don't eat my friends."

Isaac Bashevis Singer: "If we ask for the mercy of God, then we have no right to be merciless to creatures weaker than us. Animals are also people. They also have souls."

Mahatma Gandhi: "The greatness of a nation and its moral progress can be judged by the way its animals are treated."

"I do feel that spiritual progress does demand at some stage that we should cease to kill our fellow creatures for the satisfaction of our bodily wants."

Genesis 1:29: "And God said, Behold, I have given you every plant yielding seed which is upon the face of all the earth, and every tree with seed in its fruit; you shall have them for food."

Genesis: "I have given every green plant for food."

In the book of Isaiah God says, "He who killeth an ox is as if he slew a man."

Leo Tolstoy: "A vegetarian diet is the acid test of humanitarianism."

"This is dreadful! Not (only) the suffering and death of the animals, but that man suppresses in himself, unnecessarily, the highest spiritual capacity—that of sympathy and pity towards living creatures like himself—and by violating his own feelings becomes cruel."

Leonardo da Vinci, who was known to pay the owners of caged birds for the right to buy the pet and set it free, said; "I have from an early age foresworn the use of meat, and the time will come when men will look upon the slaughter of animals as they now look upon the slaughter of men."

Albert Einstein: "It is my view that the vegetarian manner of living, by its purely physical effect on the human temperament would most beneficially influence the lot of mankind."

Persian mystic Sheikh Saadi says that because we are filled up to our noses with food, we are not able to see God's light. According to the mystic we must think of our stomachs as divided into four compartments. Two would be for filling with simple foods, one is reserved for water, and the last should remain for the light of God.

Plutarch: "The obligations of law and equity reach only to mankind; but kindness and beneficence should be extended to the creatures of every species, and these will flow from the breast of a true man as streams that issue from the living fountain."

John Wesley, eighteenth century founder of Methodism: "Dr. Cheyne advised me to leave off meat and wine, and since I have taken his advice I have been free, blessed be God, from all bodily disorders."

Paavo O. Airola

THE AUTHORITIES

PAAVO AIROLA (1919–1983)

A well-known and respected health authority. Airola believed in a well-balanced, grain-centered, vegetarian diet. He encouraged a healthy, positive mental attitude (referring to it as Vitamin X) and a well-planned exercise program. He was against the faddism and gimmickry in the health food world. His books include *Worldwide Secrets of Staying Young, How to Get Well, Hypoglycemia: A Better Approach,* and *Every Woman's Book.* His books can be purchased through Health Plus Publishers, PO Box 22001, Phoenix, AZ 85028.

PAUL BRAGG

During his lifetime, Bragg was an outstanding testament to his own theory. Living into his nineties, he remained in great physical and mental health, and looked at least 20 or 30 years younger than he was. He opened the first modern health food store in Los Angeles. He worked with Luther Burbank helping to produce organically grown fruits and vegetables. Jack LaLanne got his start with Bragg, who was the personal consultant on diet and physical fitness to many of Hollywood's great stars. His books are clearly and convincingly written. Order c/o Health Science, Box 7, Santa Barbara, CA 93102.

Paul C. Bragg

DR. JOHN R. CHRISTOPHER (1910–1983)

At the time of his death, one of the nation's leading authorities, writers, and lecturers on herbology and natural healing. Founder of the School for Natural Healing, PO Box 352, Provo, UT 84601.

PROFESSOR ARNOLD EHRET (1866–1922)

The originator and teacher of the "Mucusless Diet Healing System" (see Chapter 4, Eating Regimens). Ehret established his theories from personal experience. Diagnosed as terminally ill, he set out to cure himself. In the course of his travels in Europe and North Africa, he put together a way of eating that he claimed would cure the organism, in this case humans, without necessarily naming the ailment or disease. Ehret's cure entails eating less, eating controlled foods that do not contain mucus-forming material or albumin, and fasting. Mucus-forming foods include meat, milk, eggs, and certain grain products. Ehret's prescribed diet is essentially a raw food vegan diet.

Publications by Ehret include: *Mucusless Diet Healing System*, $2.95; *Rational Fasting for Physical, Mental and Spiritual Rejuvenation*, $2.00; *The Definite Cure of Chronic Constipation*, $1.00; *Physical Fitness thru a Superior Diet*, $1.00; *Thus Speaketh the Stomach* and *The Tragedy of Man's Nutrition*, $1.00; *Roads to Health and Happiness*, $1.00. All are available from Ehret Literature Publishing Co., PO Box 24, Dobbs Ferry, NY 10522.

Arnold Ehret

DICK GREGORY

During the 1960s Gregory was one of the most promising of young social satirists and comedians on the contemporary scene. Today he is more than that; he may very well be one of the healthiest men in the United States. Influenced a great deal by Viktoras Kulvinskas, who calls him the "200 million dollar man," Gregory has given up the night club scene, but continues to lecture, particularly on college campuses, using his humor to urge us to know the difference between nutrition and food, believing the world's hungry are desperate for nutrition, rather than nutrient-poor food-stuffs. Gregory is a proponent of a live foods regimen and judicious fasting. He has frequently made headlines with his extended fasts and cross-country treks. His book, *Natural Diet for Folks who Eat: Cookin' With Mother Nature,* is published by Perennial Library, Harper and Row, 10 E 53 St, New York, NY 10022; $2.95.

DR. BERNARD JENSEN

World traveler and lecturer. Having studied people enjoying long life all over the world, Dr. Jensen concludes that they share certain attributes in their life styles. These include ". . . a simple life, live in a moderate temperature zone, eat unprocessed food, eat no fried foods, eat a minimum of meat, live a serene, contented life, maintain good posture, and consistently live close to where the soil is black." Believing humanity needs a formula for successful living, health, and peace, he incorporates physical, mental, and spiritual elements into his teaching. Dr. Jensen's books are available from him at Rte 1, Box 52, Dept M, Escondido, CA 92025.

DR. JOHN HARVEY KELLOGG

Famous nutritionist who recommended whole-grain cereals without sugar, salt, or preservatives. Renowned as a speaker and highly respected writer on the benefits of eating only whole grains, he was the proprietor of the famous Battle Creek health spa. His brother Charles Kellogg played off John Harvey's name to build the famous Kellogg breakfast food empire. Unfortunately, however, he did not maintain his brother's ideals while making his fortune.

VIKTORAS KULVINSKAS

An accomplished proponent of live foods, he is the author of *Survival into the 21st Century* and cofounder (with Dr. Ann Wigmore) of the Hippocrates Institute in Boston. More recently Kulvinskas has started the Survival Foundation, a nonprofit research facility in Woodstock Valley, Connecticut. He is extremely active and has succeeded as a trained scientist and educator at both Harvard and the Massachusetts Institute of

Dr. Bernard Jensen

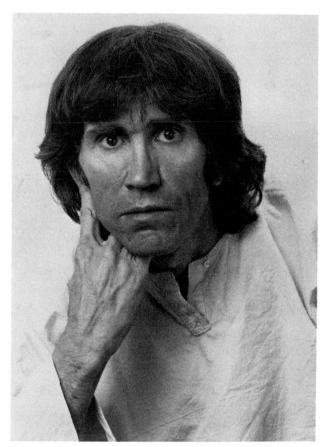

Viktoras Kulvinskas

Technology. He is a best-selling author, lecturer, and an untiring worker for world health.

Books by Viktoras include: *Survival into the 21st Century; Planetary Healers Manual; Life in the 21st Century; Sprout for the Love of Everybody; Love Your Body; New Age Wholistic Directory; 21st Century Journal;* and *Wholistic Teachings of Jesus.* All are available from Omangod Press, PO Box 64, Rte 171, Woodstock Valley, CT 06282.

MICHIO KUSHI

Founder of the East–West Foundation (see Chapter 2, Macrobiotics). A teacher, lecturer, thinker, and expert on traditional Oriental medicine and its potential impact on Western culture, life style, and disease.

Books by Kushi include: *Cancer and Heart Disease; How to See Your Health; The Book of Do-In; Natural Healing Through Macrobiotics; The Book of Macrobiotics; How To Cook With Miso.* Available from Japan Publications, Inc., 10 E 53 St, New York, NY 10022.

SCOTT NEARING (1883–1983)

After being dismissed from the Wharton School of Business in Philadelphia for advocating "socialist" views (that is, opposing child labor), Nearing moved first to Vermont and then to Maine. He said he preferred living poor in the country to poor in the city. He built more than 18 stone structures in his lifetime (symbolic of his relationship with the earth), and is considered to be the father of the "back to the land" movement. A popular speaker and author, Nearing and his wife, Helen, heartily advocated vegetarianism for both its health and ethical benefits. He died in 1983 at the age of 100 years. He authored 50 books, grew 85 percent of his own food (his diet consisted of 50 percent fruit and fruit juices, 35 percent vegetables, 10 percent fats and 5 percent proteins). His books are available from the Social Science Institute, Harborside, ME 04642: *Living the Good Life* (coauthored with his wife Helen Nearing); *Civilization and Beyond; Man's Search for the Good Life; Economics for the Power Age; United World; Black America.*

Michio Kushi   *Scott Nearing*

GARY NULL

With the untimely death of Paavo Airola, Null became America's leading popular nutritional writer. He is open-minded, receptive, yet convincing in his appeal for better nutrition for the U.S. public.

Null's books include: *The New Vegetarian, Building your Health Through Natural Eating; Natural Beauty Book; Grow Your Food Organically; Herbs for the Seventies; Body Pollution; Protein for Vegetarians; Man and His Whole Earth; Successful Pregnancy; Biofeedback, Fasting and Nutrition; Whole Body Health and Sex Book; Handbook of Skin and Hair; Alcohol and Nutrition; How to Get Rid of the Poisons in Your Body.* They are available from Dell Publishing Company. One Dag Hammarskjold Plaza, New York, NY 10017.

Gary Null

RICHARD PASSWATER

Passwater, a biochemist, has written *Supernutrition: A Megavitamin Revolution* (Dial Press, New York, 1975, $7.95), a landmark because of its marriage of orthomolecular medicine, megavitamin therapy, and antioxidant therapy. The implication of supernutrition is ''to find the optimum level of each nutrient for each individual and learn how to tell when you have reached your point of optimum health.''

LINUS PAULING

Pauling is a two-time winner of the Nobel Prize, once for chemistry, once for peace. His outspoken views, particularly against cigarette smoking and nuclear proliferation, have on occasion put him in the public eye. His 1970 book, *Vitamin C and the Common Cold,* in which he claims we can protect ourselves from colds and flu by supplementing our diets with massive doses of vitamin C, won the Phi Beta Kappa award as the outstanding scientific book of the year. Dr. Pauling is presently Research Professor at the Linus Pauling Institute of Science in Menlo Park, California, where he continues to work on the molecular basis of disease, including mental illness.

Vitamin C, the Common Cold, and the Flu by Linus Pauling. W.H. Freeman and Company, San Francisco, CA, 1976; $3.45.

GEORGE OHSAWA

Ohsawa brought the macrobiotic movement to the West, and his brilliant book *Zen Macrobiotics* started it all. Brought up as a Westernized Japanese, Ohsawa came to Zen in his search for health. Coming to realize the solid science behind the ancient teachings, Ohsawa, with a gift for language and phraseology (he coined the word macrobiotics), was able to bring modern vitality to the Zen art of selecting and preparing food to produce longevity and rejuvenation. Thanks to Ohsawa, macrobiotics caught on as a way of life, not only among many Westernized Japanese, but among people all over the world (see the section on macrobiotics in Chapter 2).

George Ohsawa Macrobiotic Foundation, 902 14 St, Oroville, CA 95965.

George Ohsawa and the Japanese Religious Traditions by Ronald Kotzsch. A study of the life and teachings of Ohsawa. Limited copies are available from Dr. Ronald Kotzsch, Hurricane

Island, Outward Bound, Box 952, Hanover, NH 03755; $21.50, including postage and handling.

J.I. RODALE

The father of modern organic farming in the United States. In 1930 Rodale observed that modern farming techniques and modern eating habits left quite a bit to be desired. Putting two and two together he came up with the revolutionary idea that the declining health of America's soil and the declining health of America's people were in some way related. He established *Organic Gardening* magazine, and on a small farm near Emmaus, Pennsylvania, set about to prove his theories. From his magazine success grew Rodale Press, which today leads the way in much organic agricultural research, and publishes a wide range of organic, health, and dietary titles. Rodale Press periodicals include *Organic Gardening, Prevention, Bicycling, New Shelter, Executive Fitness Newsletter, Body Bulletin,* and *Home Dynamics.* A series of home video cassettes reflects the entire range of Rodale subjects. Order from Rodale Press, 33 E Minor St, Emmaus, PA 18049.

DR. ANN WIGMORE

Ann Wigmore believes sickness is unnatural, that the two greatest stumbling blocks to health are deficiency and toxemia. She believes that we must build health so the body can cure itself.

Founder of the Hippocrates World Health Organization (25 Exeter Street, Boston, MA 02116), Dr. Wigmore is one of the foremost proponets of a live food diet using wheat grass and sprouts. Wigmore says, "Dead food produces dying bodies. Live foods, live bodies!" She writes, runs the health institute and the Hippocrates World Health Organization, the facilities implemented to help carry on her work, and provide onsite education, training and reinforcement. Most visitors to the health institute are cancer sufferers, as was Dr. Wigmore before she "threw away" her stove and began her programs of live foods nutrition and green drinks (chlorophyll-rich wheat grass). Her intelligence, vibrancy, amazingly youthful appearance, and energy speak for themselves. Books by Dr. Wigmore are available through the institute: *Why Suffer More?* (Wigmore's autobiography), $2.95; *Dr. Ann Wigmore's Complete Live Food Program,* $1.95; *Be Your Own Doctor,* $3.95; *New Age Child Care,* $5.95; *Recipes for Longer Life,* $8.95; *Naturama: Living Textbook,* $12.95; *Organic Soil,* $2.95; *Unity Consciousness Spiritual Diet,* $1.50; *Fat to Fit,* $2.95. Also available are a variety of pamphlets for $1.00 each, or all for $4.50. These are: *Beauty Care, Be Your Own Pet Doctor, Healthy Children Nature's Way, I See a World Without Cancer, Healing the Mind Through Food, Wheatgrass Book, Reducing Healthfully.* Order from Hippocrates Press, 25 Exeter St, Boston, MA 02116; (617) 267-9525.

4

Eating Regimens

An admirable principle to follow with regard to eating is: Eat to live, don't live to eat! You are not nourished by the food you eat, but by what you digest and assimilate into your body systems.

Dramatic weight-loss diets are dangerous. According to nutritional psychologist Dr. Arthur Hochberg, weight loss should be considered as weight control. We gain weight slowly and we should lose it at an equally slow pace, giving the body time to adjust to radical changes (e.g., chemical imbalances). Quick weight-loss regimens most often rely on high-protein diets which stress the pancreas, liver, and kidneys, thus affecting the body's calcium and phosphorus levels, and upsetting the entire mineral balance of the body. In addition, more often than not, people will gain back the weight they lose on a high-protein diet.

Controlled, intelligent eating patterns are the best way to establish the correct and natural weight for each individual. According to Hochberg, the body needs a hearty supply of the complex carbohydrates—whole grains (brown rice, millet, buckwheat, oatmeal, whole wheat, barley, and potatoes), and sufficient supplies of fruit and fresh, properly prepared vegetables. All of the above contain protein, but if you need a little more there are beans, lentils, and soy products. If you are not a vegan, protein can be obtained from dairy products and eggs.

Chickweed and nettle herbal teas will break down fat cells, as will apple cider vinegar. Vitamin B_6 is a natural diuretic; that is, it will help cleanse your body by increasing the volume of urine produced. A good source of B_6 is in brewer's yeast.

Regulate your food intake by being in tune with your body. That is, eat only when you are truly hungry, anywhere from two to six times daily, and make use of your caloric intake by releasing and burning it up through some sort of exercise.

The American Dietetic Association, 430 North Michigan Ave, Chicago, IL 60611; (312) 280-5000. The ADA is the national professional organization for dietitians. Its membership includes more than 50,000 professional people. Their chief aim is to provide direction, leadership, and service to members, while promoting high standards of practice. ADA members are nutrition professionals. Most have completed at least a bachelor's degree, have served an internship, and passed a qualifying exam. This leads to the position of registered dietitian (R.D.)

The ADA publishes a journal; a yearly subscription is $27.50. They have an extensive booklist that includes information of interest to vegetarians. Their audio-cassette, *Food for Us All— The Vegetarian Diet,* rents for $35 for a three-day period or may be purchased for $225 by nonmembers. Members receive a discount. Also available is the audio-cassette *Nutritional Misinformation and Food Faddism,* an analysis of food cultism and its implications for health food, natural food, and organic products. Also discussed are megavitamins, hair analysis, and fad diets.

The association's position paper on vegetarianism is available for $4.75. Other books of interest involve nutrition and pregnant women, athletes, old people, etc.

Airola Diet (see Chapter 3, section on Paavo Airola), a whole-foods vegetarian diet developed by Paavo Airola and described in his book *Worldwide Secrets of Staying Young.* A diet with great potential for building, maintaining, and restoring health. The diet focuses on seeds, nuts, grains, vegetables, fruits, and high-nutrient supplements, including raw or soured milk products, brewer's yeast, kelp, wheat germ, and fish liver oils. In order to protect against the increasing toxicity in the environment, the diet also calls for natural vitamin and mineral supplements.

The Cancer Prevention Diet by Michio Kushi with Alex Jack (see Chapter 3, section on Michio Kushi). A nutritional alternative to help prevent and fight cancer (which Kushi and many others believe is linked to diet), combining Western scientific thinking with traditional Oriental medicine. The book contains specific dietary recommendations for the 15 major forms of cancer, and a variety of recipes and weekly menus to help the reader. Available from St. Martin's Press, 175 Fifth Ave, New York, NY 10010; $14.95.

The Complete Scarsdale Medical Diet by Herman Tarnower and Samm Sinclair Baker. Bantam Books, 666 Fifth Ave, New York, NY 10103; $3.95. A basic weight loss plan for adults who have no special dietary needs or problems. The key: Never overload your stomach! One chapter for vegetarians. The diet hinges on a two-week time schedule.

The Scarsdale, Stillman, and Atkins diets are basically high-protein diets. Since high-protein diets encourage water loss, very often weight is regained when the diet period ends. Furthermore, high-protein diets can be unsafe if followed for too long a period. The best diet is a natural whole carbohydrate diet, maintained while reducing the intake of other foods.

Diet for Life by Francine Prince. Bantam Books, 666 Fifth Ave, New York, NY 10103; $3.50. Haute cuisine diet plan.

Dr. Atkins' Super Energy Diet by Robert C. Atkins and Shirley Linde. Bantam Books, 666 Fifth Ave, New York, NY 10103; $3.95. High-protein diet with discussions of weight loss and gain.

High Health Diet and Exercise Plan by Dr. Neil Solomon. G.P. Putnam's Sons, 200 Madison Ave, New York, NY 10016; $9.95. Solomon points out that there are two types of cholesterol, one beneficial and absolutely essential, the other dangerous. This diet is designed to make cholesterol work for you. Contains an exercise plan and a section specific to athletes.

The Hippocrates Diet and Health Program by Dr. Ann Wigmore. Avery Publishing Group, Wayne, NJ; $7.95. This is a curative diet specifically designed to enable the body to cure itself naturally at its own pace. It is a diet of fruit, vegetables, grains, nuts, sprouts, and wheatgrass juice. It involves no cooked foods. This diet has been especially effective at the Hippocrates Institute (see Chapter 3, section on Dr. Ann Wigmore) in the fight against degenerative disease. It is helpful in body cleansing, disease prevention, and perhaps life extension.

Mind Trips to Help You Lose Weight by Frances Meritt Stern and Ruth S. Hoch with Jean Carper. Two psychologists help you eliminate blocks that prevent you from losing weight effectively.

Pritikin Program for Diet and Exercise by Nathan Pritikin and Patrick M. McGrady, Jr. Bantam Books, 666 Fifth Ave, New York, NY 10103; $3.95. A high-carbohydrate diet that won't have you going hungry. It calls for eight low-calorie meals daily, but no greasy foods, sweets, or salt. Instead, Pritikin wants you to eat whole-grain bread, cereals, pasta, fruit, vegetables, soup, rice, and potatoes.

Pritikin Permanent Weight-Loss Manual by Nathan Pritikin. Bantam Books, 666 Fifth Ave, New York, NY 10103; $3.95. Four weight-loss plans using the Pritikin never-go-hungry, high-carbohydrate diet.

The Slendernow Diet by Dr. Richard Passwater. St. Martin's Press, Inc, 175 Fifth Ave, New York, NY 10010; $11.95. This diet consists of two protein milkshakes daily, one full meal, and a modest exercise program. Recommended program extends over eight-week period.

Mucusless Diet Healing System by Arnold Ehret. Ehret Literature Publishing Company, 145 Palisades St, Dobbs Ferry, NY 10522, $2.95. This book was first written in 1922 and was remarkable for its time. Since then Ehret's theories have been elaborated on and modernized by others, notably Paul Bragg. We have learned that certain foods will induce different reactions in different individuals. Ehret blames all maladies on the "clogging up of the pipes" with mucus, or constipation. He says the average person has as much as 10 pounds of uneliminated feces in the bowels, and that this waste material is continually poisoning the blood stream and the entire organism. The way to eliminate such a clog is the mucusless diet.

WEIGHT LOSS

Rutgers University professor, Dr. Paul La-Chance, rated the most popular weight loss diets. He found they were all lacking in at least one or more vitamins and minerals, mostly calcium, iron, and zinc. This is a good reason why any time you go on a diet which limits your caloric intake to less than 1,000 calories per day it may be wise to employ vitamin and mineral supplements. (This would not hold true if you were fasting to control absolutely what goes into your body.)

The best diets he found were the Pritikin 1,200 and the F-Plan. Pritikin 700, I Love New York, I Love America, Scarsdale and Atkins received intermediate ratings. The poorest diet choices were the Richard Simmons diet and the Beverly Hills. This evaluation was based on caloric intake, and ingested amounts of vitamins, minerals, protein, carbohydrates, fat, sugar, fiber, sodium, potassium, and cholesterol.

Beware of diets that tell you to eliminate whole grains from your daily food intake. These foods are rich in vitamin B_6, magnesium, and zinc. Contrary to once-popular belief, *carbohydrates are not fattening per se*. The United States Senate Select Committee's dietary recommendations call for 55% of your daily calorie intake to come from carbohydrates, 30% from fats, and 15% from protein.

DIET PILLS

According to drug industry statistics more than 10 million Americans, mostly women, take diet pills daily. In 1980 this ingestion meant a 200 million dollar a year industry.

Diet pills are not a solution, but a danger. Studies link the pills to high blood pressure, kidney failure, stroke, psychosis, and drug abuse. All this for a result that is far from satisfactory. The Federal Drug Administration reports only a modest benefit, and then only over a short period, according to *Consumer Reports,* which had access to transcripts from closed FDA hearings. Two studies performed at the University of Pennsylvania show behavior therapy to be a far more realistic and successful means of controlling weight. "Those [dieters] who underwent behavior therapy alone regained significantly less weight than those who had drug therapy, either alone or in combination with behavior therapy."

There are two basic types of drugs used in diet pills. They are: (1) Benzocaine, a local anesthetic, usually used in diet-aid gum, candy, and lozenges. Benzocaine numbs the taste buds, making eating a lot less interesting. Benzocaine is the same anesthetic often found in first-aid sprays and creams. Although serious side-effects have not been reported, scientific research has not found it as effective as advertising would lead us to believe. (2) Phenylpropanolamine (PPA) closely resembles amphetamine, a stimulant to the central nervous system. Users are advised to have their blood pressure checked regularly, and those with high blood pressure, mental depression, diabetes, or heart, thyroid, kidney, or other diseases are warned *not* to use the drug. It is also not recommended for those under the age of 18 or over the age of 60. It is not recommended for women who are pregnant or nursing because the drug can affect the fetus and appear in breast milk. The fight against PPA has been led by the Center for Science in the Public Interest (see Chapter 1).

According to the *Lancet,* a leading British medical journal, "Some of the most serious adverse reactions to PPA have arisen in previously healthy people after ingestion of modest doses."

An intelligent diet choice would not include pills of any type!

FASTING

Allowing your body to rest from eating is a good thing. Fasting is not a penance, it is a benefit to your body. Fasting can be used not only to lose weight, but also to cleanse your body.

Digestion takes its toll on body organs and your body's energy. Giving the body a rest can have surprising results. After an initially difficult period, people often experience strong renewals of energy levels. You want to do things. You begin to feel tranquil, yet capable. There can be feelings of euphoria.

Do not attempt to fast without thoroughly researching the different methods of fasting, and *never* fast for more than a few days without consulting your doctor or health practitioner first.

The Miracle of Fasting by Paul C. Bragg. Health Science Publishing, Santa Barbara, CA; $4.95. A guide to physical, mental, and spiritual rejuvenation through short time-distilled water fasting. Bragg's program calls for weekly 24- to 36-hour fasts. Four times a year he recommends slightly longer fasts of 4 to 7 days.

Fasting, the Ultimate Diet by Allan Cott. Bantam Books, 666 Fifth Ave, New York, NY 10103; Cott recommends fasting only with a doctor's permission and supervision. He recommends fasting for better eating habits, to reduce tension, improve sleep, and sex.

The Fasting Cure by Upton Sinclair. Health Research, Lafayette St, Mokelumne Hill, CA, 153 pp; $4.00. A facsimile of an original manuscript by the writer. The fasting cure is not a new concept. Pythagorus fasted as did many others throughout history. The Russian "hunger cure" of up to 45 days has been reported to cure all

kinds of ailments including problems with metabolism and skin, bronchial asthma, hypertension, gallstones, tumors, pancreatic disorders, and early forms of hardening of the arteries and arthritis.

Fasting Can Save Your Life by Herbert M. Shelton. Natural Hygiene Press, 698 Brooklawn Ave, Bridgeport, CT 06004, 185 pp; $4.50. A serious manuscript that clearly voices Shelton's views. He stresses the difference between pure fasting and fasting with fruit juices, vegetable juices, or wheat grass. His fast has nine basic steps:

- *Preparation.* A faster should understand what he is about to do, but there is no need to gradually cut back food intake, have trial fasts, etc.
- *Rest.* Reduce activity during the fast, mental, sensory, physical.
- *Activity.* In some cases moderate exercise, but in most cases Shelton believes even moderate exercise to be a needless expenditure of energy and a waste of reserves.
- *Warmth.* During fasting a person may experience cold and chills. This is why warm weather is often recommended for fasting, although Shelton says it can be performed in any climate. Be especially careful to keep your feet warm.
- *Water.* Drink water as you feel the need. Don't drink mineral water or tap water, but the purest water available. Soft spring water, rain water, distilled water, and filtered water are best.
- *Bathing.* Keep clean as you normally do. Baths should be short and lukewarm.
- *Sunbathing.* Some sun is good, imperative, but not too much.
- *Purges.* Shelton is very much against the unilateral taking of enemas and diuretics. Some people feel that without enemas the feces remain in the large intestine and tend to be reabsorbed, thus poisoning the body. Shelton argues the bowels will empty themselves as many times and as often as necessary.
- *Suffering.* Shelton warns that when suffering is greatest during a fast, and the faster is tempted to break it because he or she cannot stand it anymore, this is the very time when a fast should not be broken. It is precisely then when digestive and assimilative powers are at their lowest. The discomfort will pass. Your

doctor or practitioner will tell you when it is time to break the fast.

Shelton is the most rigid of the fasting authorities. His book is not the best for the novice, but excellent for experienced natural hygienists and their ilk.

How to Keep Slim, Healthy and Young with Juice Fasting by Dr. Paavo Airola. Health Plus Publishers, PO Box 22001, Phoenix, AZ 85028; $4.95.

Juice fasting can be easier on you than a pure fast. Dr. Shelton would argue that a juice fast is not a fast at all, but a diet of fruit and vegetables in juice form. The truth is that few of us are disciplined and single-minded enough to maintain a prolonged pure fast. Furthermore, a pure fast should never be pursued without the keen eye of an expert practitioner upon us. Airola's diet is much more realistic for the average person. His fast is milder, but many of the same results will be achieved. It can also be successfully undertaken at home, for short periods, without danger. Airola is a clear writer, offering straightforward advice and guidance. He recommends enemas and plenty of water along with the juice when you fast for regeneration and rejuvenation. Airola believes the main reason to fast is to rid the body of accumulated toxic wastes. The enemas and water will cleanse the alimentary canal. Beware, however, since enemas can be habit forming, and they are not natural. The only time they should be used is during fasting, and only during short periods.

THE ARGONNE ANTI–JET LAG DIET

Designed to help travelers quickly adjust to new time zones. The diet was designed by Dr. Charles F. Ehret at the Argonne National Laboratory (9700 South Cass Ave, Argonne, IL 60439).

Step 1. Determine breakfast time at destination on the day of your arrival.

Step 2. Feast/Fast/Feast/Fast. Starting four days before your projected breakfast time in Step 1, feast. Eat heartily with high-protein breakfast and lunch and a high-carbohydrate dinner. If you drink coffee, take none except between 3 and 5 p.m.

On day two, *fast* on light meals of salads, light soups, fruits, and juices. (NOTE: The word fast in the context of this diet is actually used to connote a system of light eating.) Again, no coffee, except between 3 and 5 p.m.

On day three, feast again.

On day four, fast again. Today, if you have been drinking caffeinated beverages take them in the morning if you are traveling west, or between 6 and 11 p.m. when traveling east.

Step 3. Break the final fast at destination breakfast time. Don't drink alcohol on the plane. If you can sleep on the flight do so, but just until normal breakfast time at your destination, and no longer. Wake up and eat a high-protein breakfast. Remain awake and active. Continue the day's meals according to the mealtimes at your destination.

LIQUID PROTEIN DIETS

Liquid protein diets are fad diets. They can be extremely dangerous, and their health claims are misleading. Many liquid protein diets proclaim fasting as the perfect diet, save for the fact that after a time the body begins to use up its stored protein and then begins to eat itself up. It therefore follows that fasting with liquid protein is logically the perfect diet. Not so. Much of the liquid diet products are overly expensive, poorly made, and unsafe. Some are made with animal protein, many times simply from hooves and hides. Usually they don't even contain complete proteins, but merely a haphazard amalgam. Even those purportedly supplemented with "high quality" protein deserve your suspicion. A juice fast with a variety of fresh juices and vegetable broth would be a far wiser choice, not to mention infinitely less expensive.

NIGHTSHADE-FREE DIET

Originated by Norman F. Childers, professor at Rutgers University. The nightshade family, which includes tomatoes, white potatoes, eggplants, peppers, and tobacco, and derivatives of the nightshade family such as potato starch, paprika, and cayenne pepper, contain a substance called solanine to which some people can be extremely sensitive. Solanine and some other substances present in nightshades can interfere with enzymes and cause arthritis or similar problems in nightshade-sensitive people. Not all arthritis is caused by nightshade sensitivity, but by maintaining a nightshade-free diet for a period of 3 to 12 months a correlation may be detected.

WINTER DIET

Like a bear preparing to hybernate, the human body makes adjustments for winter weather. As weather grows cooler we begin to store fat as insulation. In colder climates we find ourselves craving hot soups, warm drinks, and heartier foods to fight the chill our body feels. According to the teachings of the macrobiotics, the fall and winter are times of lessened activity. The body relies more heavily on stored energy and fats. In the spring and summer, when renewal is the key, the body cleanses itself. The liver flushes the system and this is the best time for herbal cleansing regimens and fasts. A natural hygienist or raw food enthusiast who lives in a cold climate but neglects to make adjustments during the winter months more than likely will find himself or herself the possessor of cold hands and feet. Add bulk to your diet or wear an extra sweater and thick socks.

5

Preventive Medicine Through Nutrition

Except for nuclear holocaust, cancer and heart disease may be our greatest personal fears.

Unfortunately, our nuclear destiny is linked with politicians, and although we can protest, sit in, and write letters, we know in our hearts that our fate is ultimately in their hands. In a similar way, politicians also control the food we eat. The government allows our food industry to poison us by infiltrating our foodstuffs with antibiotics, pesticides, toxins, poison, and hormones.

Diet affects life, and the chances of contracting certain types of cancer and heart disease rise dramatically with the ingestion of various chemicals and fats. Vegetarians as a whole are less susceptible to these great killers, because the further down the food chain one eats, the less likely the predominance of chemicals in the food. By eliminating fat-saturated fast foods from our diet, by cutting back or eliminating our meat intake, we are increasing our chances for survival. Remember, no food we eat that originated in the plant world contains artery-clogging cholesterol!

Diet should take into account what we know intuitively—that nobody in their right mind wants to eat DDT, EDP, or BHT. Yet chemicals are alive in our environment. Incredibly, DDT has crept into every corner of our globe. Researchers have found polar bears with substantial amounts of chemicals in their bodies, even though the animals lived hundreds or even thousands of miles away from the nearest sprayed areas. Even a carrot grown organically can have the same amounts of pesticide deposits, chemicals, and toxins that a similar vegetable grown on a corporate farm has. For the longest time commercial farmers thought there was no escape from chemical fertilization and chemical insect and pest control. The decimation of our environment has only recently become clear to most of us, and still has not dawned on many. Pioneer organic researchers and farmers are beginning to make an impact. We, the public, must make it known that we demand quality, uncontaminated food!

What can you do? Sproutarians (see Chapters 2 and 20) are able to grow most everything they eat in their own home. They thus control the circumstances of what they eat. But the sproutarian diet may not be for everyone. The average person should try to eat the freshest food possible; eat food that's grown in your immediate area, making sure it's as chemically free as possible. And if you can possibly keep a garden, do so.

NUTRITION RULES FOR DISEASE PREVENTION

This list has been adapted from *Nutrition Applied Personally* by the International College of Applied Nutrition (available from the Cancer Book House, 2043 North Berendo St, Los Angeles, CA 90027, $3.00 plus $1.00 postage).

- Eat natural foods. Eat them raw whenever possible. Don't eat foods that have been highly processed, such as sugar, white bread, cookies, cake, crackers, TV dinners, and so on.

- Eat only foods that will spoil, and see that you eat them before they do. Don't eat foods that are laden with chemical preservatives, dyes, artificial coloring, etc.

- Don't eat products that are advertised as "foodless" snacks! Plan for a balanced diet.

- If you must eat meat, use meat, fish, and poultry that have been naturally raised. Don't eat commercial meat containing chemicals such as stilbestrol (DES). Don't eat meat from animals that have been inhumanely raised (e.g., veal or commercial chickens).

- Use organically grown fruits and vegetables whenever possible. Grow your own! Don't use fruits and vegetables that have been sprayed, waxed, dyed, or fumigated.

- Try to use fresh produce in season. Freeze it for later use. Sprout your own seed at home and use the sprouts daily. Avoid canned fruit and vegetables.

- Whenever possible use fertile eggs. They provide more nutrients and are less likely to contain antibiotics, chemicals, and sprays. Eat the eggs of free-ranging chickens. Don't use eggs produced by hens that have been confined to small, crowded cages, force-fattened, and treated with chemicals.

- Try to make your own bread and bakery products at home. Buy a flour mill and make your own flour. Avoid commercially made white bread and other products made with white flour.

- For shortening in baked goods use soya, sesame, peanut, or cold-pressed safflower oil with no preservatives. Do not use oil that has been heat-treated or has preservatives. Don't use hydrogenated shortenings.

- Fry as little as possible, but if you must, use oils such as sesame or safflower. Avoid foods that have been deep-fried.

- Carob has its own sweetener and is a better choice than chocolate, which interferes with mineral utilization. People are also frequently allergic to chocolate, and often do not realize it.

- It's better to make your own ice cream, yogurt, and cottage cheese than to use commercial products which often contain artificial coloring, flavoring, emulsifiers, and sweeteners.

- Drink raw milk whenever possible. Avoid processed milk such as pasteurized, homogenized, dried, and canned.

- Drink spring water, milk, and natural unsweetened juices instead of other beverages. At all costs avoid soft drinks, with or without sugar, and avoid caffeinated drinks that stimulate because they exhaust the adrenals and pancreas.

- Drink herb teas and coffee substitutes rather than caffeinated teas and coffee. If you must drink coffee limit your intake to two cups per day. Do not drink instant coffee. Do not use coffee lighteners and other such products.

- Shop in health food stores. If you shop in a supermarket, be smart and scrutinize labels. Don't buy junk food!

- Cook only in stainless steel, Corning, enamel, or glassware. Do not use aluminum pots, pans, or pressure cookers. Too much aluminum in your body is not good for you and has been linked to Alzheimer's disease.

- Use butter, not substitutes. If you want to make a spread high in unsaturated fats blend one-half pound of sweet cream butter with one-half cup of sesame oil.

- Drink lots of clean, pure water. Preferably not tap water.

- Use a natural sea salt, but use it sparingly. Check labels for hidden salt in your food.

- Cook with a variety of herbs and spices. This creates food interest and stimulates not only the appetite, but also the gastric juices.

- Apple cidar vinegar will help maintain good gastric acidity.

SOCIETIES AND ORGANIZATIONS

American Academy of Medical Preventics. 2811 L St, Sacramento, CA 95816. Dedicated to the alternative possibilities of preventing and treating chronic degenerative disease in our society, this educational organization stages conferences, symposia, and workshops for both the layman and the health professional. Information referrals are freely given.

Health and Nutrition Resources. PO Box 258, Syosset, NY 11791. Workshops, fairs, seminars conducted by professionals to help the public prevent disease through intelligent nutritional choices.

Integral Health Services. 245 School St, Putnam, CT 06260. An organization that encourages the individual to take charge of his or her health through the awareness of the potential for preventive action.

International Academy of Preventive Medicine. 10409 Town and Country Way, Ste 200, Houston, TX 77024. IAPM is a professional organization interested in furthering discussion and research into the possibilities of prevention in not only medicine, but dentistry, psychiatry, and podiatry. Also concerned with nutrition and holistic healing systems. The academy will supply a membership directory for referral purposes.

Linus Pauling Institute of Science and Medicine. 2700 Sand Hill Rd, Menlo Park, CA 94025. Delving into the mysteries of vitamin C and cancer, aging, orthomolecular medicine, and prevention, the institute is dedicated to the alleviation of human suffering. They will provide information and a bibliography to both professionals and laypersons (see Chapter 3).

Northwest Academy of Preventive Medicine. 15650 North East 24 St, Bellevue, WA 98008. Working to educate the professional on the possibilities of treating and preventing disease through nutrition, this organization produces both videos and audio cassettes of seminars and publishes a newsletter and the *Northwest Academy of Preventive Medicine Journal*. They maintain a referral list of doctors throughout the United States and Canada.

Southern Academy of Clinical Nutrition. 1045 East Atlantic Ave, Delray Beach, FL 33444. The sponsor of yearly conferences, this organization attempts to help the public understand what good health is, how to attain it, and how to maintain it.

The Vegetus Foundation. 5744 Market St, Philadelphia, PA 19139; and 143 Madison Ave, New York, NY 10016. The Vegetus Foundation is nonprofit. It promotes improvement of the general welfare through proper nutrition. The foundation supplies teaching aids, supports a lecture series, subsidizes writers and book publications, and is interested in developing radio and television programming that supports the idea of preserving health through proper nutrition. All contributions to the Vegetus Foundation are tax-exempt.

MAGAZINES AND REVIEWS

Black Health. 28 St. James Place, Brooklyn, NY 11205. Ralph A. Johnson, editor; subscription rate, $6 per year. Shoestring budget operation trying to bring good health guidance to the black community.

Joy Gross's Health Hotline. Box 401, Hyde Park, NY 12538. Subscription rate, $15.00 per year for 12 issues. A newsletter with a warm personal touch. Much reader interaction. Informative updates on government action in relation to food and health issues, case histories, questions and answers, tips on child health, smoking, losing weight, allergies, and other issues.

Nutrition Health Review. 143 Madison Ave, New York, NY 10016. Subscription rate; $8.00 for 8 issues (2 years). "A journal devoted to the principle of optimum nutrition as the basis of mental and physical well-being." Published quarterly by the Vegetus Foundation.

Nutrition Today. PO Box 1829, Annapolis, MD 21404. Subscription, $17.75, including membership in Nutrition Today Society. Conservative magazine for nutrition and health professionals, supported by the food industry.

The People's Doctor. PO Box 982, Evanston, IL

60204. Subscription, $24 per year. Dr. Robert S. Mendelsohn runs a medical newsletter for consumers. Decidedly not of the establishment bent, Mendelsohn answers questions posed by his readers. He also has a column in the *Whole Life Times* magazine. Helpful and interesting.

Tuft's University Diet and Nutrition Letter. PO Box 2465, Boulder, CO 80322. Monthly publication, $24 per year. Conservative journal.

BOOKS

Guidelines for Your Total Health by Dennis and David Sinksank. The Sinksanks emphasize a take-charge attitude in regard to one's personal health. They detail current thinking in health and nutrition. It is an understandable primer full of helpful information. The Sinksanks are also the originators of the computerized *Personal Health and Nutrient Assessment*. Available from American Health and Nutrition, 6409 Odana Rd, PO Box 4421, Madison, WI 53711.

The 1984 Guide to Health-Oriented Periodicals by Jeff Breakey. Sprouting Publications, PO Box 62, Ashland, OR 97520; $3.95. Comprehensive listing to more than 250 magazines, journals, newsletters, newspapers, and related publications. A superior tool covering ecological and environmental health, fitness and exercise, gardening, health (general and holistic), nutrition (including vegetarian, raw foods, natural hygiene, general), self-care and preventive medicine, women's issues, regional and international periodicals, and networking.

Nutrition Against Disease by Dr. Roger J. Williams. Bantam Books, 666 Fifth Ave, New York, NY 10103; $1.95. One of the classic books in the field of diet and nutrition.

Well Body, Well Earth by Dr. Mike Samuels and Hal Zina Bennett. Sierra Club Books, PO Box 3886 Rincon Annex, San Francisco, CA 94119; $12.95 paper, $22.50 hard-bound. How to function and flourish in a troubled environment.

CANCER

Lots of meat, lots of fat, and little fiber add up to an increased chance of contracting cancer of the breast, colon, prostate, rectum, ovary, and pancreas. Vegetables, beans, and whole grains are suspected of actually containing elements that *protect* you from cancer. Vitamin A, vitamin C, and lignan, a substance found in fiber foods, all have been linked to cancer prevention.

Foods that Fight Cancer, by Patricia Hausman. Rawson Associates, 597 Fifth Ave, New York, NY 10017; $16.95. What to eat, what to cut back on, what to avoid. Suggests vitamins, minerals, and supplements that will help prevent cancer in high-risk people.

HEART DISEASE

Fat levels in your blood dictate your chances for heart disease. Vegetarians, under scientific scrutiny, have proven time and again to have reduced levels of blood fats, cholesterol and triglycerides, compared to meat eaters of similar background.

Lacto-ovo vegetarians have consistently higher levels than vegans. The more dairy products such as hard cheese, cream cheese, sour cream, ice cream, and eggs the greater the risk of having a heart attack.

A way to fight cholesterol is to include soy protein in your diet. Soybeans and foods made from soy products, such as tofu and tempeh, have a marked effect in lowering cholesterol levels in the blood. Tests in Italy have proven that even when substantial amounts of cholesterol are added to a diet (500 milligrams daily), the added soybean keeps cholesterol levels low.

HIGH BLOOD PRESSURE

High blood pressure exists more in meat eaters than in vegetarians. Recent scientific research in Israel, Finland, and Australia confirms this. A low-fat diet using polyunsaturated vegetable oil rather than highly saturated animal fats will lead to a substantial reduction in blood pressure. Even healthy meat eaters who have switched to lacto-ovo diets for limited times have had noticeable drops in blood pressure, which, incidently, rose after they went back to meat eating. Meat consumption has a more significant effect on blood pressure than salt consumption, even though the latter is in no way good for you. Salt is not a food, nor is it a nutrient, and its intake should be kept to a minimum.

There is speculation among certain researchers that it is actually the potassium level of vegetarians that keeps their blood pressure down. This has not been scientifically borne out, and it remains controversial, but fruit contains a high level of this protective nutrient, and since vegetarians consume more fruit on the whole than meat eaters, they naturally consume more potassium. If you remain a meat eater, *cut back!* Vegetarians are significantly less polluted than their meat-eating counterparts.

TOOTH DECAY AND GUM DISEASE

According to Dr. David Ostreicher, professor of preventive dentistry at Columbia University, contrary to common belief, in many cases plaque may not be the cause of gum disease. Instead, Dr. Ostreicher says, a typical American diet, heavy in meat, fish, flour, and poultry provides more phosphorous than is necessary to the body and not enough calcium. This adds to the risk of periodontitis. Periodontitis destroys gum tissue and attacks the bone that surrounds the teeth and anchors them to the jaw. When calcium intake is too low and phosphorous intake too high, the body pulls calcium from the bones in order to balance the phosphorus in the body. This of course is not good for the bones. The doctor suggests limiting meat consumption, limiting the intake of soda and colas and consuming more dark-green, leafy vegetables, which are rich in calcium.

The best defense against cavities and gum disease also includes an adequate cleaning regimen. Flossing, gum massage, and proper cleaning help your teeth and gums.

Human Ecology Research Foundation. 505 North Lake Shore Dr, Chicago, IL 60611. For dental care the foundation publishes a 20-tape series, an educational tool for the patient and a teaching aid for the dental practitioner. In addition there is a three-part series of instructional manuals dealing with comprehensive environmental control.

6
How To Get Well

Self-treatment is a tricky business and should not be entered into without intelligent investigation. Nothing in this book is meant as a cure for any disease and/or ailment; just because a source is mentioned, it does not mean that it is recommended. Before you begin *any* course of therapy consult your physician and discuss it thoroughly with him or her. Research is your best tool; look into everything. There is a new wave of health practitioners who are not necessarily medically trained doctors. Often members of the medical field lack knowledge when it comes to nutrition. Nutritional specialists may have new and interesting perspectives on illness.

BOOKS

The Complete Book of Natural Medicines by David Carroll. Summit Books, 1230 Avenue of the Americas, New York, NY 10020; $17.95. This volume anthologizes all the tried and true remedies that have endured through the ages. Calling on cures from other cultures as well as our own, this book deals with natural healing methods, acupressure, herbal medicine, homeopathy, massage, and vitamin and nutritional therapy.

Dr. Mandell's 5-Day Allergy Relief System by Dr. Marshall Mandell and Lynne Waller Scanlon. Pocket Books, 1230 Avenue of the Americas, New York, NY, 10020; 1979; $2.95. Unsuspected allergies may be the cause for many health problems. This book offers dietary, environmental, and nutritional programs to identify and deal with any allergic conditions.

Dr. Wright's Book of Nutritional Therapy by Jonathan V. Wright. Rodale Press, Emmaus, PA; $18.95. Case history descriptions of a wide variety of medical afflictions by *Prevention* magazine's medical columnist. Book's subtitle is *Real-Life Lessons in Medicine without Drugs.*

Do-It-Yourself Medical Testing by Cathey Pinckney and Edward R. Pinckney. Facts on File, 460 Park Ave S, New York, NY 10016; $14.95. More than 160 different medical tests that you can perform on yourself at home.

The Encyclopedia of Common Diseases by *Prevention* magazine staff. Rodale Press, Emmaus, PA; $19.95. Up-to-date information on most any disease you're likely to encounter.

Foods for Health and Healing by Yogi Bhajan. Spiritual Community Publications; $6.95. Remedies and recipes outlining how to use food to balance the organism.

The Healing Handbook by Jade Easter. Orenda/ Unity Press; $8.95. A reference book focusing on "the empty-handed method" of healing, that is: the art of healing exclusive of tools, relying rather on the healer's knowledge of life force, body manipulation, and natural substance. More than 40 types of healing techniques are dealt with.

The Practical Encyclopedia of Natural Healing by Mark Bricklin. Rodale Press, Emmaus, PA 18049 1976; $21.95. Mark Bricklin, executive editor of *Prevention* magazine, runs through an alphabetical list of over 140 natural healing techniques and their application.

The *Prevention* Guide to Surgery and Its Alternatives by the editors of *Prevention* magazine. Rodale Press, Emmaus, PA 18049; $8.95. Gives you a chance to avoid unnecessary surgery, or, at worst, helps you to recover after required surgery.

Rodale's Encyclopedia of Natural Home Remedies by Mark Bricklin. Rodale Press, Emmaus, PA 18049, 1982; $19.95. Case histories of over 800 people and the natural home remedies they used to cure themselves of everything from foot odor to dysentery.

You Can Do Something About Common Ailments by Siri Khalsa. Nutrition News Publishing, PO Box J, Pomona, CA 91769; $3.00. Using nutritional supplements to help ward off and cure many of today's most common disorders.

SOCIETIES AND ORGANIZATIONS

Health Writers, Inc., 1127 University Ave, Madison, WI 53715. A consumer-oriented organization "helping health consumers help themselves." They publish the *Health Newsletter* which is distributed free in Wisconsin area hospitals and clinics, but can be obtained by mail. Subscription and membership is $15 per year and includes the *Health Writers Cookbook*.

People's Medical Society, 33 E Minor St, Emmaus, PA 18049. A project of the Rodale Soil and Health Society, the People's Medical Society has been established as a national citizens' group that promotes preventative health practices while it fights the exorbitant cost of medical care. Annual, tax-deductible dues are $20 and include a newsletter.

MAGAZINES, PERIODICALS, JOURNALS

American Health: Fitness of Body and Mind, Published by American Health Partners, 80 Fifth Ave, Suite 302, New York, NY 10011. Bimonthly; subscription rate for 6 issues is $12. Not strictly of a vegetarian bent, this well-produced magazine offers a variety of clearly presented, helpful information.

Current Nutrition and Therapeutics, PO Box 5277, Berkeley, CA 94705. Bimonthly journal. Sample issue upon request with a stamped, self-addressed envelope.

Harvard Medical School Health Letter, PO Box 2436, Boulder, CO 80321. A one-year subscription is $15.

Health and Diet Times, Published by Human Research Laboratories, Inc, 202 W 14 St, New York, NY 10011. Sold in the New York, New Jersey, Connecticut area, this 75-cent newspaper is packed with good information. Often focuses on a single topic per issue. Plentiful local advertising, including medical practitioners, diet and beauty care, health centers, holistic centers, health foods and supplies, supplements, physical fitness, restaurants, more.

Kup's Komments, Written and published by Dr. Roy Kupsinel of the Lost Horizon Health Awareness Center, Shangri-la Lane, PO Box 550, Oviedo, FL 32765. Free to Center patients, this holistic newsletter is packed with information. It's $12.00 for a year's subscription (4 issues), but an introductory issue willl be sent upon request with a stamped, self-addressed envelope.

Metabolic Update, by Jeffrey Bland, 15615 Bellevue Redmond Rd, Suite E, Bellevue, WA 98008. A 12-month subscription is $200.00 for this 90-minute audio cassette journal detailing the latest trends in nutritional healing. For the health professional.

Natural Health World and the Naturopath, 1920 North Kilpatrick, Portland, OR 97217. Yearly subscription rate is $7.50. Small informative newspaper, with items of interest from the National College of Naturopathic Medicine.

Prevention Magazine, 33 E Minor St, Emmaus, PA 18049. Monthly magazine, subscription rate is $11.97. A "cure-yourself" attitude best describes this publication. It contains personal stories of people conquering wide varieties of illness and affliction through unconventional means.

THE MAGAZINE FOR BETTER HEALTH

Vitamin E, When It's Sink or Swim... 132
Use This Easy Food Guide... 20
Break the Stranglehold of Asthma... 92

CONSUMER MEDICAL LIBRARIES

Usually established with the help of grant aid, these centers help the public in their quest for medical knowledge. With the aid of your local librarian, there will be no excuse for not knowing what your doctor's saying.

Center for Medical Consumers, 237 Thompson St, New York, NY 10012; (212) 674-7105. This center attracts some 3000 visitors annually, but it doesn't compare to the thousands who call in to help themselves to the recorded advice offered on 140 different subjects. The center's newsletter "Health Facts" is available for $18 per year (12 issues).

Consumer Health Information Center, 680 E 600 South, Salt Lake City, UT 84102; (801) 364-9318. CHIC, as it is called, answers questions, offers resources, and will perform routine screenings (blood pressure, etc.). They will respond to questions over the phone, but only for those unable (because of medical reasons) to come in themselves.

Health Education Center, 200 Ross St, Pittsburgh, PA 15219; (412) 392-3160. A library that also offers classes and workshops, and a telephone information service for medical and legal problems (412-281-4664). The center has a tape library on over 660 different subjects, and they have established health substations in three local branches of the Carnegie Library, where registered nurses will answer questions and provide health counseling one day per week.

Health Library, Kaiser-Permanente Medical Center, 280 W MacArthur Blvd, 12th Floor, Oakland, CA 94611; (415) 428-6569. Classes, plus library, film privileges, and free pamphlets.

Planetree Health Resource Center, 2040 Webster St, San Francisco, CA 94115; (415) 346-4636. In addition to a library, there is a health care reference service, a bookstore, classes, and a research service for people unable to visit the center.

ALTERNATE PHYSICIAN REFERRALS

American Biologics, 111 Ellis St, San Francisco, CA 94102. Worldwide access to alternate treatment doctors.

American Chiropractic Association, 2200 Grand Ave, Des Moines, IA 50312. A professional organization that will make referrals to association members in your area. Publishes the *Journal of Chiropractic,* as well as *Healthways* magazine.

American Holistic Medical Association, 6932 Little River Turnpike, Annandale, VA 22003. This organization, which is dedicated to educating and expanding the horizons of health professionals, will make referrals to holistic doctors in your area.

American Holistic Nurses Association, PO Box 116, Telluride, CO 81435.

International Academy of Biological Medicine, PO Box 31313, Phoenix, AZ 85046. This organization shares the responsibility of educating both the public and its professional members on all types of healing. This includes nutritional, preventive, naturopathic, orthomolecular, holistic, chiropractic and osteopathic, and spiritual counseling. Will make referrals through a published list of its membership.

National Health Federation, 212 W Foothill Blvd, Box 688, Monrovia, CA 91016. This group advocates health freedom—the right of people to choose their own means of health care, services, and products as long as it does not infringe on the rights of others. They are against health care monopolies and large pharmaceutical concerns, and advocate a clean, safe environment for all. They publish the journal *Health Freedom News.* Membership in the federation is $15.00 annually and includes a subscription. There are 34 local chapters nationally.

Spears Chiropractic Hospital, 927 Jersey St, Denver, CO 80220. World's largest chiropractic hospital. Uses nutritional therapy.

HOMEOPATHY

A systematic form of medicine developed by Dr. Samuel Hahneman in the early nineteenth century in Germany. Homeopathy treats the mental, emotional, and physical symptoms as a unit rather than as disassociated parts. Homeopathic remedies involve healing the system itself, rather than attempting to rid the body of some disorder or bacteria. Homeopathy does not treat symptoms. These are recognized as signals of the organism attempting to recreate a balance or homeostasis—the cure itself. Homeopathic medicine tries to help the body by stimulating the immune system, thereby helping the body's capacity to fight and rid itself of disease. Homeopathic cures are not toxic, and they have no side effects. In homeopathy "a remedy can cure a disease if it produces in a healthy individual symptoms similar to those of the disease." More than 600 homeopathic remedies are in use.

International Foundation for Homeopathy, 1141 NW Market St, Seattle, WA 98107. Dedicated to educating, developing, researching and maintain-

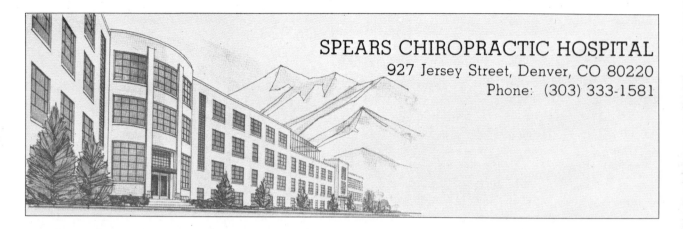

 SPEARS CHIROPRACTIC HOSPITAL
927 Jersey Street, Denver, CO 80220
Phone: (303) 333-1581

ing homeopathy. Annual membership is $25.00 and includes the *IFH Newsletter*.

National Center for Homeopathy, 1500 Massachusetts Ave NW, Suite 41, Washington, D.C. 20005. Directory of homeopathic practitioners ($3.00), subscription to *Homeopathy Today* ($12.00), homeopathic home remedy kit ($35.00), *Homeopathic Medicine at Home* ($10.95). Annual membership includes subscription to *Homeopathy Today* ($25.00).

HOMEOPATHIC SUPPLY HOUSES

CALIFORNIA

Homeopathic Educational Services, 2124 Kittredge St, Berkeley, CA 94704.

Mylans Homeopathic Pharmacy, 222 O'Farrell St, San Francisco, CA 94102.

Norton & Converse, 621 W Pico Blvd, Los Angeles, CA 90015.

Santa Monica Drug, 1513 Fourth St, Santa Monica, CA 90401.

Standard Homeopathic Company, 204 W 131 St, Los Angeles, CA 90061 or PO Box 61067, Los Angeles 90061.

ILLINOIS

Ehrhard and Karl, Inc., 17 North Wabash Ave, Chicago, IL 60602.

MISSOURI

Luyties Pharmaceutical Company, 4200 Laclede Ave, St. Louis, MO 63108.

NEW JERSEY

Humphries Medicine Company, 63 Meadow Rd, Rutherford, NJ 07071.

NEW YORK

Freeda Pharmacy, 36 E 41 St, New York, NY 10017.

United States Homeopathic Research, c/o Homeopathic Center, 107 E 38 St, New York, NY 10016.

PENNSYLVANIA

Boericke and Tafel, 1011 Arch St, Philadelphia, PA 19107.

Borneman and Sons, 1208 Amosland Rd, Norwood, PA 19074.

VIRGINIA

Annandale Apothecary, 7023 Little River Turnpike, Annandale, VA 22003.

CANADA

D.L. Thompson Homeopathic Supplies, 844 Yonge St, Toronto, Ontario, Canada.

ENGLAND

Nelson's Pharmacy, 73 Duke St, Grosvenor Square, London W1, England.

BACH FLOWER REMEDIES

Dr. Edward Bach's theory, formulated during the 1930's, claims that a variety of 38 flowering trees, plants, and special waters are instrumental in treating certain negative states of mind such as uncertainty, impatience, and fear. Practitioners attempt to ascertain state of mind, mood, and personality type then treat with the appropriate flower remedy.

Ellon Company, PO Box 320, Woodmere, NY 11598. National and Canadian distributor for the Bach Centre of England.

HERBS

Herbs have value for both nutritional and medicinal purposes. Herbs were our first medicines. In *Back to Eden,* a book that is a cornerstone in herbology, author Jethro Kloss claims as much as 80% of the world population relies on herbalists for their medical treatment, and it is only in modern times that it has shrunk to this level. Garlic, golden seal, and rose hips are still staples in many household medicine kits. Beyond your grandmother, an experienced herbal practitioner is essential for the uninitiated.

It is important to buy your herbs fresh whenever possible. If you cannot get them fresh, then at the very least, buy them from a reputable dealer. Herbs may be adulterated, or sometimes they are so old they have lost their potency.

HERBAL CRYSTALLIZATION ANALYSIS

A saliva test that reveals the herbs the body may be lacking. Many holistic healers administer this test. A sample of saliva is placed on a slide then coated with copper chloride. The slide is analyzed in a lab, where technicians match chemical deficiencies to ascertain a person's primary and secondary herbal needs.

Herbal Tracers, Ltd, PO Box 343, Woodmere, NY 11598. This laboratory will supply a list of herbal crystallization analysis practitioners.

HERBAL BOOKS

Back to Eden by Jethro Kloss. Lancer Books, NY. The late Jethro Kloss's classic guide to natural healing with traditional herbal medicine. Simple, inexpensive, homemade treatments for hundreds of ailments. The most important book in the field.

Nature's Medicines by Richard Lucas. Award Book, NY. The folklore surrounding some of the better-known herbs such as ginseng, garlic, gotu kola, fo-ti-tieng, lemon, papaya, licorice, and many more, and their application and acceptance in the modern world.

Using Plants for Healing by Nelson Coon. Rodale Press, Emmaus, PA. A guide to more than 250 medicinal plants.

HERBAL NEWSLETTERS

Dr. Christopher's Natural Healing Newsletter, PO Box 412, Springville, UT 84663. Suscription rate, $25.00 for 12 issues. Topics include growing herbs successfully, advice from the teachings of Dr. Christopher (before his death one of the foremost herbologists and teachers in the coun-

try), expert opinions, updates on the latest studies, and readers' questions and answers.

Potpourri from Herbal Acres, Pine Row Publications, Box 428, Washington Crossing, PA 18977. One-year subscription, $12.00. A quarterly newsletter with gardening tips, recipes, and crafts. "Herb Blurbs" provides a network for herbal enthusiasts: ask questions, get answers, buy–sell, pen pals.

HERBAL OUTLETS

ARIZONA

The Herb Hut, 101 West Grant, Tucson, AZ 85705. Services, products, classes. Herbology, nutrition, oral chelation therapy (a means to remove mineral deposits, especially calcium, from circulatory system), weight loss. Nutritional testing.

CALIFORNIA

The Herb Shop, 415 North Highway 1, Solana Beach, CA. Live plants, dried herbs (bulk available), books.

Herb Trade Association, PO Box 409, Santa Cruz, CA 95016.

House of Quality Herbs, PO Box 14, Woodland Hills, CA 91365.

Lhasa Karnak Herb Co. (two locations), 2513 Telegraph Avenue, Berkeley, CA; and 1938 Shattuck Avenue, Berkeley, CA. More than 500 herbs and spices in stock, including Chinese, Korean, and American ginseng. Lhasa Karnak carries herbs in capsules, herbal extracts, herbal formulations, tea blends, oils, smoking mixtures, herbal baths, toiletries, and books.

Medicine Wheel, PO Box 1121, Idyllwild, CA 92349.

Nature's Herb Company, 281 Ellis St, San Francisco, CA 94102.

CONNECITCUT

Heartrest Herb and Spice Company, PO Box 65, Darien, CT 06820. A mail-order business that stocks over 400 different herbs, spices, and essential oils. Heartrest specializes in rare bulk botanicals and herbal formulas. Their catalog is free.

ILLINOIS

Herbs for All Seasons, 3056 North Lincoln Ave, Chicago, IL. Fresh herbs year round.

INDIANA

Indiana Botanic Garden, PO Box 5, Hammond, IN 46325. Catalog, $1.00.

MICHIGAN

Harvest Health, 1946 Eastern Ave, SE, Grand Rapids, MI 49507. More than 275 herbs in stock. Available in bulk or in 4-, 8-, and 16-oz. packages. Their catalog is free.

NEW HAMPSHIRE

Attar Herbs & Spices, Playground Rd, New Ipswich, NH. Catalog, $1.00.

NEW JERSEY

Meer Corporation, 9500 Railroad Ave, North Bergen, NJ 07047.

NEW YORK

Aphrodisia, 28 Carmine St, New York, NY 10014.

Arach Herbal Research, 39 Bowery, Box 111, New York, NY 10002. Chinese herbs.

Bio-Botanica, 2 Willow Park Center, Farmingdale, NY 11735.

Caswell–Massey, 111 Eighth Ave, Room 723, New York, NY 10011. Catalog, $1.00.

Natural Herbal Extracts, George Benner, Ltd., 871 Montauk Highway, Oakdale, NY 11769. Catalog, 50 cents. Active herbal ingredients preserved in alcohol.

OHIO

No Common Scents, Kings Yard, 220 Xenia Ave, Yellow Springs, OH 45387. Herbs, spices, botanicals.

OREGON

Nature's Pantry, PO Box 349, Oregon City, OR 97045.

PENNSYLVANIA

Druid Herbs, PO Box 41, Philadelphia, PA 19105. Roots, barks, berries, seeds, leaves, oils, books.

Fund-raising arm of the International Druid Society.

The Herb Man, James W. Berry, RD 1, Box 297, Shippensburg, PA 17257. Hand-picked herbs, teas, spices, seeds, and botanicals.

Penn Herb Company, 603 North 2nd St, Philadelphia, PA 19123. Catalog, $1.00

TEXAS

Hilltop Herb Farm, Box 866, Cleveland, TX 77327.

UTAH

The Herb Shop, PO Box 352, Provo, UT 84601. This is Dr. John Christopher's retail outlet (see Chapter 3).

VIRGINIA

Tom Thumb Workshops, PO Box 10258, Alexandria, VA 22310. Catalog, $1.00.

CANADA

For Your Health, Box 307, Willowdale, Ontario, Canada. Catalog, $1.00

CANCER

What causes cancer?

Based on the reserach of Dr. Richard Doll, British epidemiologist:

Diet	35%
Cigarette smoking	30%
Occupation exposure	4%
Pollution	2%

It is much, much easier to prevent cancer than to cure it!

To fight cancer: (1) Reduce the fat content of your diet while increasing the fiber content. (2) Improve your life style by making it healthier. Stop smoking, avoid excessive exposure to the sun, and maintain good personal hygiene. (3) Take charge of your emotions, eliminate avoidable stress. In Fred Rohé's book, *Metabolic Ecology: A Way to Win the Cancer War* (see book list, below), he lists eight early warning signs of cancer. "Killer diseases seldom arrive suddenly to someone who never showed any signs of ill health. It is usually a downward evolving spiral from the simple to the more complex." The signs are: gas on the stomach or bowel, sudden weakness of the eyes, tired feeling most of the time, muscle weakness and cramps (first in the back, later in the chest), extreme mental depression, sudden change in hair texture and color, development of various hernias (only in slow-growing tumors), confusion (difficulty in making even simple decisions).

BOOKS

The Macrobiotic Approach to Cancer by Michio Kushi and the East–West Foundation. Avery Publishing Group, 1981; $6.95. The first book to actually point the finger at diet and nutrition and their relation to cancer and other degenerative disease.

Metabolic Ecology: A Way to Win The Cancer War by Fred Rohé. Wedgestone Press, PO Box 175, Winfield, Kansas 67156; $5.95 plus $1.00 handling cost. How to detect cancer early, how to surround it, how to win. (see description of early warning signs, above).

The Miracle of Living Foods by Dr. Kristine Nolfi. New Medical Books, 218 Randoph Ave, Elins, WV 26214; $5.95. Dr. Nolfi, who claims to have cured herself of breast cancer, offers insight into what she discovered: that certain foods can cause cancer and excluding them from the diet can only help your health.

Recalled by Life: The Story of My Recovery from Cancer by Anthony J. Satillaro and Tom Monte. Houghton-Mifflin, New York, NY, 1982; $12.95. An eminent Philadelphia doctor, dying from cancer, confronts and, to his surprise, conquers his disease through a macrobiotic diet. Satillaro has received a lot of criticism from the medical community for even suggesting that diet could *cure* cancer, yet his voyage back from death could be a learning and revitalizing experience for the open-minded.

Vitamin C Against Cancer by H.L. Newbold, M.D. Stein and Day Publishers, New York, NY, 1979; $10.95. Dr. Newbold, one of the foremost medical nutritionists, describes his experience in treating cancer with vitamin C. Drawing on the research of Linus Pauling, Ewan Cameron, Allan Campbell, and William Saccoman, Newbold makes a case for vitamin C's effectiveness. He also interviews doctors with a more conservative point of view. In understandable language Newbold discusses the importance of diet and the necessity for added vitamins and minerals in the everyday regimen.

SOCIETIES

Cancer Control Society, 2043 North Berendo, Los Angeles, CA 90027. Promotes the knowledge, prevention, and cure of cancer and other nutritionally related diseases, and reports on nutritional and metabolic research. They publish the *Cancer Control Journal* and are a major source of information on alternate therapies and testing that show promise but are not sanctioned by the medical establishment. A one-year membership is $15.00 and includes journal subscription.

People Against Cancer, RFD #1, Box 415, Mashpee, MA 02649. International directory to alternate therapy. Suggested donation for their 23-page directory is $10.00.

Project Cure, 2020 K Street NW, Suite 350, Washington, D.C. 20070. Five years ago Chairman Robert DeBragga was given what he terms a "death sentence"—36 weeks to live. He had a tumor in his lung and was given little information or choice of treatment. Still alive, DeBragga is now asking the question, Why? Not why did he get cancer, but why were his choices of fighting the disease so limited? (He used nutritional and trace mineral therapy in his battle.) Project Cure is a watchdog committee, trying to urge the

National Cancer Institute (NCI), the American Cancer Society (ACS) and the American Medical Association (AMA) to find new methods to fight the disease that now may strike one of every three Americans during their lifetime. Project Cure asks for donations so that they can distribute petitions "to force the investigation [into the scandal of cancer research], to continue their lobbying efforts in Washington, and to help pay the cost of Project Cure's TV and radio public awareness campaign."

HOSPITALS AND TREATMENT CENTERS

American Biologics Mexico, 111 Ellis St, San Francisco, CA 94102. In-hospital treatment of cancer and degenerative disease by every alternate method, including laetrile. Treatment costs run $2800 per week, but most U.S. health plans will cover the costs.

AMERICAN BIOLOGICS — MEXICO, S.A.
Research Hospital and Medical Center
Tijuana, B.C., Mexico

American International Hospital, Shiloh Blvd and Emmaus Ave, Zion, IL 60099. The clinic is located at 1911 27 St, Zion, IL 60099. Stresses the importance of personal responsibility for health. Nutritional emphasis in treatment of cancer and degenerative disease.

DIRECTORY OF ALTERNATIVE THERAPIES AND DIAGNOSTIC TESTS FOR CANCER

The following list is furnished by the Cancer Control Society (see above). Note that the society makes this statement, "Most non-toxic independent cancer therapies are in limited supply. Persons seeking unorthodox and orthodox help for cancer are urged to investigate carefully the doctor, the product and the price before deciding on a course of action. Please remember that C.C.S. does not recommend or endorse in this instance, nor does it assume any responsibility.

"Frequently a combination of more than one non-toxic therapy renders a more complete approach for a given individual and thus offers a greater protection and range of benefits."

Tours of The Mexican Cancer Clincs can be arranged for public and private viewings. Contact: 777 South Main St, Ste 57-335, Orange, CA 92668.

LAETRILE THERAPY (also known as Vitamin B$_{17}$ or Amygdalin)

ARIZONA

Robert Wickman, D.O., 1525 North Granite Reef, Scottsdale, AZ 85257

CALIFORNIA

Mario Soto, M.D., PO Box 5129, San Ysidro, CA 92073

MARYLAND

Ahmad Shamim, M.D., 200 Fort Meade Rd, Laurel, MD 20707

NEVADA

Health Medical Center, 1245 Las Vegas Boulevard South, Las Vegas, NV 89104

PENNSYLVANIA

Sidney Auerbach, M.D., Clymer Rd, R.D. #3, Quakertown, PA 18951

DISTRICT OF COLUMBIA

Hellfried Sartori, M.D., 4501 Connecticut NW, Ste 306, Washington, D.C. 20008

GERMANY

Hans Nieper, M.D., 21 Sedanstrasse, 300 Hanover, Germany

HOLLAND

Hans Moolenburgh, M.D., Oranjeplein 11, Haarlem, Holland

MEXICO

Clinica Cydel S.A., Harold Manner, director, Apartado 3437, Tijuana, B.C., Mexico. In U.S. contact: PO Box 4290, San Ysidro, CA 92073.

Ernesto Contreras, M.D., Centro Medico Del Mar, Paseo de Tijuana 1-A, Playas de Tijuana, Mexico. In U.S. contact: PO Box 1561, Chula Vista, CA 92012.

PHILIPPINES

Manuel Navarro, M.D., 3553 Sining Morningside Terrace, Santa Mesa, Manila 2806, Philippines 2070-21

SCOTLAND

Jan de Vries, Ph.N.D., Auchenkyle Southwoods, Monkton, Ayrshire, Scotland, Troon 311414 (0292)

METABOLIC THERAPY

ALABAMA

Ray Evers, M.D., Evers Health Center, PO Box 587, Cottonwood, AL 36320

ARIZONA

Arthur Davis, Jr., M.D., Carefree Health Services, 37417 Tom Darlington Dr, Carefree, AZ 85377

CALIFORNIA

William Bryce, M.D., Plaza Del Logo, 17220 Newhope St, #9, Fountain Valley, CA 92708

Bruce Halstead, M.D., 1330 Cooley Dr, Colton, CA 92324

CONNECTICUT

Joseph Kaplowe, M.D., 131 Dwight St, New Haven, CT 06511

DISTRICT OF COLUMBIA

Howard Lutz, M.D., 2139 Wisconsin Ave NW, Ste 400, Washington, D.C. 20007

FLORIDA

Daniel Clark, M.D., 800 South Nova, Ste H, Ormond Beach, FL 32074

Maurice Kaye, D.O., 735 49 St North, St. Petersburg, FL 33710

Lauderdale Medical Center, 1421 East Oakland Park Blvd, Fort Lauderdale, FL 33334

W.W. Mittelstadt, D.O., 1736 East Commercial Blvd, Fort Lauderdale, FL 33334

GEORGIA

William Douglas, M.D., 41 Perimeter Way NW, Ste. 501D, Atlanta, GA 30339

MARYLAND

Paul Beals, M.D., 14300 Gallant Fox Lane, Ste. 114, Bowie, MD 20715

MASSACHUSETTS

William Girourd, D.C., 27 Salem St, Woburn, MA 01801

NEVADA

W. Douglas Brodie, M.D. 848 Tanager, Incline Village, NV 89450

NEW JERSEY

Antonio Chan, M.D., 670 Sanford Ave, Newark, NJ 07106

John Pung, M.D., 607 West St. George Ave, Linden, NJ 07036

NEW YORK

Harold Markus, M.D., 161 Avenue of the Americas, 14th Floor, New York, NY 10014

Michael Schachter, M.D., Mountainview Medical Association, Mountainview Ave, Nyack, NY 10960

NORTH DAKOTA

Brian Briggs, M.D., 718 6th St SW, Minot, ND 58701

OHIO

John Baron, D.O., 3103 Euclid Ave, Cleveland, OH 44115

David Goldberg, D.O., 4444 North Main St, Dayton, OH 45405

Jack Slingluff, D.O., 5850 Fulton Rd NW, Canton, OH 44718

OKLAHOMA

Bob Gibson, M.D., 215 North 3rd St, Ponca City, OK 74601

OREGON

Brian MacCoy, N.D., 8904 North Ivanhoe, Portland, OR 97203

Joel Wallach, N.D. DVM, 1235 South Hemlock, Cannon Beach, OR 97110

PENNSYLVANIA

Harold Buttram, M.D., R.D. No. 3 Clymer Rd, Quakertown, PA 18951

P. Jayalakshmi, M.D., 6366 Sherwood Rd, Philadelphia, PA 19151

Donald Mantel, M.D., Preventive Medicine and Nutrition, R.D. 1, Box 286, Evans City, PA 16033

SOUTH CAROLINA

Raymond Hillyard, M.D., Rte. 2, Rolling Green Circle Dr, Greenville, SC 29607

TEXAS

Dan Dotson, M.D., 805 Cherry, Graham, TX 76046

Owen Robins, M.D., 6565 De Moss, Ste 202, Houston, TX 77074

VIRGINIA

Thomas Roberts, M.D., 31 West Loudoun St, Leesburg, VA 22075

CANADA

R. Glen Green, M.D., 103–1311 Central Ave, Prince Albert, Saskatchewan, Canada S6V 4W2

ENGLAND

Leon K. Chaitow, D.O., 49 ST. Lawrence Ave, Worthing, Sussex BN1 47JJ England

JAPAN

Seiichi Kawachi, M.D., 7-3-8 Ginza Chuoku, Tokyo, 104 Japan

PUERTO RICO

Norman Gonzalez Chacon, N.D., PO Box 4654, Carolina, Puerto Rico 00630

WHERE TO BUY LAETRILE (B$_{17}$)

DMSO, hydrazine sulfate, orotates, digestive enzymes (pancreatic and bromalin), Vitamin B$_{15}$, etc.

ARIZONA

Laetrile Corp, 4419 North Scottsdale Road, #210, Scottsdale, AZ 85251

CALIFORNIA

American Biologics, 111 Ellis St, Ste 3000, San Francisco, CA 94102

Great Expectations, PO Box 534, Orange, CA 92666

Kem, S.A. Laboratories, PO Box 1561, Chula Vista, CA 92012

Proviso de Mexico, 223 Via de San Ysidro, Ste 7, San Ysidro, CA 92073

Professional Distributors, 115 South H St, Lompoc, CA 93436

Vita Chem International, 241 Hazel Ave, Redwood City, CA 94061

INDIANA

L & S Pharma Specialties, Attn. Frank Spolnick, PO Box 724, Hammond, IN 46320

MARYLAND

Henderson's Pharmacy, 7401 Harford Rd, Baltimore, MD 21234

MINNESOTA

Donna Schuster, 1724 Hiawatha Court NE, Rochester, MN 55901

TENNESSEE

Millet, Pit & Seed Company, R. 1, Norton Creek Rd, Gatlinburg, TN 37738

TEXAS

Laetrile Information Center and Legal Service, 3701 Fairmont, Dallas, TX 75219

GERMANY

Chem. Lab. Heinrich Kadan, Porgesring 50, 2000 Hamburg 74, Germany

CPW Rahlstedt GMBH (Ltd), PO Box 73 05 27, D-2000 Hamburg 73, Germany

MEXICO

Amygdalin Center, PO Box 1510, Tijuana, B.C., Mexico

CANCER TESTS

Immuno-diagnostic urine and blood for those who want to have a "double check" through comparative testing:

Robertson Medical Center, 221 North Robertson Blvd, Beverly Hills, CA 90211

Institute of Regeneration, PO Box 1822, Ensenada, B.C., Mexico

Manuel Navarro, M.D., 3553 Sining Morningside Terrace, Santa Mesa, Manila 2806, Philippines

LAETRILE RESEARCH

Dean Burk, Ph.D, Dean Burk Foundation, 4719 44 St, Washington, D.C. 20016

Ernst T. Krebs, Jr., D.Sc., John Beard Memorial Foundation, PO Box 685, San Francisco, CA 94101

Harold Manner, Ph.D., RE: Doctor information, Professor at Loyola University, Department of Biology, and President of the Metabolic Research Foundation, 518 Zenith Dr, Glenview, IL 60025

Andrew McNaughton, McNaughton Foundation, PO Box B 17, San Ysidro, CA 92073

CELLULAR THERAPY

MEXICO

Institute of Regeneration, PO Box 1822, Ensenada, B.C., Mexico

Wolfram Kuhnau, M.D., American Biologics Hospital Mexico, Tijuana, Mexico/ 111 Ellis St, Ste 300, San Francisco, CA 94102

Anton Schenk, M.D., Tapachula No. 7, Tijuana, B.C., Mexico

WEST GERMANY

Four Seasons, Clause Martin, M.D. (Live Cell Therapy), PO Box 244, Farberweg 3, D-8183 Rottach-Egern, West Germany

JAMAICA

Dietmar Schildwaechter, M.D., Montego Bay, Jamaica, West Indies. In U.S. contact: PO Box 748, Pompano Beach, FL 33061.

NUTRITIONAL PROGRAMS

Particularly in support of laetrile patients:

ARIZONA

Michael Cessna, D.C., 504 North 13 St, Rogers, AZ 72756

CALIFORNIA

Albert La Rusche, D.C., 131 West El Portal, San Clemente, CA 92672

James Privitera, M.D., 105 North Grandview, Covina, CA 91723

ILLINOIS

Edward Karp, D.N., 1969 John's Dr, Glenview, IL 60025

Jean Kirk, D.C., Box 53, Perry, IL 62362

IOWA

Gary Rosenberger, D.C., 1007 Morningside Ave, Sioux City, IA 51106

MISSOURI

McDonagh Medical Center, 2800 A Kendallwood Parkway, Kansas City, MO 64119

NEBRASKA

Ray Beach, D.C., 300 W 23 St, Freemont, NE 68025

NEW JERSEY

James H. Marsillo, D.C., 120 Prospect St, South Orange, NJ 07079

NEW YORK

Donald Geoghean, D.C., Elizabeth Rd, Yorktown Heights, NY 10598

OREGON

John Hurd, D.C., 1437 Esplanade, Klamath Falls, OR 97601

TEXAS

Ruth Yale Long, Ph.D., 3647 Glen Haven, Houston, TX 77025

The International Health Institute, William D. Kelley, D.D.S., PO Box 402607, Dallas, TX 75240

AUSTRALIA

Dorothea Snook, N.D., Radient Health Clinic, 17 Iverness Crescent, Menora 6050, West Australia

GERSON THERAPY

Gerson Institute, PO Box 430, Bonita, CA 92002

Totality House (Gerson diet of 13 vegetable and liver juices daily), 17 4th Ave, Chula Vista, CA 92010

HOXSEY THERAPY (Herbal)

Considered to be compatible with laetrile:

Bio-Medical Center, PO Box 727, 615 General Ferreira (Colonia Juarez), Tijuana, B.C., Mexico

IMMUNOLOGY (B.C.G. Vaccines and Nutrition)

Richard Huemer, M.D., 32144 Agoura Road, Ste 116, Westlake Village, CA 91361

Virginia Livingston, M.D., 3232 Duke St, San Diego, CA 91361

Steenblock Medical Clinic, 22821 Lake Forest Dr, Ste 114, El Toro, CA 92630

Lawrence Burton, Ph.D., Immunology Researching Center, PO Box F 2689, Freeport, Grand Bahamas Island

WHEAT GRASS THERAPY

Health Institute of San Diego, 6970 Central Ave, Lemon Grove, CA 92045

Hippocrates Health Institute, 25 Exeter St, Boston, MA 02116

THERMO THERAPY

Donald Cole, M.D., 8 South Tyson Ave, Floral Park, NY 11001

OTHER THERAPIES

Linus Pauling Institute, 440 Page Mill Rd, Palo Alto, CA 94306

Kendall Medical Arthritis Clinic, 1319 North Doheny Dr, Los Angeles, CA 90069 (clinic is in Tijuana, Mexico)

Dr. med. Josef Issels, Ringberg Strasse 36, 8183 Rottach-Egern, West Germany

ROUMANIAN GEROVITAL H3 & PLACENTA

(see Chapter 9: Vegetarianism and the Elderly):

Rejuvecenter, PO Box 3780, Beverly Hills, CA 90212 (clinic is in Tijuana)

DMSO (Dimethyl sulfoxide)

Sierra Clinics Mexico, (Tumorex), PO Box 4602, San Ysidro, CA 92073

CANCER LITERATURE

Cancer Book House, 2043 North Berendo St, Los Angeles, CA 90027

International Health Council, Walter Ermer, D.D., 204 Beeler Dr, Berea, OH 44017

HOSPICES

National Hospice Organization, 1901 North Fort Myer Dr, Ste 402, Arlington, VA 22209. Hospice care is a specialized health care program emphasizing the management of pain and other symptoms associated with terminal illness while providing care for the family as well as the patient. The aim of the hospice is to improve the quality of life remaining for dying patients and to provide support for the family through their bereavement. Hospice care is provided by physicians, nurses, social workers, therapists, clergy, and specially trained volunteers, and is given in the home whenever possible with inpatient care provided when necessary. Annual membership is $25.00. There is a newsletter and a directory of hospice programs, listed by state and city ($15 to members; $30 to nonmembers).

7

Spas, Health Farms, Travel

The best thing about spas is that they give you the opportunity to wind down and relax. The next best thing is that they can provide a great learning experience. Many spas pride themselves on their ability to rekindle your interest in good health, or spark new interest by helping you to be as healthy and vibrant as possible. Exercise, diet regimens, and classes are designed so you can go home and practice what you lived at their facility.

Some of the spas listed here have specific programs to aid people suffering from degenerative diseases, such as heart problems, cancer, and diabetes.

Virtually every program listed will give you a healthy, revitalizing, rejuvenating experience. Most are vegetarian or will accommodate a vegetarian or vegan diet.

SPAS AND RESORTS

AABA Health Hotel Klosters, PO BOX CH-7250 Klosters, Switzerland; tel: 083/4 12 13. A five-star vegetarian alpine retreat. Three restaurants serve gourmet vegetarian specialties from all over the world, including the bi'r Brugga, a restaurant specializing in cheese-based dishes like fondue and raclette. Fully equipped with Turkish bath, Kneipp bath, and over 30 different types of herbal and mineral baths. Sport and leisure programs, massage, hiking, skiing, karate, yoga.

All Life Sanctuary, PO Box 77, Woodstock Valley, CT 06282; (203) 974-2440. Part of Viktoras Kulvinskas' Survival Foundation, members invite you into their home, a large farmhouse, where they share their regimen and knowledge of their carefully researched living foods program. Stay includes consultation with Viktoras. Prices begin at $45 per day. A week-long stay can range from $195 to $275 for a private room.

Ashkelon Vegetarian Center, PO Box 341, Ashkelon, Israel 78102; tel: 051-35111/35114/35115. Located on the Mediterranean, this vegetarian hotel features organic food, spring water, medical supervision, physical therapy, lectures, and a good selection of videotapes on vegetarian cooking, vegetarian child rearing, and holistic health. Dedicated to the prevention of disease through natural healing and supervised nutrition. Travel tours can be arranged of Jerusalem, and all of Israel and Egypt.

The Ashram, PO Box 8, Calabasas, CA 91302; (213) 888-0232. A very rigorous regimen, both physically and dietetically. Raw foods and plenty of exercise in a secluded valley only 30 miles from Los Angeles. Prices are in the $1200 per week category.

ASHKELON VEGETARIAN CENTER

P.O.B. 341, ASHKELON
Tel: (051) 23706
Cables: AVC Ashkelon, Israel

Biba Hot Springs, One Cascade Dr, North Bonneville, WA 98639; (503) 233-2337. Holistic health facility set in the Columbia River Gorge near Portland, Oregon. Full health assessment, individualized treatment program, nutrition, exercise, and mineral spa facilities. Orientation is toward health self-care. Logwood guest lodges, campgrounds, including RV hookups and dormitories. French, gourmet, vegetarian meals. Conference facilities available.

Breitenbush Community Healing/Retreat/Conference Center, PO Box 578, Detroit, OR 97342; (503) 854-3501. Not a spa, but something more, a community in the Cascade Mountains, east of Salem, providing facilities and services for conferences, retreats, workshops, and seminars for individuals, families, groups, and other communities. Large and small groups can be housed in geothermally heated cabins. Vegetarian meals, child care, and hot springs. The community is experienced and will help with planning, registration, and publicity. Weekday rates are $20 for shared cabin lodging ($25 on weekends and holidays). This includes three vegetarian meals and use of the hot springs. Weekly rates are $130. For the hot springs alone, you must pay $3.50. There is a 25 percent discount for all people over 65.

Buckhorn Mineral Wells, 5900 East Main, Mesa, AZ 85205; (602) 8532-1111. Mineral baths and motel accommodations. Twenty-seven private whirlpool baths at a temperature of 106°. Massage therapist present on the premises.

Camp Akiba, East–West Foundation, Mid-Atlantic Summer Camp, 606 South 9 St, Philadelphia, PA; (215) 922-4567. Macrobiotic retreat in the foothills of the Poconos. Offers a wide variety of courses over a six-day period. The price is $395. There is also a special program for children.

Evers Health Center and Sealy Springs Spa, Cottonwood, AL 36320; (205) 691-2161. Probably the only live-in facility in the United States offering intravenous chelation therapy, a technique used to rid mineral deposits, particularly calcium, from the circulatory system. Insurance probably will not cover treatment here. Average stay is three to four weeks, and prices begin at $2250.00 per week. Cancer patients kick in an additional $350.

Feathered Pipe Ranch, Holistic Life Seminars, Yoga Vacations, Box 1682, Helena, MT 59624;

(406) 442-8196. Cradled in a bowl near the Continental Divide, the ranch offers a mountain retreat during the summer months. A wide variety of teachers, including Dr. Bernard Jensen (see Chapter 3), visits annually, write for details and a schedule. Vegetarian food is served at all meals, camping is available, and prices are generally in the $600 per week range. Holistic Life Seminars are conducted in conjunction with Timeless Travels, 323 Geary St #413, San Francisco, CA 94102; (415) 986-0622. Timeless also sponsors Mexican and Mediterranean cruises with famous nutritionists: lectures, classes, workshops with the experts in exotic ports of call.

Fineway House Natural Health Learning Center, 101 Ocean Ave, Palm Beach Shores, Singer Island, FL 33403; (305) 842-0099. Nestled between the Atlantic Ocean and Intracoastal Waterway, on 16 acres with plenty of beach frontage, two pools, nine tennis courts, massage, sauna, and shuffleboard. Occupies a wing of the Colonnades Beach Hotel. Meals are vegetarian. Fasting available, water or juice, medically supervised. Lectures and classes focus on health and nutrition dynamics.

The Golden Door, 777 Deer Springs Rd, San Marcos, CA 92069; (714) 744-5777. The spa features beautiful Japanese-style gardens, mountain scenery, and Oriental treatments. Natural foods are featured, each room has a private garden. Price, $2500 per week.

Gurney's Inn, Montauk Beach, Montauk, NY 11954; (516) 668-2345. On the beach on the South Shore of Long Island, this resort features a wide variety of treatments and therapies from all over the world, including Trager Psychophysical Integration, herbal wraps, Russian steam baths, and German Thalasso therapy (sea water hot tubs). Prices range from $525 per week for treatment plus $75–$110 a day for a room.

Harbin Hot Springs, Box 782, Middletown, CA 95461; (707) 987-2477. Mineral springs, both hot and warm, and a cold-water swimming pool. Vegetarian restaurant on site. Group facilities include rooms for retreats, workshops, and study groups. The conference center will hold up to 300 people. Group rates range from $6 to $21 per

HARBINGER

WORK-STUDY PROGRAM

at

Harbin Hot Springs

person per day, depending on the size of the group, length of stay, and whether food is provided. Individual costs begin at $4 for a soak in the springs, $6 for the day, or $8 for overnight camping. Dormitories and private rooms are also available, as is a work-exchange program. Harbin Springs is home to a resident community which includes the Niyama School of Massage, and the East–West Center for Macrobiotic Studies. If you or your group are interested in applying for residency, inquiries are invited. Financial assistance may also be available.

Hawaiian Health Hideaway of the Vegetarian Society, Inc., PO Box 5688, Santa Monica, CA 90405; (213) 396-5164. Run by Blanche Leonardo and Dr. Philip J. Welsh of the Santa Monica Vegetarian Society. Raw foods, lacto-ovo, and vegan diets. Also a reducing diet, papaya cleansing regimen, an anti-arthritis diet, a juice fast, and wheat grass on request. Weekly rates begin at $300 for a single, $250 per person for a double.

Heartwood's Island Mountain Retreat, 220 Harmony Lane, Garberville, CA 95440; (707) 923-2021. In conjunction with Heartwood College, California College of the Natural Healing Arts. A supportive isolated environment for self-healing, education, and professional training. Fourteen-day fast and cleansing available; cost, $350. Seminars available on an individual basis or as part of a three-month Spectrum Program, which gives you a taste of all of Heartwood's facilities and classes. Costs: $700 if you camp, $800 in a dormitory, $950 in a two-person room.

Heartwood Spa, 3150 A Mission Dr, Santa Cruz, CA 95065; 462-2192. Community and private hot tubs and sauna, a facility of Heartwood College. Open daily from noon.

Hippocrates Health Institute, 25 Exeter St, Boston MA, 02116; (617) 267-9525. A two-week cleansing program designed by Dr. Ann Wigmore (see Chapter 3), featuring a raw foods diet, exercise, relaxation, massage, and individual counseling to help you become responsible for your good health. Located in Boston's historic Back Bay district, prices begin at $780 for the two-week stay. In addition there is a ten-week health ministry program designed for the health professional or those seeking career opportunities therein.

Kripalu Yoga Retreat, Box 120, Summit Station, PA 17979; (717) 754-3051.Cleansing fasts, weight loss, relaxation techniques, hot tubs, in addition to extensive yoga training. Well-prepared vegetarian food is served. Two-week course runs $495.

Life Science Health School, 439 East Main St, Yorktown, TX 78164; (512) 564-3670. A facility that offers a raw-food diet and tasting as a means to weight loss, health, and well-being. Rest is emphasized—physical, mental, sensory, emotional, and physiological—in a warm, gentle south Texas climate. Prices begin at $245 per week.

Lindenhof Haus für Lebenserneuerung, 7200 Tuttlingen 74, West Germany. A beautiful, serene, vegan hotel retreat. Situated on a forest-blanketed mountaintop, the hotel is run by the Nazarians, a Christian sect that believes in vegetarianism, pacifism, and a reverence for life. Pure surroundings, organic, well-prepared food. Lindenhof also features fasting. Rates are reasonable and include all meals.

Living Springs Retreat, Rt 3, Bryant Pond Rd, Putnam Valley, NY 10579; (914) 526-2800. Seventh-Day Adventist reconditioning and health education center. Some programs offered are: anti-smoking, stress control, weight management, heart rehabilitation, disease prevention, life-style improvement, cooking and nutrition, and natural remedies seminars.

Maduro Travel, 330 Biscayne Blvd, Miami, FL; (800) 327-6709, (305) 373-3336. Offers Caribbean cruises with health experts and nutritionists, such as Edwin Flatto. All diets accommodated.

Mazdaznan Vegetarian Science Center, 15-2726 Lalakea, Pahoa, HI 96778; (808) 965-8643. Mastery of the self through good word, good deed, good thought. Adherence to glandular breathing exercises which include deep breathing, singing and energizing movement. Vegetarian meals using fruits, vegetables and produce grown in the center's organic garden. Rates are $105 per person for a week's stay.

Meadowlark Health and Growth Center, 26126 Fairview Ave, Hemet, CA 92343; (714) 927-1343. Run by Dr. Evarts G. Loomis, Meadowlark is one of the nation's original holistic retreats, and has been in operation for more than 25 years. Medical consultations, fasting, thorough lab and nutritional testing. The minimum recommended stay is one week; two weeks are recommended for greatest benefit in learning a new approach to life, diet, and exercise. The fasting program is two weeks. Prices begin at $395 per week for singles. Additional services, counseling, therapies, and testing incur charges.

Murrieta Hot Springs, 28779 Via Las Flores, Murrieta, CA 92362; (714) 677-7433. Healthful mineral springs near San Diego run by Alive Polarity. Features a lacto-vegetarian diet, but may be customized to most vegetarian needs. Murrieta offers a four-week healing program and a week long "Fit 'n' Trim" regime. Prices begin at $51 per day, but are very often discounted. Alive Polarity also runs Rancho retreat at the Sierra Inn, PO Box 90, Department 3, Emigrant Gap, CA 95715; (916) 389-8237.

Natural Healing Center, South Rte Box 10, Lavina, MT 59046; (406) 575-4487. Welcoming up to seven guests at one time, the center is located in the pine-covered hills of central Montana. Natural weight reduction and fasting program runs $65/day. Camping is available. There are also tipis and a yurt available on the premises. The environment affords solitude, and the staff prides itself on providing a loving, family atmosphere. Natural, home food cooking, hot tubs, and saunas. Visitors fees are $15 for campers providing their own shelter and sharing chores. This fee includes meals.

New Age Health Farm, Neversink, NY 12765; (914) 985-2221. A holistic retreat featuring both juice and water fasts. A compendium of courses is offered. Prices begin at $60 per day.

Northern Pines, Box 279, Rte 85, Raymond, ME 04071; (207) 655-7624. Paul Haroutunian, director of nutrition. Located on Crescent Lake in southern Maine, open summer and winter, features a holistic approach toward healing and well-being. Follows the precepts of Dr. Bernard Jensen (see Chapter 3) and Dr. Paavo Airola (also Chapter 3). Fasting, exercise, classes. A small, attentive community. From $350 per week.

Pawling Health Manor, Box 401, Hyde Park, NY 12538; (914) 889-4141. Situated on the shore of the Hudson River, administrated by natural hygienists Drs. Robert and Joy Gross. Specifically designed for weight loss. The doctors seek to re-educate the individual. The means is through a carefully administered water fast, the aim to lose 7 to 14 pounds during the first week. Rates begin at $344 per week.

Philadelphia Institute, Box 98, Sulphur Springs, AR 72768; (501) 298-3362. Christian holistic health retreat. Naturopathic doctor (i.e., one who uses

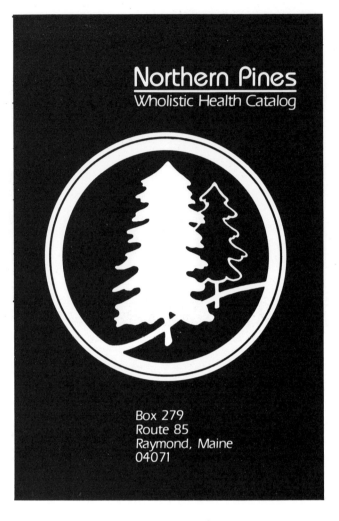

Northern Pines
Wholistic Health Catalog

Box 279
Route 85
Raymond, Maine
04071

only natural, nontoxic, nonsurgical remedies to restore health), sauna, mineral baths, whirlpool, organic gardening, nutritional testing. Rate is $30/day and includes room and board, nutritional counseling, and instruction in holistic principles.

Poland Springs Health Institute, Rte 1, Box 4300, Summit Springs Rd, Poland Springs, ME 04272; (207) 998-2894. A health reconditioning facility focusing on disease prevention. A 30-day program for those suffering from coronary heart disease; a two-week smoking cessation clinic; and individualized programs for blood pressure control, diabetes management, weight loss, hypertension, depression, arthritis, and stress. Natural, whole food, vegetarian cooking.

Pritikin Longevity Center, 1910 Ocean Front Walk, Santa Monica, CA 90405; (213) 450-5433. A 26-

day session that uses the Pritikin diet to deal with degenerative disease. Medical services are provided, as are 40 hours of educational seminars. Price is $3,850 for a 13-day stay; $5,970 for a full 26 days. There is also a Pritikin Center in Downingtown, Pa 19335; (215) 873-0123 or (800) 344-8243 featuring a "Corporate Executive Health Program" designed to help the overweight, reduce cholesterol, adult diabetes, high blood pressure, coronary heart disease and stress (see Chapter 4 for more about Pritikin diet).

Resort of the Mountains, 1130 Morton Rd, Morton, WA 98356; (206) 496-5885. In the foothills of the Cascade Mountains, this resort offers seminars, study weeks, and visiting lecturers, in addition to an individualized program featuring thorough lab testing, colonic therapy, massage, and advice on spiritual well-being. Organic food grown on the premises is the high point of the menu. Prices are about $750 per week per person.

Ringberg-Klinik, 8183 Rottach-Egern, Terernsee, West Germany. Dr. Josef Issels, medical director. A center for cancer cure. The method works through artificially induced fevers, plus special diets of raw foods, juices, and fermented lactic-acid foods. Write for prices and details.

Russell House, 415 William St, Key West, FL 33040; (305) 294-8787. A newly restored nineteenth century house in old Key West. Lose weight, stop smoking, learn good health maintenance. Features a well-supervised program of juice fasting in accordance with the teachings of Paavo Airola (see Chapter 4). Prices range from $350 per week.

Shangri-La Health Resort, Bonita Springs, FL 33923; (813) 992-3811. Devoted to natural health, this resort on Florida's Gulf Coast features an in-season fresh fruit, vegetable, and nut diet; fasting; exercise; and relaxation. In addition, nutritional

Poland Spring Health Institute

November 29, 1983

guidance and health education classes are offered. Prices begin at $32 per day for a dormitory-like accommodation. Singles range from $55 per day, doubles from $40.

Sharon Springs Health Spa, Chestnut St, Sharon Springs, NY 13459; (518) 284-2885. Mineral springs water and sulfur baths, detoxification, weight loss, education, exercise. Diet features fresh fruits, vegetables, wheat grass, juices, sprout salads, whole grains. Weekly prices are $300 for a single, $220 for a double.

Still Mountain Society, RR #1, Fernie, British Columbia V0B 1M0 Canada; (604) 423-6406. Located in Canada's Rocky Mountains, summer programs include four- and eight-week intensive courses in macrobiotic cooking and pioneer life style, a two-week summer camp, organic gardening, natural agriculture, wild plants, herb and folk medicine, dietary healing.

Swiss Bathing Cures, Swiss National Tourist Office, 608 Fifth Ave, New York, NY 10020; (212) 757-5944. 250 Stockton St, San Francisco, CA 94108; (415) 362-2260. Commerce Court West, Toronto, Ontario M5L 1E8 Canada; (416) 869-0584. Known not only for curative, but also preventative health methods, the 22 recognized health spas of Switzerland remain unsurpassed. They include: Andeer, Basen, Bad Ragaz/Valens, Bad Scuol, Bad Tarasp-Vulpera, Breiten, Lavey-les-Bains, Lenk, Leukerbad, Lostorf, Passugg, Ramsach, Rheinfelden, Rietbad, St. Moritz-Bad, Schinznach-Bad, Schwefelbergbad, Serneus, Stabio, Vals, Yverdon-les-Bains, Zurzach. Most spas have doctors and medical facilities on the premises. Some, including Baden, feature Gerovital

H-3 (see Chapter 9) and spa treatment combinations.

Turnwood Organic Gardens, Turnwood-Star Route, Livingston Manor, NY 12758; (914) 439-5702. A small organic farm situated in the Catskill Forest Preserve a few hours outside of New York City. They accept a limited number of guests for raw juice or water fasting under strict supervisory conditions. Nearby there are swimming, boating, and hiking in a beautiful, healthful environment. Rates for water fasting are $250 per week. Organic raw juice therapy is $300.

Villa Vegetariana Health Spa, Box 1228, Cuernavaca, Mexico. Tel: 3-10-44. A remote, holistic retreat an hour and a half from Mexico City (taxi pick-up can be arranged through the spa). The spa specializes in weight loss, blood pressure reduction, and alleviation of arthritis and asthma suffering. Even in summer the weather is cool and beautiful. Prices range from $180 to $250 per week.

Voie Suchness Way, Rte 3, Almonte, Ontario K0A 1A0 Canada; (613) 256-2665. Self-healing, macrobiotic rejuvenation center. Daily, weekly, and holiday group rates. Set in a country river village 30 miles from Ottawa. Rustic pine buildings, organic garden, macrobiotic cooking.

White Cloud, RD 1, Box 215, Newfoundland, PA 18445; (717) 676-3162. A quiet country inn in the heart of the Pocono Mountains. Natural, wholesome environment promotes study, meditation, peaceful communion with nature. Originally founded as a retreat for members of the Self-Realization Fellowship, the inn welcomes anyone seeking peaceful, relaxing surroundings. The restaurant features food organically grown on the grounds, salads, and home baked breads. White Cloud welcomes small groups of up to 50, as well as individuals and families. Prices for lodging begin at $21.25 per person per day. Meals are $16 for breakfast, lunch, and dinner inclusive. White Cloud is open year-round.

Wilbur Hot Springs, Wilbur Springs, CA 95987; (916) 473-2306. As traditional native American healing ground, now an international curing spa. Natural hot mineral baths in a rustic setting. Wood heat; no electricity. Seventeen private rooms and a 20-bed community room. Bathhouse temperatures range from 98° to 120° F. There is an outdoor pool, cool in summer, heated in winter. Wilbur is two and a half hours northeast of San Francisco. Private rooms are $25 per person per night. Discounts are available for groups.

Additional spas can be located through:

The Well-Being Guide to Health Spas in North America by Melissa Schnirring. Atheneum, 1982.

The Spa Book by Judy Babcock and Judy Kennedy. Crown Publishers, New York, NY; 228 pp; $14.95.

TRAVEL: THE VEGETARIAN PASSPORT

A set of cards in a miraculous array of languages enables vegetarians to travel anywhere in the world with minimum risk to their diet and state of mind. The idea is to present the passport to the waiter or whomever is dealing with your food. The little card in the appropriate language will accurately explain your diet and which foods are acceptable for you to eat. The passport will eventually be available in languages ranging from French and Spanish to Bulgarian, Farsi, Urdu, Tagalog, Korean, Pidgin, Namibian, Swahili, and so on.

It states:

I am a VEGETARIAN.
This means: because of my conviction I do not eat anything obtained from a killed animal.
I do not eat:
> *meat (including minced meat, all kinds of sausages, etc.), shrimps, mussels, poultry (including chicken), or other meat products.*
But I do eat:
> *vegetables, potatoes, tomatoes, nuts, mushrooms, rice, fruit, butter, milk, cheese, eggs, corn and corn products, etc.*
Soups and sauces may be made with vegetable stock, but not with meat or chicken extracts.
Frying and baking may only be done in vegetable oil, margarine or butter, but not in any other animal fat.

I am a VEGAN.
This means: because of my conviction I do not eat anything of animal origin.
So I do not eat:
> *meat (including minced meat, all kinds of sausages, etc.), fish, shrimps, mussels, poultry (including chicken), or other animal products such as milk, cheese, eggs, or any dairy products.*
But I do eat:
> *vegetables, potatoes, tomatoes, nuts, mushrooms, rice, fruit, corn and corn products, etc.*
Soups and sauces may be made with vegetable stock, but not with meat or chicken extracts.
Frying and baking may only be done in vegetable oil or vegetable margarine, but not in butter or any other animal fat.

The Vegetarian Passport is available from Ms. Tienke Padmos, Deliplein 89, 9715 ED Groningen, The Netherlands.

The Special Diet Foreign Phrase Book: Your Passport to Healthy Dining in Mexico, Spain, Germany, France and Italy by Helen Saltz Jacobson. Rodale Press, Emmaus, PA, 304 pp; $10.95. Simple key phrases to make yourself understood.

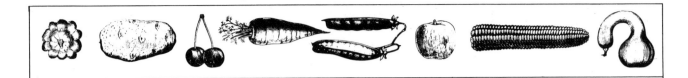

8

Vegetarianism
And The Elderly

ife extension experts today feel that it is a reasonable expectation that people should be able to live to be 100. Most feel the keys to such a long life is moderation and a positive interest in one's health and well-being. So, follow a low-calorie, high-nutrient diet; keep fit and exercise sensibly; and maintain strong friendships and social bonds. Human connections underscore an interest in life, and people who enjoy life tend to live longer.

Vegetarianism for the elderly is little different from vegetarianism for anyone else. As people grow older, their appetites often diminish, thus lessening the chance for good nutrition. As people grow older, although they need less food intake to maintain their proper body weight, they should be more careful to eat a balanced, natural, wholesome diet. Calcium deficiency, for example, often causes broken bones in older people who have cut back on calcium in hopes of reducing their arthritis suffering. Actually, we need to maintain our calcium intake later in life.

Memory loss and impaired thinking may result from nutritional deficiencies in old people, according to a study by scientists at the University of New Mexico School of Medicine. A correlation exists between low blood levels of vitamins C, B_{12}, riboflavin, and the ability to think and remember.

BOOKS

Avoid Premature Aging by Dr. Ronald L. Thayer. Loompanics Unlimited, PO Box 1197, Port Townsend, WA 98368, 300 pp, $7.95. Included are chapters on nutrition, exercise, mental attitude, cancer, vitamins, minerals, food supplements (brewer's yeast, for example) for added health benefits, virility tips, drugs, body resistance to disease, and flexibility.

Dr. Kugler's Seven Keys to a Longer Life by Dr. Hans J. Kugler. Loompanics Unlimited, PO Box 1197, Port Townsend, WA 98368, 250 pp with index, $8.95. Kugler explains how we can stay well longer mentally and physically. His discussion includes nutrition, exercise, stress, life habits, biorhythms, cell injection, nucleic acid therapy and organ-specific concentrates.

Food Enzymes for Health and Longevity by Dr. Edward Howell. Omangod Press, PO Box 64, Woodstock Valley, CT, 124 pp, $8.95. Stresses the need for a raw-food diet, because vital enzymes are destroyed by cooking. Condensed research from 435 medical and nutritional journals.

Hunza—Secrets of the World's Healthiest and Oldest Living People by Jay M. Hoffman. Professional Press Publishing Company, 13115 Hunza Hill Terrace, Valley Center, CA 92082, $10.00 including postage. Under the auspices of the National Geriatrics Society, Hoffman traveled to the Himalayas and studied the Hunza people, who claim to live 120 to 140 years. This illustrated book tells what he discovered.

Let's Stay Healthy by Adelle Davis. Signet, New York, NY, $4.95. Adelle Davis, voice for nutritional sanity in our diet, offers her knowledgeable guidance for lifelong good nutrition.

Life Extension: A Practical Scientific Approach. Adding Years to Your Life and Life to Your Years by Durk Pearson and Sandy Shaw. Warner Books, 858 pp, $22.50 hardcover/$10.95 softcover. Husband and wife research scientists explain why you age, how it works, and how science has been able to slow the aging process and sometimes even reverse it. Topics include baldness, weight control, memory and intelligence, reduction of degenerative disease, sexual function, physical appearance, strength, stamina, and anti-aging techniques. The authors suggest a comprehensive regimen of food supplements, which can be an expensive proposition, and not necessarily toward the best end. Some of the research scientists whom Pearson and Shaw cite claim their findings have been manipulated or entirely misconstrued by the two authors, and they question the advisability of taking expensive additives in hopes of living to be 120.

The Life Extension Revolution by Saul Kent. Loompanics Unlimited, PO Box 1197, Port Townsend, WA 98368, 466 pp, $12.95. A sourcebook and overview of current happenings in the life extension field. Includes references to publications, articles, scientific research, and organizations.

Living to be 100 by Osborn Segerberg. Charles Scribner's Sons, New York, NY 1982, 405 pp, $19.95. The story of 1200 people who lived to be 100, and how they did it. Everything from sex to hard work to mysterious omens to diet to genes.

Longevity: Fulfilling Our Biological Potential by Kenneth R. Pelletier. Merloyd Lawrence Book, Dell Publishing, New York, NY, 1982, 431 pp. A

work of scholarship. Pelletier isolates six factors that help to dictate how old we will become: (1) Genetic factor; how long have the people in your family lived? (2) Nutrition factor; common-sense vegetarian diet is best. Plenty of fresh fruit and vegetables, under-eating rather than over-eating. (3) Physical and mental activity factor; keep active physically, not unduly, but as you've exercised all your life. Work and challenge your mind. (4) Social factor; be with people you like. (5) Sexual activity factor; remain sexually active as long as you can. (6) Environment factor; people who live in milder climates live longer than people who must brave the elements.

Pelletier also mentions a curious seventh factor. People of the Hunza culture (whose people claim to grow very, very old), the inhabitants of the Caucasus in the Soviet Union, and also those of Vilcabamba in the Loja valley of Ecuador all drink quite a quantity of homemade alcohol daily. Pelletier allowed this might also have something to do with tickling the longevity factor.

Maximum Life Span by Roy L. Walford. Loompanics Unlimited, PO Box 1197, Port Townsend, WA 98368, 256 pp, $15.50. Dr. Walford is a life-extension researcher, and an advocate of restricted diet—undernutrition without malnutrition. (He fasts two days week.) He outlines his own plan for long life (he predicts 120 years or longer). The book includes menu plans, recipes, and a chart showing the nutritive value of a variety of foods.

Nucleic Acid and Anti-Oxidant Therapy of Aging and Degeneration by Benjamin S. Frank. Loompanics Unlimited, PO Box 1197, Port Townsend, WA 98368, 220 pp, $12.95. A research doctor analyzes the role of nucleic acid and its derivatives in slowing down the aging process.

Nutrients to Age Without Senility by Abram Hoffer and Morton Walker. Keats Publishing, New Canaan, CT, 230 pp, $2.95. The authors claim senility is a form of malnutrition. Sound nutrition planning, therapy, vitamin and mineral supplements, and exercise will reverse it.

Zen Macrobiotic Cooking by Michel Abehsera. Avon Books, New York, NY 1968; $1.75. The Zen macrobiotic way to health and youth: "Avoid industrialized food and drink; use only subtle spices; eliminate coffee; avoid any vegetable or fruit out of season; eliminate potatoes, tomatoes, and eggplants from your diet; avoid drinking while you eat.''

ORGANIZATIONS

American Association of Retired Persons, 1909 K St NW, Washington, D.C. (202) 872-4700.

Forty Plus, 1718 P St NW, Washington, D.C. 20036. (202) 387-1582.

Gray Panthers, 3700 Chestnut St, Philadelphia, PA 19104. (215) 382-3300. A national organization fighting for the rights of older people. They publish a quarterly newspaper, *The Gray Panther Network*.

Institute of Lifetime Learning, 1306 Connecticut Ave NW, #501, Washington, D.C. 20036. (202) 872-4800.

Operation Pep (Protection of Elderly People), 200 L St NW, Ste 307, Washington, D.C. 20036. (202) 676-5790.

Retired Senior Volunteer Program, 95 M St SW, Washington, D.C. 20024. (202) 488-2138.

LONGEVITY AND LIFE EXTENSION CENTERS

Anti-Aging Diet of the Hippocrates Health Institute. Hippocrates Health Institute, 25 Exeter St, Boston MA 02116; (617) 267-9525. Dr. Ann Wigmore (see Chapter 3, section on vegetarian authorities) believes there is only one disease—malnutrition. According to her it may take many different forms: cancer, diabetes, heart disease, mental illness, or even premature aging.

Wigmore believes the means to combat sickness is within our grasp. She believes in Hippocrates' philosophy that the body can act as its own doctor, that it can cure itself if it has the right tools. These tools come in the form of nourishment, and, in Wigmore's opinion, the nourishment should come from eating live, unprocessed, uncooked foods.

"Dead food cannot be digested easily," says Wigmore. Rather than passing quickly through the body's digestive tract it collects in the large intestine like thick sludge, decays, and becomes a breeding ground for bacteria.

The focus of Wigmore's diet is living food, especially sprouts. Second, she recommends, drink a small amount of wheatgrass juice (the liquid squeezed from young wheat plants, rich in vitamins, minerals, and especially chlorophyll) every day, because the chlorophyll cleanses the blood. Lastly, rather than drink simple water, substitute *rejuvelac,* which is the water that has been used to sprout the seeds. It is loaded with helpful bacteria and enzymes (see Chapter 20: Grow Your Own to learn how to make rejuvelac.)

The final step in Wigmore's anti-aging program is to maintain internal cleanliness. To this end she recommends colonic irrigation, so that the impacted waste that has collected inside of you (some studies say as much as 10 pounds of feces glued in the folds of your large intestines), is loosened and washed away.

Life Extension Institute, 11 E 45 St, New York, NY 10017. (212) 575-8300. A diagnostic center.

Longevity Research Institute, 1121 E Cabrillo Blvd, PO Box 40570, Santa Barbara, CA 93103. (805) 969-5935. A medically supervised rehabilitation center for people suffering from cardiovascular or other degenerative diseases. Program runs 26 days, and costs approximately $2000. Patients are taught to combat their disease through a reorientation program of nutrition and exercise.

NEWSLETTERS

Health and Longevity Report, Agora Publishing, 2201 St. Paul Street, Baltimore, Maryland 21218. Monthly newsletter with most current information in the field of life extension, old age and their relation to optimum health. No advertising and some useful information. $36.00 subscription rate for 12 issues.

THERAPIES

Dr. Ana Aslan's Gerovital H3 (GH3) Therapy. Eighty-two year old Dr. Aslan directs a staff of 1000 in over 200 anti-aging clinics in Roumania. Thirty years ago, by adding buffering agents and chemicals to novocaine, she developed the controversial rejuvenating drug, Gerovital H3 (GH3).

Tests at the University of Chicago and the University of California at Los Angeles have supported Dr. Aslan's findings, but other testing has proved inconclusive. According to Aslan, GH3 is effective in reversing the debilitating effects of arthritis, bronchial asthma, rheumatism, angina pectoris, Parkinson's disease, and more.

H3 In the Battle Against Old Age by Henry Marx. Loompanics Unlimited, PO Box 1197, Port Townsend 98368, 199 pp, $12.95. The book includes a discussion of what old age is, and what can be expected from rejuvenation. Also discussed are the effects of H3 on diseases of the nervous system, muscles, joints, skin, allergies; diseases of the cardiovascular system; gastrointestinal disease; and diseases of the endocrine glands. There is also a discussion of novocaine and its ability to postpone old age.

Where to get Gerovital H3 (GH3):

Vita, Inc., P.O. Box 756, Playas de Rosarito, B.C.N. 22710, Mexico. Twenty-five tablets for $22.00; 12 vials for $60.00 A cream is available for $20.00.

World Institute of Health, PO Box 970, Cayman Islands, Grand Cayman, British West Indies; or GH3, PO Box 9494, San Diego, CA 92109; (619) 282-9316. A three months' supply of GH3 is $80.00; a one-year supply is $275.

CELL THERAPY (Organ-specific Ribonucleic Acids)

Cell therapy was initiated by Dr. Paul Niehaus during the 1930s in Switzerland at the LaPraire Clinic. The idea is to stimulate the growth and proper functioning of healthy cells with RNA, tricking older cells into behaving like younger cells, which purportedly leads to increased zest. In time optimun vitality can allegedly be restored.

American Biologics–Mexico, S.A., Tijuana, Mexico/111 Ellis St, Ste 300, San Francisco, CA 94102; (800) 227-4458 or (415) 981-8384 (call collect). Most complete live-cell therapy–based program in North America. Total treatment for early and advanced aging.

IMMUNE REVITALIZATION SERUM THERAPY

Immune revitalization serum therapy originated at the Pasteur Institute in the 1930s. Bogomolet's serum is a facsimile, named after its developer, of an improved reticular endothelial system, which is the body's main line of defense against all disease. Introduced into the body, the serum seeks out the weakest cells in organs and glands (the ones that supposedly are causing premature aging in the individual), and destroys them while encouraging the growth of new, healthy cells.

VEGETARIAN OLD AGE HOMES

Helping Hand, 1050 Lemon Ave, El Cajon, CA 92020.

Vegetarian Retirement Home, Dr. Anton Kraak, PO Box 2254, San Diego, CA 92112.

Homes for Elderly Vegetarians, Ltd., 159 Clapham High St, London SW47SS, England. They run four homes: two in Sussex, one in North Wales, and one in Yorkshire.

9
Women: Menstruation, Pregnancy, and Vegetarianism

Scientific research has shown that babies born to vegetarian mothers are as healthy as babies born to omnivore mothers. Still births, premature deliveries, birth defects, and incidents of underweight infants occur with no more or less frequency in vegetarian women than they do in any other particular group.

It is every woman's duty to eat with care and intelligence while pregnant. It's the old saw: You're eating for two. Vegetarian women, especially vegans, must plan their daily, weekly, and monthly diet. This should be implemented with the help of a trusted health practitioner, preferably someone experienced in the birthing process.

During pregnancy it's best to eat a variety of foods daily. In order to get enough protein, vegan women must combine consumption of plant foods with grains, legumes, nuts, and seeds. Vegetarian women who use dairy foods should drink plenty of milk. Women who drink goat's milk rather than cow's milk should take a vitamin B$_{12}$ supplement. Vegan women should not only take the B$_{12}$, but also a calcium supplement, vitamin D, and riboflavin. All women should take an iron supplement as well as a folacin supplement, which is instrumental in maintaining a satisfactory blood supply by aiding red blood cell formation and in maintaining healthy sex organs. Good sources of folacin are in whole grains, leafy green vegetables,

nutritional yeast, dairy products, and root vegetables.

Iodine is also important during pregnancy. The use of an iodized salt (as opposed to sea salt which contains no iodine,) can take care of the need.

Never diet during pregnancy. As a matter of fact, expect to gain about 25 pounds. A baby developing in your womb uses your nutrients. If you have a good supply at the time of conception and maintain it throughout pregnancy, you'll be protecting yourself as well as your child.

ORGANIZATIONS

American Academy of Husband-Coached Childbirth, PO Box 5224, Sherman Oaks, CA 91413; (213) 788-6662. This birthing program, developed by Dr. Robert A. Bradley, has a strong nutritional bent. The idea is to remain focused and relaxed during labor, avoid drugs, and depend on the assistance and support of a birthing partner. The academy trains instructors and develops material to be used in classes.

Cooperative Childbirth Network, 14 Truesdale Dr, Croton-on-Hudson, NY 10520; (914) 271-6474. Diverse birthing resources. They have national referrals for cooperative childbirth courses and specialists expounding a full spectrum of birthing philosophies. Also available are course outlines, a newsletter, tapes, slides, instructor-training seminars, and reprints focusing on the health needs of expectant mothers.

Feminist Women's Health Centers, 1112 Crenshaw Blvd, Los Angeles, CA 90019; (213) 936-6293. Referrals to women-run health clinics throughout the U.S. They'll send self-help material through the mail.

Institute for Childbirth and Family Research, 2522 Dana St, #201, Berkeley, CA 94704; (415) 849-3665. Scientific investigatory group studying alternatives in childbirthing. Local branches nationwide.

National Association of Parents and Professionals for Safe Alternatives in Childbirth (NAPSAC), PO Box 267, Marble Hill, MO 63764; (314) 238-2010. In and out of hospital family-centered birthing. Yearly conference well attended by the childbirth reform community.

National Midwives Association, 1119 East San Antonio Ave, El Paso, TX 79901; (915) 533-8142. Informational clearinghouse and active directory of midwife services.

Society for the Protection of the Unborn through Nutrition, (SPUN) 17 North Wabash Ave, #603, Chicago, IL 60602; (312) 332-2334. This agency networks nationwide to counsel pregnant women about nutrition. They provide speakers, train nutritionists, publish a newsletter, and provide educational material.

BOOKS

Birth by Caterine Milinaire. Harmony Books (Crown Publishers), New York, NY, 1974, 304 pp. A good introductory childbirth book with intimate, reassuring case studies.

Building Better Babies: Preconception Planning for Healthier Children by Dr. Daniel Elam. Celestial Arts Publishing, 231 Adrian Road, Millbrae, CA 94030, 141 pp, $6.95. Concentrates on the period prior to conception in both male and females, stressing the need for excellent nutritional states in prospective parents in order to ensure the creation of a healthy infant. A biochemist who focuses on nutrition, Elam discusses the effects of radiation, drugs, caffeine, alcohol, smoking, virus, disease, stress, environment, chemicals, and pets on prospective parents and their future offspring.

Everywoman's Book by Paavo Airola. Health Plus Publishing, 638 pp, $12.95. Addresses the questions that specifically affect women, ranging from pregnancy and natural childbirth to menopausal distress and varicose veins. It outlines a complete and effective program to be started one year before conception, and will help ensure optimal health in your baby.

The Los Angeles Birth Directory. 16545 Ventura Blvd, Ste 23, Encino, CA 91436, $5.79 including postage; (213) 990-6188. A comprehensive guide to childbirth, parent needs, and services in the Los Angeles area. Over 80 categories of products and services including resources, classes, child care, health care, play groups, natural fiber clothing, and more. Updated annually. Available at local bookstores as well.

Mega-Nutrition for Women by Dr. Richard A. Kunin, McGraw-Hill, 1221 Avenue of the Americas, New York, NY 10021, $14.95. This book, focusing in large part on pregnancy, argues that women suffer by eating the same diet as men. Kunin finds it hard to believe that doctors treat men and women the same by not taking into account the facts that women menstruate (thereby loosing valuable nutrients) and become pregnant. The medical profession, he argues, has taken certain manifestations of nutritional deficiencies, such as moodiness, unhappiness, and general despair, dubbed them typical "women's syndromes," and has over-prescribed drugs to women as a consequence.

The Pregnancy After 30 Workbook: A Program for Safe Childbirthing—No Matter What Your Age, edited by Gail Sforza Brewer. Rodale Press, 33 E Minor St, Emmaus, PA, 18049, 1978, 233 pp, $10.95. A helpful book designed to deal with fears real and imagined that one may encounter before, during and after pregnancy.

To Parent or Not by C. Norman Shealy and Mary-Charlotte Shealy. The Dunning Company, Virginia Beach, VA, 1981, 299 pp. Not only the question of parenting, but the full spectrum of responsibility to the child. Shealy runs the Pain and Rehabilitation Center, La Crosse, Wisconsin.

Total Nutrition During Pregnancy by Betty and Si Kamen. Appleton-Century-Crofts, 25 Van Zant St, East Norwalk, CT 06855, 1981, 234 pp, $6.95. Discusses the pros and cons of vegetarianism for pregnant women. Stresses the need for a sensible, individually tailored diet plan during pregnancy.

Woman's Almanac, 211 E 51 St, New York, NY 10022, $6.95. Includes a women's directory, listing over 1500 services, organizations, and resources, both locally and nationally. The almanac itself is geared to the active woman in today's society, offering advice on how to, encouragement, and knowledge.

GUIDE TO VEGETARIAN EATING DURING PREGNANCY

The following recommendations are based on a food guide created by the California Department of Health. The indications of serving size will provide only minimal recommended daily allowances. Individuals may choose to eat more from certain groups (e.g., protein).

Food group	What to eat	Nutrients involved
Protein	Cooked dry beans, peas, lentils, nuts, seeds, nut butters, tofu	Protein, iron, thiamine, folacin, vitamin B_6, vitamin E, phosphorus, magnesium, zinc

You must eat at least two cups of peas, lentils and beans each day, as well as a quarter-cup of nuts and/or seeds, a quarter-cup of nut butter, and at least one small cake of tofu.

Food group	What to eat	Nutrients involved
Grain products	Whole-grain bread, pasta, cereal, rice, etc.	Thiamine, riboflavin, iron, phosphorus, zinc, magnesium

You should eat some whole-grain bread, muffins, or crackers at each meal, in addition to at least one serving of grain as a centerpiece to a daily meal.

Food group	What to eat	Nutrients involved
Leafy green vegetables	Asparagus, bok choy, broccoli, brussels sprouts, cabbage, chicory, endive, red leaf lettuce, romaine, escarole, beets, collard greens, kale, mustard, spinach, swiss chard, turnips, scallions, watercress	Folacin; vitamins A, C, E, B_6, and riboflavin; iron, magnesium

Twice a day you should eat at least a cup of raw or cooked vegetables.

Eat some of these fruits, drink some juice and eat some of these vegetables at least two or three times a day:

Food group	What to eat	Nutrients involved
Fruits (rich in vitamin C)	Oranges, grapefruit, mangoes, berries, tangerines	Vitamin C

Vegetables (rich in vitamin C)	Tomatoes, green pepper, greens, cauliflower, broccoli, cabbage, bok choy	Vitamin C

Choose from this group at least once a day, unless you are a vegan; then you must eat from this group three times a day:

Fruits	Apples, apricots, bananas, pears, peaches, cherries, dates	Vitamins A, C, B_6, and E; zinc, magnesium, phosphorus, riboflavin
Vegetables	Other vegetables, not mentioned previously, such as root vegetables, or more exotic ones, such as artichokes	

Dairy products	Milk, yogurt, hard and soft cheeses, ice cream, eggs	Calcium, phosphorus, vitamins D, A, E, B_6, and B_{12}; zinc, protein, riboflavin, magnesium

Anyone who does not use animal products (milk, eggs, etc.) must take a food supplement of calcium, B_{12} and riboflavin. They should also eat more from the other recommended categories. You should be eating from this category at least four times per day.

EXERCISE

For many years pregnant women were told not to exercise because it was thought the exertion would rob the fetus of oxygen-rich blood. Now, however, doctors are realizing that exercise is good for pregnant women, and they should trust their own instincts regarding their limitations. Doctors feel that stress is actually the key factor. If a woman regards exercise as a punishment, she will not feel comfortable exercising while pregnant; but if she enjoys it, then it will more than likely be good for both her and her child. Use caution! Always consult your physician before attempting any stressful exercise during pregnancy.

MORNING SICKNESS

The Pregnant Woman's Comfort Guide by Sherry Lynn Mims Jiminez. Prentice-Hall, Englewood Cliffs, NJ 07632, 1983; $14.95. If at all possible don't take chemicals to combat morning sickness. The intake of chemicals may not be good in the very best of times, and when you're pregnant you and your developing child are most vulnerable. Don't take risks! In the *Pregnant Woman's Comfort Guide* author Ms. Jiminez has a lot to say about combating nausea. First, she says, know what may cause it. During pregnancy the body needs more protein due to the demands of the developing fetus. In the morning, because a woman has not eaten all night, her level of blood sugar is at its lowest, which augments the problem. Adding to the difficulties is the excess acid secreted by the stomach while she has slept, causing further nausea. Neutralize acids by drinking milk, eating an apple, or a potato without the peel. Jiminez suggests if you cannot face food take two calcium tablets. This ought to settle your stomach so that you can eat about 30 minutes later. It is best to snack lightly and frequently on protein-rich foods. This will keep blood sugar levels up and hopefully stave off the nausea. Other recommendations include: sucking or chewing on ice chips; a cold compress to the throat; slow, regular breathing; and acupressure, specifically to points in the ear.

Another source of possible relief is offered by John Heinerman, a medical anthropologist, who writes an herbal column for *Vegetarian Times.* He says ginger root can be quite effective in alleviating discomfort from morning sickness. Try two or three capsules when you wake up in the morning, or at any time during the day when you're feeling queasy. Be sure the ginger is encapsulated, otherwise it may cause an irritation to the digestive tract.

Wish Garden, Box 1304-N, Boulder, CO 80306; (303) 449-0059. Catalog, 50 cents. An extensive selection of herbs for pregnancy, labor, and family care.

PRE-MENSTRUAL TENSION

Scientists, medical doctors and nutritionists agree that changing hormone levels during the menstrual cycle cause nutritional deficiencies in the body. These deficiencies result in the emotional and physical discomfort that as much as 40% of the women in our population suffer.

Pre-menstrual tension (PMT) can be dealt with nutritionally. How? First, one must have a proper diet. A well-rounded eating regimen of sufficient protein, with plenty of fresh fruit, vegetables, and fiber is essential. In addition to this, dietary supplements of certain vitamins and minerals can be an enormous benefit. Coffee, tea, chocolate, and any other caffeine-containing food or drink must be eliminated because they add to the problems of PMT, rather than alleviating them. Gentle exercise is in order, as well as plenty of rest.

What affects PMT? According to an article in *Vegetarian Times,* deficiencies of calcium, magnesium, zinc, iron, and vitamins B_6, E, and C. Therefore, while maintaining a balanced diet throughout the month, it's important to change your diet about 5 days before your period. Start to include foods rich in these vitamins and minerals, or you can take supplements if your deficiencies are more severe.

Vitamin B_6 will help by reducing water retention and may even instill a degree of calmness, according to research physician Guy E. Abraham, who studied PMT and published his findings in the *American Journal of Clinical Nutrition.* Vitamin B_6 can be taken in supplements or found in foods such as cabbage, avocadoes, split peas, brown rice, wheat germ, peanuts, walnuts, raisins, and prunes. Try asparagus, parsley, watermelon, and strawberries as well. They are all natural diuretics, and will help alleviate water retention. Be careful, however, because eating those foods depletes potassium levels as well. Again, take a supplement or eat bananas, figs, dates, or other foods that are potassium-rich.

Women who take birth control pills are particularly susceptible to iron deficiency. To boost iron levels, eat wheat germ, blackstrap molasses, dried fruit, beans, and leafy green vegetables. It is the iron in your blood that carries oxygen. If you have an iron deficiency at the time of menstruation, this is probably the reason you feel fatigued no matter how much you rest.

Vitamin E and zinc control the amount of prostaglandins in the blood. Prostaglandins are a hormone-like substance that causes the uterus to contract, resulting in cramps. With added zinc and E, prostaglandins production willl remain at a minimum and cramping will not occur.

Vitamin E is contained in nuts, fruits, wheat germ, green leafy vegetables, and corn, peanut, and soy oils, as well as other vegetable oils and margarine.

Zinc is found in wheat germ and wheat bran, milk, nuts, yeast, lima beans, and dried split peas. Calcium can be obtained by eating milk products, eggs, cheese, kelp, and brazil nuts.

Magnesium is available from leafy green vegetables, fruit, dairy products, wheat germ, wheat bran, nuts, and kelp.

Vitamin C is particularly good in the battle against PMT because it reduces stress. According to *Vegetarian Times* women have found vitamin C in the form of calcium ascorbate, which is a calcium/vitamin C combination, to be particularly effective.

10

Vegetarianism For Newborns, Babies, Children, and Adolescents

The best advice for a child nutrition program is to start them early on the healthiest diet possible. Recent reports from the American Health Foundation confirm what many have known for a long time. Children should be taught to eat a low-fat, low-cholesterol diet from the very beginning of life to lessen the risk of heart disease. These scientists said, "Efforts to reduce blood levels of fats and cholesterols cannot begin early enough."

Breastfeed your child if at all possible. Don't be dissuaded. And once your child is eating solid foods, chose a diet that will benefit her or him for their entire life. Eating well can be simply a case of establishing good habits. Remember that grandparents, a never-ending source of discussion and frustration with regard to children's diets, can be trained! Just say, "Ma, no more lollypops!" then hand over a copy of *Yuk to Yum Snacks* (see page **74**).

BREASTFEEDING

Formula manufacturers would like to have people believe that breast milk is not as good as formula for babies. The following organizations work very hard to let people know otherwise. Mother's milk is the diet best for newborns. The less polluted the mother, the purer the milk.

Human Lactation Center, 666 Sturges Highway, Westport, CT 06880. This research center studies breastfeeding nutritionally, culturally, and developmentally.

La Leche League International, 9616 Minneapolis Ave, Franklin Park, IL 60131; (312) 455-7730. An organization that now is worldwide, supporting good mothering through breastfeeding. They publish *The Womanly Art of Breastfeeding* as well as pamphlets and a newsletter. They work on a local level as well. Most communities have leaders trained to teach and encourage breastfeeding.

FOR NON-BREASTFEEDING MOTHERS

NATURLAC An all-natural infant formula made with barley, whole milk, maple syrup, and a small vitamin/mineral core so that FDA specifications are met. The approximate cost is $1.10 per 8-ounce serving (compared to 85 cents for commercial formula, which contains preservatives and coconut oil, mono and diglycerides, denatured milk, chemicals, corn syrup, and sugar). NATURLAC is carried by most health food stores or you can obtain it from Nutripathic Formulas, 6821 East Thomas Rd, Scottsdale, AZ 85251; (800) 321-6917 or (602) 946-5515. Price: $24.45 including shipping. Mixed with water it makes 21 8-ounce servings. A NATURLAC packet is available for $3. It provides background information about NATURLAC as well as pertinent information concerning the dangers of commercial infant formulas.

Tofu is a terrific source of protein, and can make a fantastic baby food. Puree a little fruit or vegetable, and mix it with an equal amount of tofu. Serve it warm or at room temperature. Remember to introduce tofu gradually into your child's diet, as you would any other food in case of allergic reaction.

BOOKS AND PAMPHLETS

The Complete Guide and Cookbook for Raising Your Child as a Vegetarian by Michael and Nina Shandler, Ballantine, 201 E 50 St, New York, NY 10022, 370 pp, 1981, $3.50. A book by parents who became vegetarians when their child was born. Follows their development, and what they learned they pass on to you. Interesting, helpful.

Feed Your Kids Right by Lendon Smith. Dell, One Dag Hammarskjold Plaza, New York, NY 10017, 304 pp, 1982, $3.50.

Feeding Your Vegan Baby, American Vegan Society, Box H, Malaga, NJ 08320. The society's experience offers knowledge and helpful suggestions in this pamphlet.

Food is Your Best Medicine, H.G. Bieler, Random House, 201 E 50 St, New York, NY 10022, 1966, $8.95. Preventive medicine for your child through intelligent eating habits.

Going Vegetarian: A Guide for Teenagers by Sada Fretz, William Morrow & Co, 105 Madison Ave, New York, NY 10016, 278 pp, $11.50. An earnest discussion of the whys and hows of vegetarianism, especially designed for the young novice. Ms. Fretz is careful to explain that vegetarianism is not a panacea, but there is no reason to prolong the agonies of slaughterhouse animals, nor is there any reason to continue to ingest chemicals and additives into our bodies. Included are recipes designed for those new and unaccustomed to the kitchen.

Hygiene Care of Children by Herbert M. Shelton. Natural Hygiene Press, Bridgeport, CT. Respected natural hygienist gives his views.

I Like Fruit by Ethel Goldman and **I Like Vegetables,** by Sharon Lerner. Lerner Publishing, 241 First Avenue North, Minneapolis, MN, 31 pp, $4.95 each. Condition your kids the right way. Picture books with text describing individual fruits and vegetables.

Improving Your Child's Behavior Chemistry by Lendon Smith. Pocket Books, 1230 Avenue of the Americas, New York, NY 10020, 1976, 270 pp, $3.50. Orthomolecular medicine tries to balance the chemical content of the body. Lendon Smith is one of its foremost advocates and this book encompasses his approach to kids. Hyperactivity, bedwetting, allergies, colds—all are related to diet and body chemistry imbalance in this discussion.

The Keats Publishing Company, 27 Pine Street, Box 876, New Canaan, CT. Their "Good Health Guide" series contains a number of books especially interesting to parents: *Stress Test for Children* by Jerome Vogel; *The Bircher–Benner Children's Diet Book* by M. Bircher–Benner; *Better Food for Better Babies and their Families* by Gena Larson; and *Parents' Guide to Better Nutrition for Tots to Teens* by Emory Thurston.

Let's Have Healthy Children by Adele Davis. New American Library (Signet), 1633 Broadway, New York, NY 10019, 386 pp, $3.95. A guide to the nutritional needs of the young. A valuable standard for many years.

Macrobiotic Child Care by Cornelia Aihara. GOMF Press, 902 14 St, Oroville, CA 95965. Macrobiotic philosophy is sometimes misconstrued. No one wants to take a chance where the health of their child is concerned. An important instructive manual.

Natural Baby Food Cookbook by Margaret Elizabeth Kends and Phyllis Williams. Avon, 1790 Broadway, New York, NY 10019, 212 pp, $4.95. Natural yes, vegetarian no. Still contains useful information.

Vegetarian Baby by Sharon Yntema. McBooks, Ithaca, NY, 1980, 224 pp, $6.05. Sensibly done, macrobiotic, discusses people and groups who've raised babies with good results. Talks of pregnancy, lactation, development, gear you'll need, selection and preparation of food, and recipes.

The Vegetarian Child by Joy Gross with Karen Freifeld. Lyle Stuart Inc., Secaucus, N.J., 1983. $12.00. Personal book by one of the most intelligent of new vegetarian movement voices. Speaking from experience, Gross touches every base with the right combination of common sense, intelligence, and love. Excellent starting place.

NUTRITIONAL AID FOR CHILDREN

If your child is a bedwetter, Dr. Lendon Smith (see his book, *Improving Your Child's Behavior Chemistry,* above) suggests feeding her or him protein before bedtime. Smith says certain blood sugar levels are imperative for normal brain function, but when the level drops off during sleep, sometimes the brain does not receive the necessary response from the bladder. The solution is some peanut butter, cheese, or tofu pudding before bedtime. Because the body takes several hours to convert protein into sugar, the bedtime snack will help the child get through the night without incident.

Dr. Smith's prevention diet for kids *(Vegetarian Times Magazine):* (1) Eliminate all the "antinutrient" junk food in the child's diet, as well as as many commercial food products as possible.(2) Eat instead natural foods: plenty of raw, steamed, and stir-fried vegetables, eggs, white cheese (lowfat), nuts (almonds are highly recommended), seeds, nut butters, legumes, and fruit. (3) Have the child eat four to six times a day, in small meals, with nibbling allowed. (4) Give vitamins and mineral supplements daily. (Smith calls them concentrated food.)

Finally, what is left? Smith says: "Walk or exercise daily, believe in a higher Being, and say something nice about yourself and someone else daily."

NUTRA Program, Sara Sloan, Fulton County Schools, Box 13285, Atlanta, GA 30324; (404) 634-5264. The NUTRA program is the work of practicing school nutritionist Sara Sloan. In 1976 she lobbied the school board of the Fulton County schools in Georgia to implement a natural foods alternative for the traditional public school lunchroom fare. Her "Nutra Lunch," which incorporates a whole-grain, high-fiber, low-fat, minimum sugar diet free of chemicals, features fresh fruits and vegetables, yogurt, sprouts, wheat germ, tofu, nuts, seeds, raw dairy products, and carob instead of chocolate.

Today, the program has met with such great success that Sloan has answered over 15,000 pieces of mail, tours the country lecturing school officials and nutritionists, health professionals, business and parent groups, and government officials. Her thesis that good food directly affects health and learning abilities may sound old hat, but it's actually revolutionary. Her food programs have also found their way into the classroom, initiating activities in organic gardening, diet charting, cooking, kitchen tours, plate-waste surveys, label reading, advertising analysis, and Friday afternoon sprout parties.

Publications by Sara Sloan:

A Guide For Nutra Lunches and Natural Foods. $8.95. A tool for homes, schools, camps, daycare centers, hospitals, and institutions that wish to convert to whole, natural foods. Tested recipes, tips, how to incorporate USDA foods, fun projects, sprouting parties, more.

Children Cook Naturally. $10.95. A "fun" cookbook using natural whole ingredients. Full of projects proven successful in the Fulton County schools. "Children who learn to cook naturally become nutrition wise adults."

From Classroom to Cafeteria. $8.95. A curriculum resource guide for food service personnel working with parents, students, and teachers on nutrition education. Grade-level projects for kindergarteners through high school, ethnic and special occasion meals, with recipes, activities, decorations, classroom cooking for kids, more.

Nutritional Parenting. $2.00. How to get your child off junk foods and into healthy eating habits.

Turn Can't Into Can. $2.00. How to get healthy meals into your local school.

Yuk to Yum Snacks. $3.50. They are a rare breed— people who don't like to snack. So here's a little book that teaches how to snack in the "raw." Here are recipes for snacks that contain no refined sugar, no white flour, no chemical additives, and no food colorings. A great idea for grandparents who can't live without tempting the little ones: "Fruit Pops": "Here's a way to use fruit that's either hung around the house too long or is on special sale at the fruit stand. Use overripe bananas, peaches, plums, nectarines (alone or in combination). Skin and pit the fruit, place the pulp in a blender and blend to puree consistency. Then pour into popsicle forms, ice trays or paper cups and freeze."

NEWSLETTER AND INFORMATION PACKS

Mini Nutra Packet. $3.50. Includes Nutra information sheet, "Nutrition Letter to Parents," *Nutra Blurbs* (school PA announcements), and more.

Nutritioning Parents Newsletter. $12.00. Promotes family health awareness with regard to diet, good nutrition, and physical fitness. Made especially for parents, teachers, health professionals, and institutions. Contains recipes, nutritional know-how, product information, more.

TAPES

Better Food for Better Learning. $8.00. Cassette tape program. Running time: 1 hour and 45 minutes.

FILMS AND VIDEO

Nutrition Naturally. A 16-mm film telling the story of nutrition classroom projects with elementary and high school students. Contains interviews with a parent, board member, food service manager, principal, and a noted pediatrician. Designed to be used by parents, teachers, food service administrators, churches, day-care centers, and other institutions. Running time: 25 minutes.

Come Alive Fun Classroom projects. Video cassette. Running time: 22 minutes.

VEGETARIAN ORGANIZATIONS FOR CHILD HELP

Jersey Vegetarian Home for Children, Quarrywood, 23 Grange Rd, Hastings, East Sussex, England. English vegetarian orphanage.

New England Salem Children's Trust, Salem Village, PO Box 56, Stinson Lake Rd, Rumney, NH 03266. Vegetarian home for children who might otherwise be in an orphanage, correctional facility, or hospital. Some children are mentally, physically, or socially handicapped. Branches in England, Germany, Greece, and Israel. In order to make money the Children's Trust sells greeting cards and posters designed by Susan Nardine. They represent a natural way of life, and are printed in two colors on quality paper. A package of ten cards and envelopes costs $6.00.

CHILDREN'S GARDENS ORGANIZATIONS

Children of the Green Earth, c/o Michael Soule, Environmental Education Center, PO Box 751, Portland, OR 97207. An organization encouraging children to help heal the earth by planting trees.

Universal Children's Gardens, PO Box 2698, Grand Central PO, New York, NY 10163; (212) 445-2365. The Universal Children's Gardens seeks to encourage and network gardens throughout the world. Feeling that through soil, water, sun, and seed, there are many lessons to be learned, the organization offers all kinds of resources from advice to funding to seeds. The gardens are organic, and nutrition is one of the primary focuses of the group. They seek contact from people everywhere. Even already established gardens are encouraged to join their network. Their newsletter is $10.00 for the year.

POSTERS

Children's Garden Poster, Transition Graphics, PO Box 30007, Eugene, OR 97403. A poster depicting children's gardens as a "sensible alternative for growing food, flowers, and friendships on our planet." Artists are Diane and Joel Schatz. They produce posters focusing on nature, society, and whole systems.

ANIMAL RIGHTS

Kids and Others for Animals, Paula van Orden and Evan Dagher, 5429 Baldwin Ave, Temple City, CA 91780. Educates and involves kids in the plight of some animals in our society. They have available a list of hundreds of organizations pertaining to the animal rights movement and children's issues. Organization list, $7.50.

11

Vegetarianism, Exercise, and Athletics

There is only *one* solution to the problem of overweight. I repeat: *only one.* And that is: *eat less and exercise more.*

Paavo Airola

Many times at vegetarian congresses, I see a vegetarian who is obese. This isn't good: diet alone is not enough; you must have exercise also.

Peter Burwash, tennis professional

Nowadays there are vegetarians in every major sport, from boxing to badminton. Athletes are finding strength, endurance, and clarity of purpose through a vegetarian regimen. In an experiment recently conducted in Sweden, nine athletes were fed a meat diet (high-fat, high-protein). After three days they were tested for endurance on a stationary bicycle. Their average time on the cycle was 57 minutes. Using a conventional mixed diet (lower in meat, fat, and protein), the athletes rode for 114 minutes. Finally, a diet high in grains and vegetables resulted in 167 minutes on the cycle. This diet, rich in natural carbohydrates, gave the athletes triple the endurance of the high-protein meat diet conventionally thought to be the best for the modern athlete.

In light of the untimely death of running guru, Jim Fixx (*The Complete Book of Running,* Random House, 201 E 50 St, New York, NY 10022, 1977, $10.00), people must re-examine their exercise regimens. Over-exercising can create dan-gerous, life-threatening situations. A good rule to follow is if you've been active throughout your life, then a full, strenuous program may be in order. But, if you've been sedentary, and suddenly get the exercise bug, you must take it easy, work gradually, don't debilitate, but build. In any case, before starting *any* exercise program, everyone *must* consult their physician.

Exercise carried out in moderation should be enervating for body and mind. In accordance with a well thought out vegetarian diet, the average person as well as the athlete will surely benefit.

The strongest animals with the greatest endurance, the horse, the ox, the elephant, are all vegetarians. In fact the human physical apparatus is not that of a carnivore. Carnivores have sharp talons and large teeth for tearing flesh, but the teeth of humans more closely resemble those of vegetarian animals who have flat molars for grinding. Furthermore, carnivores have short intestines, usually no more than three times the length of the trunk of the body, so that meat can be quickly absorbed and eliminated from the body before it has time to putrefy. But human intestines are huge, 12 times the body length, giving the meat time to turn rank inside the intestinal tract and poison the consumer.

VEGETARIAN ATHLETES

Vegetarian athletes include Chris Evert Lloyd, Johnny Weissmuller, Buster Crabbe, Bill Walton,

Ralph Sampson, Austin Carr, Connie Hawkins, Roger Brown, Dave Cash, Pete LaCock, Jim Katt, Edwin Moses, Amby Burfoot (winner of the 1978 Boston marathon), Siegried Bauer, Paavo Nurmi, Murray Rose, Chip Oliver, and three-time world wrestling champion Lee Kemp.

BOOKS

The Athlete's Kitchen by Nancy Clark. Bantam Books, 666 Fifth Ave, New York, NY 10103, 1983, $3.95. Sports nutritionist tells how to eat to win. Includes some discussion of the vegetarian athlete.

Peter Burwash's Vegetarian Primer by Peter Burwash and John Tullius. Atheneum, 597 Fifth Ave, New York, NY 10017, $14.95. A former professional tennis player, Burwash now manages other professional athletes. Burwash relates his own experience as a vegetarian, then becomes more philosophical as he recounts the spiritual side of vegetarian eating; its beauty, its peace, its health-saving qualities.

The Complete Book of Walking by Charles T. Kuntzleman and the editors of *Consumer Guide*. Pocket Books, 1230 Avenue of the Americas, New York, NY 10020, 1979, $3.50. One of the best exercise systems, especially for older people, is serious daily walking.

Hatha Yoga by Sanskrti and Veda. The Himalayan International Institute of Yoga Science and Philosophy, RD 1 Box 88, Honesdale, PA 18431, 1977, $6.95. This manual, in two volumes, is based on the hatha yoga teachings of Sri Swami Rama. Wide variety of exercises.

How to Eat to Win: Food for Champions by Ned Bayra and Chris Qualter. Berkley Books, 200 Madison Ave, New York, NY 10016, 1984, $3.50. Some discussion of vegetarianism and its positive impact on athletes in training.

Joints and Glands Exercises by Sri Swami Rama. Simple book of yoga stretches to increase circulation and flexibility.

The Long Run Solution by Joe Henderson. World Publications, PO Box 366, Mountain View, CA 94040. 1976. $3.95. Running with intelligence, instead of compulsion. Henderson's philosophy is strength, not debilitation. Everyone at their own pace, the gradual and steady, enjoyable means to health and physical well-being.

The Massage Book by George Downing. Random House, 201 E 50 St, New York, NY 10022, 1972, $8.95. Practical, simple instructions for massage regimen.

The Second Book of Do-In by Jacques de Langre. Happiness Press, 14351 Wycliff Way, PO Box DD, Magalia, CA 95954, 1981, $10.00. Healing and rejuvenation through self-massage techniques calling upon the axioms of an ancient system.

SportsFitness for Women by Sandra Rosenzweig. Harper and Row Publishers, 10 E 53 St, New York, NY 10022, 1982, $9.95. Includes an excellent discussion of the vegetarian woman athlete in the context of a complete resource book.

Stretching by Bob Anderson.

AUDIO TAPES

The Main Ingredients: Positive Thinking, Exercise and Diet by Susan Smith Jones. Health Unlimited, 332 Gretna Green Way, Los Angeles, CA 90049, $10.00. Exercise and fitness columnist for *Vegetarian Times* tells all.

NEWSLETTERS

Executive Fitness, Rodale Press, 33 E Minor St, Emmaus, PA 18049. Bimonthly; one year (26 issues), $27.00. Health news and information for the busy man or woman on the go: how to eat in the executive dining room.

NUTRITIONAL SUPPLEMENTS

A vegetarian athlete really needs no supplements. A well-balanced diet will give her or him a complete spectrum of vitamins, minerals, and nutrients. Proteins, derived from a variety of legumes, and other sources, will be complete. Some authorities suggest a vitamin B_{12} supplement. However, some athletes don't feel comfortable without the added cushion of a nutritional supplement.

SportScience Laboratories, PO Box 390, Essex Junction, VT 05452. Makers of Competitive Edge vitamins, minerals, and food supplements—nine formulas designed to make you tough! Not all are vegetarian. Send for information.

SAMPLE REGIMEN

The first place baseball finish of the Chicago White Sox during the 1983 season has been in part attributed to this diet that could easily be converted to a totally vegetarian diet.

Ann Grandjean, associate director of the Swanson Center for Nutrition at the University of Nebraska Medical Center, originated the diet. She has worked with the University of Nebraska football team, and has worked as a consultant to the United States Olympic Committee.

Breakfast: Heavy in carbohydrates (whole bread, pancakes or waffles)

Lunch: Big meal of the day, eaten between 2 P.M. and 3 P.M. Pasta, bread, baked potato, fish or fowl for the White Sox, but you could substitute vegetarian sources of protein. No red meats! They make the player sluggish because digesting it eats up the oxygen in his or her system. Every vegetarian athlete who describes his or her diet comments on the feeling of competitive lightness that accompanies their eating regimens.

Dinner: The light meal of the day. Grandjean doesn't want the player going to sleep with a heavy stomach. Fruits, vegetables, salad, nuts.

Players are advised to sleep 8 hours.

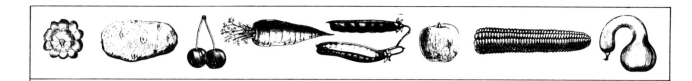

12

What's To Eat?

WHAT IS NATURAL FOOD?

The United States Department of Agriculture's definition of a natural product is any food item that "does not contain any artificial flavoring, coloring ingredient, or chemical preservative, or any other artificial or synthetic ingredient and the product and its ingredients are not more than minimally processed."

In today's supermarket, however, natural has come to mean virtually anything. Many chemical additives are presumed to fall under the "natural" heading simply because they or their facsimiles occur in "nature." The consumer's one recourse is to become a careful and prudent label reader. If there is any doubt, don't buy.

WHAT IS ORGANIC FOOD?

Organic food is produced in a fertile, self-regenerative soil, rich in organic matter. Through soil management, crop rotation, composting, animal manures, and a variety of biological controls to maintain crop productivity, these soils are crafted to generate their own nutrients without the use of synthetic additives. Pest control is achieved through the use of predatory insects or natural substances, such as caffeine. Chemical pesticides are not used. Some states (e.g., California) have established regulatory commissions that affix an "organic" label on produce, but most do not. Deal with a retailer who you trust, and ask

questions about the food that you buy. Remember also that it is always best to eat what is locally grown.

According to the United States Department of Agriculture, vegetable consumption is at its highest level in 30 years. Between 1981 and 1982, fresh vegetable consumption climbed from 105 pounds per capita to 110 pounds per capita.

In India food is categorized into three groups according to the effects it has on the eater. The first is known as *satvik* or pure foods. Satvik foods include vegetables, grains, legumes, beans, fruits, nuts, milk, butter, and cheese. Such a diet, taken in moderation, is said to keep the head and heart pure, producing serenity and balance. The second category is *rajsic,* energizing foods, such as pepper and all kinds of spices, condiments, and sour and bitter foods. A diet including such things will produce restlessness. The final category is stupefying foods, *tamsic.* These foods are meat, fish and fowl, alcohol, eggs, and all stale foods. Such a diet produces inertia.

ORGANIZATIONS

California Agrarian Action Project, PO Box 464, Davis, CA 95617; (916) 756-8518. Citizen organization working with growers, consumers, and government agencies to modernize farming techniques and cut down the use of dangerous chemicals. Send for pamphlets "What is Organic Food?" available at $4.00 per 100.

California Certified Organic Farmers, Statewide Chapter, 1920 Maciel Ave, Santa Cruz, CA 95060; (408) 476-0504. Group set up to assure consumers that the food grown in California under the Organic Food Act of 1979 is indeed organic.

Friends of the Earth, 1045 Sansome Street, San Francisco, CA 94111; (415) 433-7373. Environmental group that strongly supports pesticide-free organic farming. They use extensive lobbying efforts to help their cause. Membership fee ($25.00) includes a subscription to *Not Man Apart,* the FOE environmental newspaper.

Greenmarket, c/o Council on the Environment, 51 Chambers St, New York, NY 10007; (212) 477-3220. The aim of the Greenmarkets, which have been springing up all over New York City these last few years, is to bring fresh, locally grown produce to city neighborhoods. Champion of the farm-to-city movement, Greenmarket has a three-fold purpose. First, they want to establish a marketplace in the city for local farmers. Second, they want to provide fresh, healthful food to city dwellers. Third, they have hopes of revitalizing urban areas that are currently run down and ragged. For example, Union Square, once the home of political movements and soap box speakers, was until recently the home of drug pushers and addicts. Greenmarket set up two dozen trucks on a Saturday morning, and, astonishingly, the junkies moved aside and organic cabbages moved in. You can buy corn, apples, freshly baked bread, rennetless cheese, fresh spices, jams, pretzels, melons, tomatoes, lettuce, all according to season, all fresh, and cheaper than at the supermarket. Not all the farmers produce organically grown goods, but more than a few do. Greenmarkets presently take place in Brooklyn, East Harlem, Clinton (Hell's Kitchen), Greenwich Village, and they're spreading. Their newsletter, *Greenmarket News,* is published six times per year (subscription rate, $5.00). Included is news of where and when the markets take place, a "Farmer of the Month" feature, and a "Vegetable of the Month," too. There are articles on preservation techniques, farm survival, community gardens, and recycling. Helpful to those thinking of setting up a similar program in an urban blighted community.

International Federation of Organic Agricultural Movements (IFOAM), Postfach, CH 4104, Oberwill/BL, Switzerland. Coordinates and monitors the development of organic agriculture on a worldwide basis, providing a forum for growers, merchants, and academicians to discuss international standards and evaluation procedures.

BOOKS

The Complete Book of Natural Foods by Fred Rohé. Shambhala Publications, PO Box 271, Boulder, CO 80306; $12.95 plus $1.50 shipping. Helps to get you on track for smart eating in the 1980s. Loaded with helpful tips and useful information.

Food Combining Made Easy by Herbert Shelton. Natural Hygiene Press, 698 Brooklawn Ave, Bridgeport, CT. A handbook telling how to eat for optimum nourishment and health. Shows how incompatible foods lead to difficulties in the digestive tract. Classifies food and offers menu ideas. For example, fruits should not be eaten with vegetables at the same meal. Acidic fruits such as oranges, lemons, grapefruit, strawberries, and pineapple do not mix well with sweet fruits like bananas, papayas, dates, and figs. Foods rich in protein such as nuts, seeds, and legumes do not do well with high-starch foods such as potatoes, grains, corn, and carrots. On the other hand, green leafy vegetables are excellent with both protein-rich food and carbohydrate-heavy food.

Food Co-ops in New York City: An Organizing Handbook and Resource Guide by the Community Food Resource Center. 17 Murray St, 4th Floor, New York, NY 10007, $4.25 through the mail; $3.00 at their office; (212) 349-8155. How to organize a food co-op, and how to work together with friends, neighbors, and co-workers to get high-quality food at low prices. Help in buying wholesale, keeping records, and sizing crates and cases. Useful particularly in New York, but could be helpful to others.

Nutrition Sourcebook for the Eighties by Gary Null. Macmillan, 866 Third Ave, New York, NY 10022; $7.95. A listing of thousands of different foods referenced by nutrient values. Cross-indexed for protein, carbohydrates, fat, fiber, cholesterol, sodium, vitamins, and minerals.

The Psychobiology of Human Food Selection edited by Lewis M. Barker. Avi Publishing Company, Westport, CT; $27.50. This book makes a study of what humans would eat if they were stripped of socialization and relied on instinct alone. Living in a society that relies on inspiration rather than need, people have adulterated his diet. The book tries to get back to what Paavo Airola (see Chapter 3) called "eating at your roots." That is, not only eating what is native to your area, but eating what is common to the part of the world where your ancestors originated.

Shopper's Guide to Natural Foods. Shopper's Guide, East–West Journal, PO Box 1200, Brookline Village, MA 02147; $3.95 per copy. Compilation of articles from the macrobiotic magazine, *East–West Journal* (see Chapter 2, Section on macrobiotics). An informed and comprehensive handbook on basic foods.

NEWSLETTERS AND MAGAZINES

Natural Perspective, PO Box 22424, San Francisco, CA 94122. Edited by Fred Rohé, an outgrowth of the *The Complete Book of Natural Foods*. What Rohé wants to do with this newsletter is "set up an information flow and filing system, and *stay* on top of things." A constant update of his book. A ten-issue subscription is $15.00.

Raisin Consciousness, 849 South Broadway, #310, Los Angeles, CA 90014. Any editorial correspondence goes to Mike Cluster, editor, 4071 W 130 St, #F, Hawthorne, CA 90250; (213) 676-3205. Food alternative newsletter primarily for the Los Angeles area, but these helpful articles can be pertinent anywhere. The group is "basically educational, working to inform people of the alternatives to supermarkets as well as providing information about what's wrong with our nation's corporate-controlled food system." For a one-year subscription (six issues) they ask for a donation of between $2.50 and $10.00, according to your income level.

POSTERS

Nutrition Scoreboard, Center for Science in the Public Interest, 1779 Church St NW, Washington, D.C. 20036; $1.75. This poster shows the nutritional values of many common foods. The more nutritious the food, the higher the rating.

FOOD DISTRIBUTORS

Arrowhead Mills, PO Box 2059, Hereford, TX 79045; (806) 364-0730. Wholesale suppliers of grains, cereals, whole-grain flour, mixes, oils, peanut butter, cake and cookie mixes, granolas, beans, seeds, nuts, condiments, the *Deaf Smith Country Cookbook,* the *Deaf Smith Farms Cookbook,* the *Simpler Life Cookbook,* and *Menu Planner.*

Chico-San Products, PO Box 810, Chico, CA 95927. Brown rice and rice products, including rice cakes, whole grains, seeds, beans, condiments, imported seaweeds, herb teas, and traditional oriental cookbooks. Free catalog and natural food newsletter, *Crackerbarrel.*

Country Life Natural Foods, Box 163, Harrisville, NH 03450; (603) 827-3389. Bulk food distributor associated with the Seventh-Day Adventists. Easy to prepare, ready-made soyfood dinners and meat substitutes.

Eden Foods, 701 Tecumseh Rd, Clinton, MI 49236; (800) 248-0301, (517) 456-7425. Wholesale organic food distributors: whole grains, beans, flour, pasta, cereals, granolas, ready-made dinners and beans, mixes, unrefined oils, vinegars, shoyu-tamari, miso, seaweed, oriental vegetables, *ume* plum products, nuts and seeds, dry roasted nuts, snacks, nut and seed butters, fruit jams, juices and drinks, sweeteners, condiments, sauces, pickles, baking and cooking goods, crackers, chips, rice cakes, teas, candies, cheese, herbs, ginseng, body care products, vitamin and mineral supplements, cooking utensils, and books.

Erewhon Natural Foods, 236 Washington St, Brookline, MA 02146. Whole grains, flour, pasta, beans, seeds, nuts, dried fruit, sea vegetables, miso, tamari, macrobiotics (they offer a macrobiotic starter kit: 15 food items, recipes, and sample menus for $45.00), condiments, oils, sweeteners, snacks, sweets, beverages, herbs, spices, natural cosmetics, cookware, appliances, books, gifts.

Granum Company, Department J, PO Box 14057, Seattle, WA 98114; (206) 323-0892. Japanese macrobiotic staples and specialty items. Wholesale inquiries encouraged.

Mercantile Development, 274 Riverside Ave, PO Box 2747, Westport, CT 06880. A major supplier of organic food products throughout the United States and most of Western Europe.

Organic Farms, Inc., 10714 Hanna St, Beltsville, MD 20705; (301) 595-5151, 52, 53, 54. Wholesalers of organically grown food: nuts and seeds, dried fruit, pasta, cereals, legumes, grains, sweeteners, juices, produce, cheese, dairy, tempeh, tofu, coffee, teas, more.

Suncloud Distributing, 2102 NW 15 Ave, Miami, FL (305) 325-1106. Organic produce, tofu products, raw milk and cheeses, juices.

Walnut Acres, Penns Creek, PA 17862; (717) 837-0601. Five hundred-acre organic farm in business since 1946, supplier of everything from brown rice to tree-ripened olives to corn chutney. Their catalog is a delight.

Wildwood Natural Foods, 135 Bolinas Rd, Fairfax, CA 94930; (415) 459-3919. Wildwood makes natural, ready-to-eat foods for over 80 stores in the San Francisco Bay area. They make their own cauldron-style tofu daily with organic soybeans, filtered water, and nigari for curdling. They use this tofu in their tofu steaks,, avocado tofu sandwiches, tofu vegetable salad, dill tofu salad, etc. They make natural sushi, hummus, tabouli, and hijiki rice pie as well. They welcome all wholesale inquiries.

FOODSTUFFS

CHEESE AND MILK

Cresset Farms, RD 1, Route 34B, Aurora, NY 13026; (315) 364-7286. Cheese made from raw milk on an organic farm. A six-pound wheel is $18.00 plus shipping.

GOAT MILK

Dairy Goat Journal, PO Box 1908, Scottsdale, AZ 85252. Journal of the goat industry. Interesting

for the farmer as well as the consumer. One-year subscription, $9.00 (12 issues).

Hoegger Supply Co, Dept O, PO Box 331, Fayetteville, GA 30214. Dairy goat supplies.

FRUIT/DRIED FRUIT/FRUIT JUICES

Ahler's Organic Date, Grapefruit Garden, Box 726, Mecca, CA 92254.

Jaffe Brothers, PO Box 636, Valley Center, CA 92082; (619) 749-1133. Thirty-four-year-old family business. Produce originates from their ranch. Organically grown, untreated foods, including dried apples, apricots, dates, figs, peaches, pears, raisins, bananas, pineapple, papayas, and mangoes. Also, nuts, almonds, peanuts, cashews, pecans, walnuts, macadamias, pistachios. Gift boxes of fruits and nuts. Seeds: sunflower, sesame, flaxseed, pumpkin, chia, and alfalfa for sprouting. Cold-pressed, unprocessed olive oil from organic olives ($15.25 per gallon). Grains, brown rice, pasta, peas, beans, honey, bee pollen, and vegetarian food supplements.

Lee's Fruit Company, PO Box 450, Hobby Hill, Leesburg, FL 32748. Oranges and grapefruits, chemically free, composted ($23.75/bushel; $16.80/half-bushel; $19.25/three-quarter bushel). Add $4.00 west of the Mississippi.

Life Support Systems, 6034 Rose St, Houston, TX 77007. Aloe Vera Juice, $20.00/gallon; case (4 gallons), $75.

Starr Organic Produce, 2926 "C" Road, Loxahatchee, FL 33470; (305) 798-0399. Wholesale distributors of organically grown tree-ripened fruit and vegetables. Avocadoes, papayas, oranges, grapefruits, tangelos, and more according to season.

Sunshower Orchards, RR1, Box 56, Lawrence, MI 49064; (616) 674-3103. Apple, apple blends with grape, cherry, strawberry, and pear. Fresh and frozen. Also apple butter and apple sauce.

Swampfox Vineyards, Box 148 Waskom TX 75692; (214) 687-2617. Six miles south of Waskom on Farms Market Road 9. Features grapes, blueberries, sweet corn, purplehull peas, herbs, and vegetables (in season only).

Timber Crest Farms, 4791 Dry Creek Rd, Healdsburg, CA 95448; (707) 433-8251. Dried organic apples, apricots, dates, figs (both black Mission and Calmyna), peaches, pears, prunes, Monukka and Thompson raisins, pineapple, almonds, cashews, brazil nuts, pistachios, filberts. Gift boxes, trays, and baskets.

GRAINS

Diamond K Farms, St. Charles, MN 55972. Grains, stone-ground flours, wheat, rye, corn, buckwheat, soybeans, brown rice, roasted soybeans, sunflower seeds.

Clarke Whetham, 11230 West Mt. Morris Rd, Flushing, MI 48433; (313) 659-8414. Organic. Late July and August. White wheat for food storage and home flour grinding.

HERBS FOR COOKING (see also Chapter 6)

Fox Hill Farms, 444 West Michigan Ave, Box 7, Parma, MI 49269; (517) 531-3179. Twelve-bunch herb assortment includes: sweet basil, French fine leaf basil, thyme, Greek oregano, rosemary, French tarragon, French sorrel, watercress, chervil, savory ($20.00). For pesto lovers, *Basil Annonymous* membership (which equates to a pound of fresh basil sent once a month), is $200.00 for the year. Half a pound is $135.00.

Rafal Spice Company, 2521 Russell St, Detroit, MI 48207; (313) 259-6373. Hard-to-find spices for regional and ethnic cuisine. Send for a list.

LIVING FOODS

Fresh and potent vitamins and energy are bursting forth from sprouts! Dr. Ann Wigmore of the Hippocrates Health Institute in Boston lives on 35 cents worth of living food per day. Here's some tips:

Salad: Sunflower seed sprouts make an especially delicious salad. Soak the seeds overnight, then given them a day to sprout. Use a shallow plastic cake platter, and spread a thin layer of quality soil on the bottom. Cover with plastic wrap. In seven days you'll have the makings of a beautiful green salad.

Soup: Put several well-scrubbed potatoes, avocado, water and herbs in a blender. Liquefy, but don't cook. Just eat.

Milk: Put coconut strips and water in a blender. After they're nicely blended, strain and drink.

Bread: Soak wheat berries for about 12 hours, then allow them to sprout for a day or two. Blend with water until you get a paste approximately the consistency of cereal. Spread on a plastic sheet and let it dry naturally. Unleavened, but delicious.

Dr. Wigmore suggests "drinking" your solid food; "chewing" your liquids. That is, chew your solid foods until they become like juice, and swish around your juice in your mouth several times before you swallow.

LIVE FOODS NEWSLETTERS

The Sproutletter, PO Box 62, Ashland, OR 97520; (503) 482-5627. If Jeff Breakey, a very active man, gets even half his energy from his live food, sprout-centered diet, then that's endorsement enough. Jeff works hard to put information about sprouts out in the real world. *The Sproutletter* is full of innovative tips, recipes, and book reviews which focus on sprouts, raw foods, and nutrition. There is also a networking feature. Back issues full of excellent material on topics such as wheat grass, chlorophyll, indoor gardening, equipment, and tools are available. A one-year subscription (6 issues) is $14.00.

Also available from the *Sproutletter* are sprouting charts, providing detailed information regarding sprouting 39 different seeds, grains, and legumes. These are only 25 cents. A variety of hand-painted buttons and bumper stickers are also sold.

You can also order books from Breakey. Add 10% handling charges for orders under $30.00.

Love the Sunshine in with Sprouts by Sita Ananda. 130 pp, $4.50. This book deals with indoor gardening and sprouting. Included are recipes and information about seed storage.

The Miracle of Sprouting by Stephen Blauu. 73 pp, $3.95. A basic book dealing with sprouts, their cultivation and use. Includes recipes.

The UNcook Book by Elizabeth and Elton Baker. 210 pp, $5.95. Breakey calls this the best, most complete sprout, live food book he has seen.

Wheatgrass Juice—Gift of Nature by Betsy Russell Manning. 26 pp, $2.00. A booklet devoted to the growing, juicing, and health-giving properties of wheat grass.

SPROUTING ORGANIZATIONS

The Sprout House, 210 Riverside Dr, New York, NY 10025; (212) 864-3222. The "Sproutman," Steve Meyerwitz holds weekly meetings, courses, workshops, and cooking instruction classes, all on the topics of live foods and sprouts. He sells a complete line of sprouting supplies, juicers, and other equipment.

NUTS

Ace Pecan Company, PO Box 747, 900 Morse Ave, Elk Grove Village, IL 60007; (312) 364-3278 or 3279 (call collect). Retailers can buy cases of pecans, cashews, almonds, pistachios, peanuts, brazil nuts, raisins, dates, and dried apricots. One-pound samplers are $3.75 for pecan halves, $4.75 for cashews.

San Saba Pecan Company, 2803 West Wallace, San Saba, TX 76877. Native nuts that grow wild along Texas rivers and creeks. They are never sprayed or fertilized. First pound $5.75, each additional pound $5.25. Over five pounds, $4.50.

Virginia Diner, Inc, PO Box 310, Wakerfield, VA 23888; (804) 899-3106. Water-blanched, salted or unsalted peanuts. Crisp with deep flavor. Two-and-a-half-pound can is $6.95 plus shipping. One pound is $2.60.

OILS

Arrowhead Mills (see distributors) guide to natural oils:

Sesame: Light oil for sauteeing or stir-frying vegetables, grains, noodles; good for homemade salad dressings. Best all-around oil with excellent stability.

Safflower: Light oil. One of the best for frying; also good for sauteeing and the preparation of mayonnaise, but tends toward rancidity.

Corn: A rich oil fine for baking pie crusts and breads and popping corn.

Soy: An especially strong-tasting oil fine for baking, but may go rancid quickly.

Peanut: Another strong oil good for frying.

Olive: Best for classical salad dressing and sauces for pasta. Strong in flavor and aroma.

SALT-FREE FOOD

Salt Free Gourmet Company, 215 E 49 St, New York, NY 10017; (212) 759-5991. Kosher dills pickled in cider vinegar and spices, among other salt-free items.

SOY PRODUCTS

Soy products are some of the best sources of vegetarian protein. Historically, soybeans are one of the American farmer's best crops (they can be grown in a variety of different climates and soils). But most of the soybean crop is either fed to livestock or exported to the Orient. It is only recently that Americans are finding uses for soybeans in their daily diet.

Tofu is becoming a common product in many dairy cases although it is not truly a dairy product. Tofu is made by boiling soybeans, mashing them, and then pressing out the "milk" through a strainer. A coagulant is then added, and the water is squeezed out. The resultant curd resembles cheese, and can be used in a variety of ways. Mixed with pureed fruit or vegetables, tofu makes an excellent baby food. Tofu "ice cream" has taken over as a summer time craze that threatens to outstrip frozen yogurt. Tofu acts like a sponge, soaking up the flavor of anything it is cooked with. Tofu's use is virtually unlimited for the creative cook.

Recent studies by the Connecticut Agricultural Experiment Station have found high levels of bacteria in soy products, including tofu. *Soy Foods* magazine warns consumers that they must buy only soy products that are kept cool, preferably refrigerated, but at the least, below room temperature. Cooking soy products for at least two minutes will kill most of the bacteria that may cause gatrointestinal discomfort associated with improperly prepared or stored soy products.

STORING TOFU

Tofu is stored in water. To reduce bacteria growth it is best to keep tofu in the refrigerator. After you buy tofu, rinse it off and place it in a plastic tub with a tightly fitting top. If you change the water daily, tofu will keep in the refrigerator for about one week.

Tofu can be kept in the freezer for months, and after freezing you wil find it firmer and drier. Its changed texture will enable you to use the tofu in a variety of creative and different ways. You may also wish to dehydrate it following defrosting. In this way the tofu may be kept at room temperature for weeks.

How to freeze tofu: Rinse and drain well. Tofu that has been in the refrigerator for a while (which you think you might have to throw out in a few days) is a prime candidate for freezing. Wrap the tofu well in freezer wrap, place it in a zip-lock storage bag or in any air-tight container. The tofu can be frozen in a block or cubes. Defrosting takes 3 to 4 hours. Defrosted tofu's texture will be firm but grainy. Any excess water can be squeezed out.

How to dehydrate tofu: The oven should be preheated to 250° F. Flavor with tamari or garlic salt if you desire. Cut the tofu into chunks and place on a cookie sheet. Bake until very dry and crisp. Store in an air-tight container. If you crumble the tofu instead of cubing it your end result will be a very versatile vegetable protein.

Tempeh is fermented soybeans. Originating in Indonesia, (whereas tofu comes from Japan), tempeh is made in a process similar to that in yogurt making. A microorganism is introduced to the hulled, cooked beans, and these are allowed to ferment. Tempeh is a cultured food that comes in 8-ounce cakes, one-half inch thick. The texture is sometimes compared to that of chicken or veal. Tempeh is rich in protein, vitamin B_{12}, and iron; it contains no cholesterol and little fat. It can be all soybeans, but sometimes the soybeans are combined with grains. Tempeh is made from a combination of rice, wheat, millet, oats, and barley, and has a most delicate flavor. It is especially good with cheeses and cream sauces, soaking up their flavors. For a mushroomy flavor try soy–rice tempeh. For Mexican food and curries use soy tempeh, the tempeh with the strongest flavor. (From the *Tempeh Primer* by Robin Clute and Juel Anderson, Creative Arts Communications, 833 Bancroft Way, Berkeley, CA 94701.)

How to make soy milk: Rinse and then soak 3 cups of whole soybeans in 6 cups of cold water for about 10 hours. Drain, then resoak the beans in hot water for another four hours. By this time the beans will have doubled in size. Then, in a blender combine 1 cup of beans with 2½ cups of fresh water. Blend for about 1 minute. Put the result in a holding container, then repeat the process until all the soybeans are blended. Now bring the soymilk to a boil in a kettle. Beware: soymilk will boil over quickly; watch it carefully. Lower the heat and simmer for 20 minutes. Cool. Strain the milk through cheesecloth. Squeeze out the last of the milk from the pulp. Sweeten slightly to taste.

The Soyfood Center, PO Box 234, Lafayette, CA 94549 Industry promoter, information supplier for the soyfood industry. Send for pamphlets. Books available from them include:

The Book of Miso by William Shurtleff and Akiko Aoyagi. Ballantine Books, 201 E 50 St, New York, NY 10022; $2.95.

The Book of Tempeh by William Shurtleff and Akiko Aoyagi. Harper and Row, 10 E 53 St, New York, NY 10022; $6.95.

The Book of Tofu by William Shurtleff and Akiko Aoyagi. Ballantine Books, 201 E 50 St, New York, NY 10022; $2.95.

Books published by the Soyfood Center: *Miso Production*, $9.95; *Tempeh Production*, $15.95; *Tofu and Soymilk Production*, $17.95.

TOFU AND TEMPEH MANUFACTURERS

South River Miso Company, South River Farm, Conway, MA 01341; (413) 369-4057. Makers of several varieties of miso, available in one-pound packaging and in bulk.

Soyfoods Unlimited, 14670 Doolittle Dr, San Leandro, CA 94577. Tempeh makers.

OTHER SOY PRODUCTS

Quong Hop and Company, 161 Beacon St, South San Francisco, CA 94080; (415) 873-4444. Egg-free, low-calorie, non-dairy, creamy tofu salad dressing. Since 1906.

SWEETS AND SWEETENERS

Most every one of us has been brought up in a sugar-rich environment, full of candies, cookies, cakes, and sweet drinks. We all hear the cry to stay away from refined white sugar, but for those of us with a sweet tooth, what to add?

ORGANIZATIONS

Fructose Freeze, 309 Spring St, Herndon, VA 22070; (703) 437-9090 or (800) 336-3388. Organization campaigning to make the public aware that fructose, the supposed natural sweetener, is actually a refined sugar made from corn syrup. They are seeking "integrity and quality" in the health food industry.

HONEY

Hackenberg Apiaries, RD #5, Box 11, Lewisburg, PA 17837; (717) 524-9592. Honey, pollination service, bee removal.

Lang Apiaries, Gasport, NY 14057. Clover, fall-flower, and buckwheat honeys: 5 lbs., $7.50; 60 lbs., $55.00.

Thousand Islands Apiaries, RD 2, Box 212, Clayton, NY 13624. Liquid honey, comb honey, honey creams. Honey cookbooks, gifts.

MAPLE SYRUP

Warren Allen, Beaver Falls, NY 13305; (315) 346-6706. Organic maple syrup, no formaldehyde pellets used in their trees or other chemicals used. Five gallons, baking grade, $55.00; 5 gallons, medium amber, $77.00.

Droster Sugar Bush, Cottage Grove, WI 53527. One gallon, $19.50. Shipping, $2.00.

Red Fox Farm, Bonita Klemm, Box 6A, Sharon Springs, NY 13459. Free brochure. A small producer of organic maple syrup. Red Fox Farm uses no formaldehyde pellets in their trees and they take great care in filtering and evaporating their syrup. They do it the traditional way with a wood-fired evaporator, but make use of modern filtration. They take pride in the making of their syrup, which is heat-sealed (vacuum-packed). One pint, $6.50; one quart, $8.00; half gallon, $15.00; gallon, $25.00. State if you want light, medium, or dark amber syrup.

William Seale, Alstead, NH 03602; (603) 835-6722. $4.00/pint; $6.25/quart; $19.50/gallon.

The Wright Farm, Donald and Carol Wright, Rolling Ledge Maple Orchard, Enosburg Falls, VT 05450; (802) 933-4070 or 933-4775. Free brochure; $3.60/pint; $5.45/quart; $18.75/gallon.

SUGAR-FREE COOKIES AND CANDY

Cookies from Home, 418 South Mill Ave, Tempe, AZ 85281; (602) 894-1944. They call their cookies "super naturals"—made with sun-sweetened raisins, English walnuts, whole-wheat flour, chopped dates, and sweetened with dessert flower honey. They deliver locally and ship cookie gifts worldwide.

Yosef's Mama's Carrot Cakes, 250 Decatur St, Brooklyn, NY 11233; (212) 756-8885. Three-pound cakes.

NON-DAIRY ICE CREAM

Heller Enterprises, 395 Atlantic Ave, East Rockaway, NY 11518; (516) 593-3557. Tofu frozen desert. Wholesale.

Ice Bean from Farms Foods, Summertown, TN 38483. Non-dairy ice cream made with soymilk and honey. Cholesterol free. No animal products.

Robinson Foods, PO Box 1041, Fairfield, IA 52556. Natural, sugar-free candy bars and confectionery. Wholesale.

SUGAR-FREE SOFT DRINKS

Ginseng Up, Empire State Building, Suite 6103, New York, NY 10118. Ginseng Up is a sparkling herb drink made from organic Korean ginseng root. It retains all its natural minerals and vitamins. Not only is it refreshing, but the ginseng is supposed to keep you young.

Honey Pure Corporation, 309 Spring St, Herndon, VA 22070; (800) 336-3388 or (703) 437-9090. Fructose-free beverage in six flavors: root beer, English ginger, wild black cherry, lemon, orange, and cream cola.

CONVENIENCE FOODS

Bioforce, 21 West Mall, Plainview, NY 11803; (516) 420-1600 or (800) 645-9135. Coffee substitutes, herb teas, seasonings, condiments, preserves and fruit spreads, cereals, grains, seeds, crisp breads, food supplements, soy products (burgers), spaghetti sauce, curry, lasagne, cannelloni, ravioli, cosmetics, herb tinctures, vitamins, supplements.

Fantastic Foods, 106 Galli Dr, Novato, CA 94947; (415) 883-7718. Convenience mixes with no animal products or chemical additives, such as falafal preparation, grain and legume burgers, etc.

Grainaissance, 800 Heinz Ave, Berkeley, CA 94710; (415) 849-2866. Manufacturers of mochi and amazake. (See the glossary at the end of this section.)

Light Foods, Inc., 6144 Bartmer, St. Louis, MO 63133; (314) 721-3960. Manufacturer of soy hot dogs, sausage, and bologna made from tofu. Also tofu spinach pies, tofu tamale pies, tofu apple pies. Wholesale only.

Laughing Moon Food Company, 220 Third Ave, Venice, CA 90291; (213) 396-8616. Non-dairy, meatless, soy-based frozen convenience foods. Tofu vegetable and fruit turnovers.

New Age Naturals, 3500 Clayton Rd, Ste B #127, Concord, CA 94519; (415) 827-5626. Celestial Seasoning and Traditional Medicinal teas. Lifeline vitamins, Earthrise Spirulina. Free home delivery.

Oak Feed, 3030 Grand Ave, Coconut Grove, FL 33313; (305) 448-4370 or 448-7595. Makers of macrobiotic convenience foods, such as amazake, seitan burgers, mochi, and packet-wrapped brown rice dinners. (See the glossary at the end of this section for an explanation of amazake and seitan.)

Vegetarian Health Society, PO Box 11291, Chicago, IL 60611; (800) 323-4092 or (312) 547-1700. Food distributing club. (They ask for a $10.00 membership that entitles subscribers to a 10% discount on vegetarian meat substitutes, vegetarian cookies, fruit pies, vegetarian ice cream mix, etc.). Besides the food, they distribute vitamins, minerals, books, tapes, educational material, lectures, newsletter. The society itself is located at 2154 W Madison St, Bellwood, IL 60104.

GLOSSARY

aduki beans   Small red, dried bean. Because of its low fat content a remarkably digestible bean.

agar-agar   A gelatin made from eight kinds of red seaweed that is said to benefit the heart by dissolving cholesterol in the blood vessels.

amazake   Rice nectar. A rich, sweet, refreshing drink fermented from whole-grain brown rice.

arame   A black, mild seaweed.

arrowroot powder   A vegetable starch used as a thickener.

black turtle beans   A bean good in soups and Mexican dishes.

brown rice   Brought to the West by Alexander the Great, it has a balance of sodium and potassium remarkably similar to that of our blood. Can be stored indefinitely.

burdock   A long, dark root vegetable with an earthy flavor. Often found growing wild.

chickpeas (garbanzo beans)   Staple of Middle Eastern fare, including hummus.

daikon   Oriental white radish.

dulse   Seaweed, rich in taste, good cooked or in salads.

fu   Dried wheat gluten.

gomasio   Sesame sea salt. Roast sesame seeds in a dry, heavy skillet. When they're golden put them in a mortar with salt. Grind until most of the seeds are broken and the salt is coated with the seed oil. Good on rice.

hacho miso   Miso made from plain soybeans.

hijiki   Stringy black sea grass. Best when sauteed in light oil before cooking in water.

jinenjo powder   Wild mountain yam known for its strengthening properties.

kanten   Sea vegetable gelatin used in molded fruit and vegetable salads.

kidney bean   Red bean primarily used in chili.

koji   Rice or grain mold culture introduced to miso, shoyu, and tamari which produces enzymes that help the body digest starches and proteins.

kombu   Deep-sea kelp. Has thick wide leaves. Great when cooked with root vegetables or to make dashi, a flavorful soup stock. Put one piece of 3-inch by 6-inch kombu in two cups of slightly salted water. Remove the kombu before serving. Add tamari to taste.

kome miso   Miso made from soybeans and rice.

kuzu   A thickener made from a wildroot starch used in sauces, gravies, soups, and pies.

mirin   A liquid sweetener made from sweet brown rice, koji, and water.

miso   Paste made by fermenting soybeans with whole wheat and sea salt over a 3-year period. Because of the anti-disease bacteria present in miso, it is known for its powers to cure ailments and aid digestion. People who eat miso every day supposedly have a much lower rate of stomach and intestinal cancer. Miso paste is most commonly used to make soup.

WHAT IS MOCHI?

MOCHI

It Puffs Up!

mochi   Pounded sweet brown rice that puffs as it bakes. Broken up pieces are often put in soup.

mu tea   Tasty, aromatic herbal tea that blends ginseng and 15 medicinal plants and herbs.

mugi miso   Miso made from soybeans and barley.

mugwort leaf   A blood builder with a delicate taste.

mung bean   An excellent sprouting bean.

navy bean   Used in soups, particularly popular in England.

nigari   The natural coagulant that is used to make tofu.

nori   A seaweed. Lightly toast nori over open flame, cut into strips, and crumble. Nori can also be eaten with shoyu. Often used to wrap rice balls. Sometimes known as *laver* or *sloke*.

ramen   Noodle and soup stock combination.

seitan   Wheat gluten used as a base to make other foods, such as mock burgers.

shiitake mushroom   This is a large, dark, wide-capped mushroom. Rich in character, they are used in sauces and can be broiled, sauteed, or grilled. Frequently dried.

shoyu   Soy sauce made from soybeans, wheat, water, sea salt; fermented for many months, then pressed.

soba   Japanese whole wheat and buckwheat noodle introduced from China more than 1200 years ago.

tamari   Noncommercial soy sauce, named by George Ohsawa when he first introduced it to North America. Called it tamari to distinguish it from commercial product. Traditionally known as shoyu, which Ohsawa thought too difficult a word for Western tongues.

tekka   A condiment made from burdock root, lotus root, carrot, ginger, iriko, miso, and sesame oil. Used on rice.

triticale   A modern grain that is a cross between wheat and rye. Can be used in bread, crackers, etc.

udon   A light, sifted wheat flour noodle.

umeboshi   Japanese plum, preserved in salt for three years.

umeboshi vinegar   Brine from Japanese salted plum.

wakame   Seaweed, long and feathery, great in miso soup or raw in salad with a light sprinkle of rice vinegar.

yinnie syrup A thick sweet syrup made from brown rice and barley.

FOOD ALLERGIES

Do you know that many health problems may stem from food intolerance? You may be allergic to the food you eat. The best way to find out is to be tested cytotoxically. Blood is placed on a slide with an enormous array of foods, then analyzed under a microscope to see how it reacts.

The following is a list of insurance companies that cover all or part of the cost of cytotoxic food allergy testing:

American Life of New York
Blue Cross/Blue Shield (check in your area)
Champa, California
Constitution Life Insurance Company, Park Ridge, Illinois
Electrical Unions
Equitable Life Assurance Society of the United States
Farm Family Life
General Electric
Golden Rule Insurance, Lawrenceville, Illinois
Guarantee Reserve, Calumet City, Illinois
Liberty Life Assurance Company, Boston, Massachusetts
Life Insurance of North America, Philadelphia, Pennsylvania
Maccabus Mutual, Southfield, Michigan
Phoenix Mutual
Provident Mutual Life Insurance Company
State Farm Insurance, Bloomington, Illinois
Sun Life of Canada, Wellesley, Manitoba
Travelers
Union Central Life Insurance Company, Cincinnati, Ohio
Washington National Insurance Company

This list was supplied by Cambridge Diagnostics, Cambridge, MA 02139, a cytotoxic testing lab.

Allergy Research Group, 2470 Estand Way, Pleasant Hill, CA 94523; (415) 685-1228. Dr. Stephen A. Levine believes that many chemical hypersensitivity reactions (allergy-like reactions) may be caused by deficiencies in anti-oxidant nutrients. After extended research, he now makes supplements to help chemically hypersensitive individuals improve their chemical tolerance.

Klaire Laboratories, PO Box 618, Carlsbad, CA 92008; (619) 438-1083. Distributors of allergen-free vitamins, supplements, and beauty formulas for the hypoallergenic person.

RENT A CYTOTOXIC LAB

American Biologics, 111 Ellis St, Ste 300, San Francisco, CA 94102; (800) 227-4473 or (415) 981-8384. Attention health professionals: for $350.00 a month, health professionals can check two hundred food sensitivities in two hours. A trained person can complete up to 10 tests a day using reliable and advanced techniques. It takes 30 days to get started. American Biologics will send a trained, certified technician to your office to initiate your lab program. The equipment comes with or without video; it can be leased or purchased.

American Biologics charges $195.00 for a cytotoxic allergy test. Their instructions before taking the test are: Four days before taking the test, no steroids or cortizone. Forty-eight hours before, no medications, vitamins, supplements, or herbs. Twelve hours before, no food, drink, toothpaste, nothing. Only spring or distilled water.

13

Water

To ensure clean water, you'll have to do it yourself!
—American Health Magazine

Water is a purifying element. Most of us should drink six to eight glasses a day. Do not drink water that is too hot or too cold. Immediately upon awakening, drink two glasses of water. It will quickly enter the intestines and give them a nice cleaning. It is not a good idea to drink water while eating, since the water dilutes the digestive juices and impedes proper digestion.

The cells of the brain are particularly sensitive to dehydration. Many people unknowingly suffer from headaches simply because there is not enough water in their system.

The skin also needs water for cleansing. Waste materials emitted from the pores will be reabsorbed into the body if they are not washed away.

With more than 63,000 synthetic organic chemicals on the market and 51,000 toxic dumping sites spread across the country, the contamination of ground water is the greatest environmental horror story of the 1980s, according to Eckardt Beck, former official of the Environmental Protection Administration. Today we find more than 2,000 wells shut down nationwide, many due to these carcinogenic organic chemicals, which cause anywhere from 5 to 20 percent of all cancers in the country. Even though only 1 or 2 percent of all ground water is affected thus far, this translates into poisonous drinking water for more than 5 million people. A tainted aquifer cannot be scrubbed clean and replenished. More than likely, it will be poisoned for geological time, according to Robert Harris of Princeton University, and the problem is growing. In hopes of cleaning their aquifer, Bridgeport, New Jersey decided to try to remove contaminants by pumping out their polluted water. They've been pumping for more than ten years, and are still not sure how much longer it will take.

There is little sign of our government cleaning up our water for us. Once again we must take charge of our lives. Many believe that water purifiers, distillers, and so on must be part of everyone's kitchen appliance *now*!

What you can expect to find in your water:

· If you live near a gas station: benzene, toluene, and similar petroleum components emanating from leaking gasoline storage tanks.

· If you live near heavy industry or landfill: solvents like trichloroethylene (TCE).

· If you live in a farming community: nitrates from fertililizer and pesticides.

· If you just live: bacteria, or heavy metals such as lead and mercury.

ORGANIZATIONS TO HELP WITH YOUR WATER

The Soil and Health Society, 33 East Minor St, Emmaus, PA 18049. Will test your water for you, analyzing heavy metals and trace minerals. Cost: $28. Write for details.

BOOKS

Coronaries, Cholesterol, Chlorine by Joseph M. Price. Jove Publications; 100 pp; $1.95. The premise of this book is that it is the chlorine in our drinking water, placed there to kill bacteria, that is the major cause of coronary disease, not cholesterol as is commonly thought.

BOTTLED WATER

According to testing done in Suffolk Country, New York, there are impurities in commercial bottled water. When they tested 110 brands, authorities found only that average tap water was no worse than the average bottled water. Yet Americans spent more than $700 million on natural bottled water in 1982. The average price of bottled water per gallon is 70 cents.

Mountain Valley Bottled Water. Mountain Valley has been bottling their water for 114 years. According to scientists at the University of Arkansas Water Resource Center who have analyzed this water, it contains some natural minerals (mainly magnesium, calcium, and some trace elements), but is virtually salt-free. Basing their calculations on carbon-14 dating, they estimate the water's age at more than 3500 years.

BOTTLED WATER DISPENSERS

SpringWell Dispensers, PO Box 8180, Atlanta, GA 30306; (800) 241-8767. Table-top, porcelain-glazed pottery, designed to dispense five gallon jugs. Push-button faucet, natural sand color, with or without blue stripes. Price: $39.50 plus $3.00 shipping.

CATALYST-ACTIVATED WATER

The catalyst changes the molecular structure of the water by dividing it into a smaller structure, which is said to be more easily absorbed by the body's cells. The catalyzing agent is meant to be used with distilled water.

Bio-Line, Inc, 9201 Penn Avenue South, Ste 26, Minneapolis, MN 55431; (612) 881-7314. There are myriad healthful claims for this product. Dissolve an ounce of the catalyst in a gallon of water and either spray, soak, or drink. Spraying is supposed to cure aching muscles, acne, arthritis pains, insect bites, bruises, burns, cuts, diaper rash, poison ivy or oak, the pain and itch of psoriasis, shingles, and sunburn. Drinking is supposed to be good for acne, arthritis, diabetes, hemorrhoids, high blood pressure, indigestion, poison oak, psoriasis, shingles, and stomach discomfort. This company will refer you to dealers in your area, and will offer you a dealership of your own. A four-ounce bottle is $15.00 retail, $10.00 wholesale.

DISTILLED WATER AND DISTILLERS

Distilled water is the water of the scientific laboratory. It can be made absolutely free of all foreign elements by repeated boiling, catching the steam, condensing it, and collecting the water. Certain gases with lower boiling points than water must be allowed for and removed through a process known as fractional distillation.

Distillers boil water, turning it into steam. The steam enters a coil where it cools and condenses, dripping back into a holding tank where it is collected for later use. All impurities are left behind. But, what happens to chemicals that are in the water, but have a lower boiling point? Aren't those the first to boil away? Do the gases enter the coil and condense? Are they collected and contaminate the pure distilled water? A fractional distiller is one that makes allowances for any chemicals that will vaporize before the water. An escape vent causes these gases to exit the system, while the water vapor, heavier than the atmosphere, enters the condensing coil and collects as pure water. Fractional distillers produce the purest, least adulterated water of all water-cleansing systems.

The best way to rate a distiller's effectiveness is to check the TDS rating (total dissolved solids). The lower the rating the better the still's capacity to remove impurities from the water.

Distilled water comes in four types:

Type I: The highest purity level. Requires pretreatment, distillation, deionization, and filtration. Used in the laboratory in procedures that require maximum accuracy.

Type II: Water free of organic contamination.

Type III: Water pure enough for general lab work and most quality control procedures. Used for rinsing analytical samples, preparations of stock solutions, and for washing and rinsing laboratory glassware.

Type IV: Moderately pure water for preparing test solutions and laboratory reagents when contaminants and impurities are acceptable.

At the very least a distiller must produce type II water for satisfactory results for home consumption.

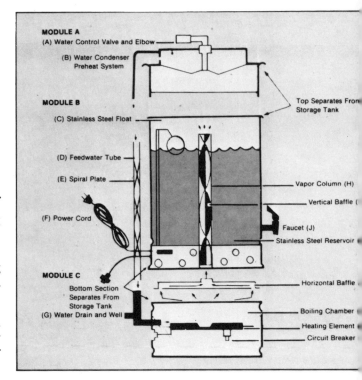

Crystal Clear, 79 Fourth St, New Rochelle, NY 10801; (914) 834-0062. Crystal Clear sells the Water Wizard no. 700, an extremely effective still that uses what the company calls the spectrum distillation method in which water is run through the distiller over and over again to produce extremely pure water. The Water Wizard 700 lists for $225.00, but Crystal Clear regularly sells the unit at excellent savings.

Pure Water Inc., Box 83226, Lincoln, NE 68501; (402) 467-2577. Pure Water Inc. manufactures eight different systems, from a portable distiller that runs with or without electricity (using a boiling pan that only requires a heat source— perfect for survival or emergency situations) to complete office systems (which will cost $1369, not including shipping.) Their most popular home unit costs $349 or $399, depending on whether you want the boiling chamber to fill automatically or you're willing to do it yourself.

Waterwise, Inc, 501 Youth Camp Rd, PO Box 459, Center Hill, FL 33514; (904) 793-5777 or (800) 874-9028. Good selection of top-of-the-line distillers, including the Hague Hydro-Clean (formerly Dennison Distillator), the Midi Still D, Distil-Clear Distiller, the portable Clean Water Machine, and others at very good prices. Lay-

away plans available. Also stocks distiller and dispensing accessories and books: *The Choice is Clear* ($2.00), *The Great Water Controversy* ($2.50), *. . . Not a Drop to Drink* ($2.00), *Your Water and Your Health* ($2.95), *The Shocking Truth About Water* ($3.95), *Water Can Undermine Your Health* ($4.95), *Water Fit to Drink* ($5.95).

FILTRATION SYSTEMS

Although filtration is the best way to remove man-made chemicals, it does have limitations. Most systems are simply canisters loaded with activated charcoal (coal, wood, or coconut shells, heated to an extreme temperature, which etches tiny holes and ruts in the carbon, thereby increasing the surface area to which chemicals contained in the water will cling). The problem is that the damp, dark carbon proves to be an excellent breeding ground for bacteria, thus making the unit effective only for biologically safe water. Filters must be replaced every 500 gallons or so (check specifictions of filter). Once they are saturated with chemicals they are useless.

General Ecology, PO Box 320, Paoli, PA 19301; (215) 363-7900. Water purification system using a cartridge with a microfiltration screen small enough to effectively remove disease causing bacteria.

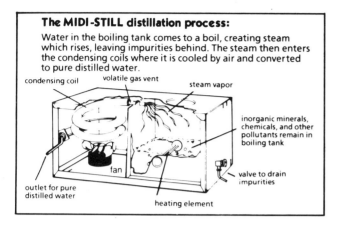

The MIDI-STILL distillation process:

Water in the boiling tank comes to a boil, creating steam which rises, leaving impurities behind. The steam then enters the condensing coils where it is cooled by air and converted to pure distilled water.

condensing coil / volatile gas vent / steam vapor / inorganic minerals, chemicals, and other pollutants remain in boiling tank / fan / outlet for pure distilled water / heating element / valve to drain impurities

WaterWise Inc.

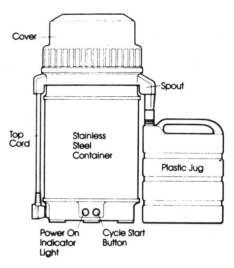

Cover / Spout / Top Cord / Stainless Steel Container / Plastic Jug / Power On Indicator Light / Cycle Start Button

Also uses activated carbon to remove chlorine, tastes, odors, and a wide range of organic chemical pollutants, including pesticides, herbicides, methyl mercury, and chlorinated hydrocarbons. The Seagull IV sells for $289.95. Replacement purification cartridges cost $39.95 each. A portable system called First Need sells for $39.95. Designed for travel, camping, emergency. Additional purification canisters are $24.95 each. Neither system removes dissolved minerals or salts.

Multi-Pure Drinking Water Systems, 15802 Arminta St, Van Nuys, CA 91406; (213) 901-0112. A three-stage solid carbon filter. The plastic counter-top model (400 gallon capacity), $123.95. The stainless steel below-sink model is $199.95.

Neo-Life Company, 25000 Industrial Blvd, Hayward, CA 94545. Makers of the Water-Dome, which is fashioned after the system used on commercial airlines. Removes unpleasant odors, tastes, colors, bacteria, chlorine, THM, and PCBs. Allows minerals to pass through the filter.

WELLS

Deep Rock, 2200 Anderson Rd, Opelika, AL 36802; (800) 633-8774 or (205) 749-3377. Well-drilling supplies: drilling pumps, hydra-drills, bits, drill stems, casings, screens, drilling gel concentrate mud kits. The basic power package sells for $495.00. Their toll-free number features a drilling consultant to answer your questions.

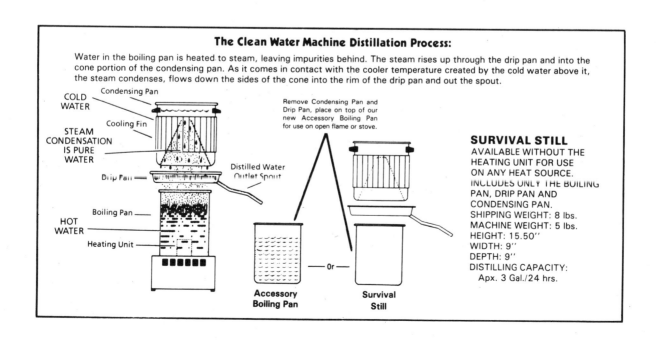

The Clean Water Machine Distillation Process:

Water in the boiling pan is heated to steam, leaving impurities behind. The steam rises up through the drip pan and into the cone portion of the condensing pan. As it comes in contact with the cooler temperature created by the cold water above it, the steam condenses, flows down the sides of the cone into the rim of the drip pan and out the spout.

COLD WATER / Condensing Pan / Cooling Fin / STEAM CONDENSATION IS PURE WATER / Drip Pan / Distilled Water Outlet Spout / Boiling Pan / HOT WATER / Heating Unit

Remove Condensing Pan and Drip Pan, place on top of our new Accessory Boiling Pan for use on open flame or stove.

Accessory Boiling Pan — Or — Survival Still

SURVIVAL STILL
AVAILABLE WITHOUT THE HEATING UNIT FOR USE ON ANY HEAT SOURCE. INCLUDES ONLY THE BOILING PAN, DRIP PAN AND CONDENSING PAN.
SHIPPING WEIGHT: 8 lbs.
MACHINE WEIGHT: 5 lbs.
HEIGHT: 15.50"
WIDTH: 9"
DEPTH: 9"
DISTILLING CAPACITY:
Apx. 3 Gal./24 hrs.

14

Vitamins, Minerals, and Food Supplements

The best way to get vitamins is in the fresh and wholesome foods one eats every day. Still, people take supplements to augment what they eat, but not all the supplements we take have their origin in what we call food. There are both natural and synthetic vitamins. Natural vitamins don't necessarily mean vegetarian. Some ingredients may be from animal sources. Any reliable vitamin firm will respond to your request for information, and assure you that their vitamins are animal-product-free. Many companies have strict vegetarian lines which they promote as such.

Vitamins are either water or fat soluble. Water-soluble vitamins cannot be stored; they must be replenished daily. Fat-soluble vitamins (A, D, E, and K) are stored by the body in fatty tissue. You can, therefore, take too much of these vitamins.

At one time it was thought that one could not take too many water-soluble vitamins. However, the August 1983 issue of the *New England Journal of Medicine* reported nerve damage in patients taking magadoses of vitamin B_6. In seven different cases individuals taking between 2 and 6 grams of B_6 per day experienced numbness, clumsiness of the hands, stamping gait, or an inability to walk at all. All symptoms ceased after the daily doses of B_6 (often recommended for relief of premenstrual syndrome) were discontinued. B_6

(pyridoxine) was taken with no other vitamin or mineral substance. Typically a vitamin B_6 capsule will contain 100 mg. In order to take toxic doses one would have to ingest 20 to 60 tablets per day.

Many experts say that granted, in a perfect world there would be no need for vitamins; but given the state of our culture, with the pollution in the soil, air and water, and the sad fact that food in many cases is lacking nutritionally, vitamin and mineral supplements are a form of nutritional insurance. Synthetic vitamins are often high-potency, but natural vitamins, which are less potent, may be more active nutritionally. Remember, in nature elements are never found in super-high doses; a delicate balance is generally better than a deluge.

According to research, enzymes contain in their nucleus certain trace minerals. If you are deficient in these trace minerals (e.g., cobalt, molybdenum, tin, nickel, fluorine, arsenic, strontium, and more), then your body is unable to absorb vitamins efficiently. Therefore, you can be spending a fortune on vitamins and be throwing away your money. In addition, trace mineral deficiencies are said to be contributors to allergies and hyperactivity. Deficiencies in trace minerals can be attributed to soil deficiencies. If the soil is depleted, the vegetables, fruits, and legumes the soil produces will be deficient as well.

NOTE: Be aware that the outer casing of capsules is always made from animal gelatin.

VITAMINS

Vitamin A. Found in green and yellow vegetables and fruits, milk and milk products. Vitamin A helps build bones and teeth and keeps the skin healthy. It's good for the mucus membranes, which shield the body from infection and pollution, and the protective skin of organs. It helps fight bacteria and infection, and helps maintain the level of visual purple production in the eyes, enabling you to see at night. Deficiencies affect vision (night blindness), cause allergic reactions, and may result in a loss of appetite and the sense of smell. The skin becomes dry, scaly, and blemished, hair becomes dry, and the body becomes susceptible to infection. Inhibitors to vitamin A are alcohol, coffee, cortisone, fluorescent light, too much iron, or lack of vitamin D. Vitamin A is a fat-soluble vitamin.

Vitamin B complex. Found in brewer's yeast and whole grains. It is important for protein, fat, and carbohydrate metabolism, functioning of the nervous system, energy levels, and muscle tonality in the gastrointestinal tract. Deficiency results in fatigue, constipation, digestive tract disorders, lack of appetite, poor sleeping, drying out and loss of hair, skin eruption, and acne. Substances and factors interfering with B-complex vitamins are alcohol, coffee, sugar, stress, infection, and a variety of medications including sulfa drugs, birth control pills, diet pills, and sleeping pills. Water soluble.

Vitamin B$_1$ (thiamin). Can be found in brown rice, brewer's yeast, wheat germ, nuts, and blackstrap molasses. Thiamin is necessary for proper carbohydrate metabolism, a healthy nervous system, muscle tone, hydrochloric acid production in the digestive tract, good energy, growth, and learning potential. A lack of thiamin results in fatigue, nervousness, digestive problems, irritability, lack of appetite, heart problems, shortness of breath, apathy, and sensitivity to pain and noise. Coffee, alcohol, sugar, tobacco, and stress (especially from surgery) interfere with the functioning of vitamin B$_1$ in the body. Water soluble.

Vitamin B$_2$ (riboflavin). Found in brewer's yeast, nuts, whole grains, milk, cantaloupe, and blackstrap molasses. Necessary for producing red blood cells and antibodies to fight disease; affects skin respiration; carbohydrate, protein, and fat metabolism; eyes; hair; and nails. Riboflavin deficiency may cause cataracts; cracks and sores around the mouth; skin problems, including acne and itching; dizziness; burning eyes; poor growth and digestion; lack of stamina and energy; and oily skin. Alcohol, coffee, sugar, and tobacco deplete vitamin B$_2$. Water soluble.

Vitamin B$_3$ (niacin). Niacin is found in brewer's yeast, milk and milk products, green vegetables, peanuts, and wheat germ. It helps keep the skin, tongue, and digestive tract healthy. It aids carbohydrate, fat, and protein metabolism, and reduction of cholesterol. It is vital for the nervous system, good circulation, and the production of sex hormones. A niacin deficiency can result in depression, nervous disorders, fatigue, headaches, bad breath, insomnia, weakness in muscles, poor appetite, nausea, indigestion, skin eruptions like canker sores, and mental illness. Alcohol consumption, coffee, too much sugar or starches, and antibiotics can interfere with niacin levels. Niacin is water soluble.

Vitamin B$_6$ (pyridoxine). Pyridoxine is found in brewer's yeast, leafy green vegetables, wheat germ, whole grains, and black strap molasses. It helps produce antibodies; digest carbohydrates, fat and protein; produce hydrochloric acid for digestion; control weight; and maintain the body's delicate sodium–potassium balance. Deficiencies result in arthritis, nervousness, depression, irritability, learning disorders, heart problems, general weakness, hair loss, dermatitis, and mouth problems. Birth control pills, alcohol and coffee consumption, tobacco, and exposure to radiation will work against vitamin B$_6$ in the body. Water soluble.

Vitamin B$_{12}$. Found in milk and milk products, including cheese; also in algae and tempeh. B$_{12}$ is necessary for the normal formation of all cells, particularly blood cells, maintenance of a healthy nervous system, and metabolism of fats, carbohydrates, and protein. B$_{12}$ deficiency results in pernicious anemia, overall weakness, nervousness, neuritis, eventual brain damage, and difficulties in walking and speaking. Alcohol, coffee, and tobacco interfere with B$_{12}$, as will laxatives. B$_{12}$ is a water-soluble vitamin.

Folic acid. Contained in green leafy vegetables, whole grains, milk and milk products, nutritional yeast, and root vegetables. Needed for the growth and division of cells, particularly red blood cells, maintenance of the nervous system, protein metabolism, and production of hydrochloric acid in the stomach. Folic acid deficiency leads to anemia, B_{12} deficiency, retarded growth, fatigue, gray hair, and digestive problems. Alcohol, coffee, tobacco, stress, and sulfa drugs hinder the body's use of folic acid. Water soluble.

Vitamin B_5 (pantothenic acid). Found in brewer's yeast, legumes, whole grains, wheat germ, peas, molasses, mushrooms, and oranges. Integral to the release of energy from carbohydrates, fats, and protein, it strengthens body resistance, helps the body use other vitamins, and works in the adrenal glands. Lack of pantothenic acid causes a myriad of digestive disorders, including diarrhea, ulcers, and stomach stress. Deficiency also causes restlessness, nervousness, loss of hair, eczema, premature aging, muscle cramps, and susceptibility to infection. Alcohol, coffee, and baking soda interfere with vitamin B_5. Water soluble.

Biotin. Biotin is found in brewer's yeast, whole grains, legumes, and egg yolks. The body uses biotin to help utilize other B vitamins, to promote cell and hair growth, to facilitate protein, carbohydrate, and fat metabolism, and to produce fatty acids. Biotin deficiency results in fatigue, depression, muscle pain, insomnia, dry grayish skin, and poor appetite. Alcohol and coffee interfere with biotin. Water soluble.

Choline. Found in legumes, brewer's yeast, soybeans, lecithin, wheat germ, egg yolks, and green leafy vegetables. Choline is good for the liver and gall bladder, transmission of nerve signals, satisfactory brain function, fat metabolism, cholesterol reduction, and lecithin production. Deficiencies result in high blood pressure, poor growth, fatty liver, hemorrhaging kidneys, stomach ulcers, and fat intolerance. Water soluble.

Inositol. Contained in citrus fruits, whole grains, brewer's yeast, milk, nuts, lecithin, and blackstrap molasses. Good for hair growth, reduced cholesterol levels, lecithin formation, brain performance, metabolism of fat and cholesterol. Lack of inositol results in high blood cholesterol levels, eye difficulties, hair loss, eczema, and constipation. Inositol is impaired by coffee and alcohol. Water soluble.

PABA (para amino benzoic acid). PABA is found in brewer's yeast, yogurt, blackstrap molasses, green leafy vegetables, and wheat germ. Its good for red blood cell formation, protein metabolism, intestinal bacteria activity, rich hair color, and natural sun protection. A lack of PABA may result in premature graying of hair, fatigue, depression, nervousness, irritability, headaches, digestive problems, and constipation. Water soluble.

Vitamin C (ascorbic acid). Found in citrus fruits, green peppers, cantaloupe, papaya, cherries, broccoli, rose hips, berries, alfalfa sprouts, and tomatoes. Vitamin C helps heal wounds and fractures, fights infection, strengthens blood vessels, and helps produce red blood cells. Massive doses of vitamin C have been associated with fighting colds. Vitamin C helps to conserve iodine, absorb iron, and promote bone and tooth formation. Vitamin C deficiency can result in anemia, frequent nose bleeds, poor healing, low resistance to infection, bad gums, cavities, painful and swollen joints, and poor digestion. Vitamin C can be destroyed in the body by tobacco, antibiotics, stress, cortisone, toxic chemicals or fumes (petroleum), surgery, aspirin, baking soda, high fever. Vitamin C is a water-soluble vitamin.

According to Dr. W. M. Ringsdorf, people can increase their recovery time from surgery or injury by 75 percent if they take 500 to 3000 mg of vitamin C daily. (Oral Surgery/Oral Medicine magazine).

According to Dr. C. Alan Clemetson, vitamin C may give protection to pregnant women from premature placental separation from the womb.

Vitamin D. Sunlight stimulates the manufacture of vitamin D in the body. It is also found in eggs and butter. Vitamin D is important for the utilization of calcium and phosphorus in the body, healthy bone formation, good nervous system maintenance, blood clotting, skin respiration, and heart function. Tell-tale signs of vitamin D deficiency are poor condition of bones and teeth, burning sensation in nose and mouth, inability to sleep, myopic vision, nervousness, and diarrhea. Mineral oil also interferes with vitamin D. Vitamin D is a fat-soluble vitamin.

Vitamin E (tocopherol). Can be found in dark-green vegetables, wheat germ, vegetable oils, seeds, and whole grains. Vitamin E is known as an age retardant because it is an anti-oxidant that is said to fight baldness, arthritis, heart disease, varicose veins, and thrombosis. It also helps build red blood cells and aids cell respiration. It reduces blood cholesterol and helps the body to fight environmental pollution and poisons in the air, food, and water. Useful in the maintenance of muscles and nerves, important for fertility and male potency. Vitamin E is a fat-soluble vitamin. Excessive amounts may be fatal for people with a history of heart disease.

Vitamin K (menadione). Vitamin K can be found in green leafy vegetables, alfalfa, wheat grass, safflower oil, yogurt, blackstrap molasses, and kelp. It is imperative for blood coagulation. Without it there is an increased danger of hemorrhage, miscarriage, nosebleed, and diarrhea. Rancid fats, mineral oil, aspirin, antibiotics, x rays, and radiation are all detrimental to vitamin K. Vitamin K is a fat-soluble vitamin.

Vitamin P (bioflavonoids). Vitamin P is found in green peppers, oranges, grapefruits, lemons, apricots, cherries, grapes, and plums. It gives strength to the body's capillary system and vein and artery walls, and fights colds and flu. Deficiencies are similar to those in vitamin C deficiency, as are the factors detrimental to proper function of the vitamin. Vitamin P is water soluble.

MINERALS

Whereas we think of vitamins as chemically organic, minerals are inert substances that, once introduced into our bodies, play an integral part in human mechanical functioning. Because of deficiencies in our soil, foodstuffs may not have a full complement of minerals, making supplements necessary.

Calcium. Calcium is found in milk, cheese, yogurt, molasses, green leafy vegetables, carrots, nuts, and sesame seeds. It is absolutely essential for bones and teeth. It helps in blood clotting, proper muscle function, heart rhythm, and nerve transmission. If the body lacks calcium there may be heart palpitations, soft or brittle bones, muscle cramps, sleepless nights, nervousness, numbness in the limbs, and tooth decay. Stress interferes with the body's calcium usage, as does a lack of exercise.

Chromium. Chromium can be found in brewer's yeast, nutritional yeast, corn oil, and whole grains. It helps insulin maintain blood-sugar levels. Stimulates enzymes for energy metabolism and the synthesis of fatty acids, cholesterol, and protein. Deficiencies lead to glucose intolerance in diabetics, arteriosclerosis, slow growth rate, and poor energy. Too much sugar inhibits chromium activity.

Copper. Copper can be obtained by eating nuts, raisins, pears, molasses, whole grains, legumes, and green leafy vegetables. Copper works in the body to help red blood cell and hemoglobin production. It forms a part of many different enzymes, and combines with vitamin C to form elastin, the substance that gives muscle tissue its stretch. Copper plays a part in hair and skin color, and it stimulates the healing process. If the body is low in copper, one feels general weakness, and can become anemic, because copper is necessary for the absorption and utilization of iron. Impaired respiration and heart palpitations may result, and sores may break out on the skin.

Iodine. Found in kelp and other sea vegetables, as well as in vegetables grown in iodine-rich soil. Iodine is also added to some commercial salt. Iodine is essential to proper thyroid function (preventing goiters). Iodine helps regulate body energy and the rate of metabolism, which plays a part in both physical and mental development. A lack of iodine may be characterized by cold extremities, an enlarged thyroid, protuberant eyes, dryness of the skin and hair, lack of energy, nervousness, irritability, and obesity.

Magnesium. Sources are whole grains, bran, nuts, green vegetables, honey, figs, apples, kelp, and algae. Magnesium acts as a catalyst in the body's use of carbohydrates, fats, protein, calcium, phosphorus. It helps to metabolize blood sugar, balances the body's pH levels, maintains numerous enzyme systems, and helps nerves to function properly. A lack of magnesium will cause nervousness, tremors, rapid pulse, confusion, general weakness, breathing difficulties, poor memory, brittle nails, and it is, therefore, sometimes called the "tranquility mineral."

Manganese. Can be found in whole grains, bran, nuts, legumes, green leafy vegetables, celery, bananas, blueberries, and pineapple. Manganese is an enzyme activator, helps to produce sex hormones, and aids reproduction and growth. It facilitates tissue respiration, vitamin B_1 metabolism, vitamin E utilization, and the proper functioning of the central nervous system. Deficiencies result in dizziness, paralysis, muscle coordination failure, convulsions, ear problems resulting in possible loss of hearing, and lower back pain.

Phosphorus. Phosphorus is contained in whole grains, cheese, and all protein-rich foods. Phosphorus, after calcium, is the second most abundant mineral in the body. It is important to bone and tooth formation, proper contraction of the heart muscle, energy production, kidney function, metabolism of calcium and glucose, nerve activity, muscle activity, and vitamin utilization. Low phosphorus levels result in loss of appetite and the resultant loss of weight, irregular breathing, nervous disorders, pyorrhea (gum disorder), fatigue, and discomfort and pain in bones. Excess aluminum in the body from food or cooking, sugar, iron, and magnesium all affect the level of phosphorus in the body.

Potassium. Good sources of potassium are apricots, avocadoes, dates, figs, peaches, bananas, raisins, seeds, nuts, potatoes, green leafy vegetables, whole grains, and blackstrap molasses. Potassium is necessary for nerve and muscle function and the regulation of heartbeat. A lack of potassium could result in cardiac arrest, irregular heartbeat, muscle damage, continuous thirst, weakness, nervousness, bad reflexes, lower back pain, cramps, apathy, dry skin, and acne. Potassium is inhibited by alcohol, coffee, cortisone, diuretics, laxatives, too much salt and/or sugar, and stress.

Selenium. Selenium is found in bran, wheat germ, brewer's yeast, sesame seeds, onions, garlic, tomatoes, and eggs. It enhances the benefits of vitamin E, preserves tissue elasticity, helps heart function, is known to neutralize certain carcinogens, and, therefore, may afford some protection from cancer. Selenium helps protect your body from oxidative and pollutant damage. Selenium in large doses can be toxic.

Sodium. Sodium is found in salt, milk, cheese, whey, and kelp. It helps to regulate fluid levels in the body, and is needed to keep the musclar, blood, lymph, and nervous systems in operation. Without sodium we experience general muscle weakness and loss of appetite. We may suffer from muscle cramps, or experience intestinal gas, nausea, vomiting, and dehydration. Too much sodium has long been associated with hypertension. Studies in Japan have shown, however, that if sodium intake is augmented by high levels of potassium, hypertension may be held in check. Nevertheless, it is a good idea to keep salt use to a minimum.

Zinc. Zinc is present in pumpkin and sunflower seeds, brewer's yeast, spinach, whole grains and soybeans. Insulin and male reproductive fluids contain zinc. Zinc affects the function of the prostrate gland and proper reproductive growth and development. Zinc also contributes to carbohydrate, fat and protein metabolism. A lack of zinc can be detected by retarded growth rates, and the delaying of sexual maturation, sometimes even dwarfism. Wounds heal slowly without zinc. Fatigue may set in. There may be prostrate trouble, sterility, and joint pain. Alcohol, cadmium, excessive calcium or copper in the body or a lack of phosphorus may affect the operation of zinc.

Aluminum and Alzheimer's Disease

Too much aluminum in the body has recently been associated with the advent of premature senility and Alzheimer's disease. The body has no use whatsoever for aluminum. All aluminum cooking utensils and cookware should be eliminated from kitchen use, and foods rich in aluminum such as baking powders, individually wrapped cheese slices, pancake mixes, frozen dough and self-rising flours, and some pickled cucumbers should not be included in the diet.

GENERAL VITAMIN, MINERAL, AND FOOD SUPPLEMENT BOOKS:

The ABCs of Vitamins, Minerals, and Natural Foods by John Paul Latour. Arco Publishing, New York, 1978, 92 pp; $1.50. Passable introductory guide.

A Food Supplement Handbook by L. Fryar and A. Dickenson. Mason and Lipscomb Publishers, 1975. Home reference work with useful information.

Mega-Nutrients for Your Nerves by H.L. Newbold. Berkley Book, New York, 1978, 393 pp; $2.50. How to implement and tune your health regimen by regulating your intake of key vitamins and hormones.

Supernutrition: Megavitamin Revolution by Richard Passwater. Dial Press, New York, 1975, 224 pp; $7.95. In view of the fact that Americans generally do not eat nutritiously, Passwater outlines a program beginning with relatively low vitamin dosages that increase at two-week intervals, leading to an individually tailored, supernutrition program and peak health at the end of a ten-week period.

Vitamins and Health Foods: The Great American Hustle by Victor Herbert and Stephen Barrett. George G. Stickley, 1981; $11.95. An indictment of some practitioners in the health industry who prey on unsuspecting consumers. Forty-four percent of the adult American population take vitamins. In 1980 it was a $6 billion a year industry. Herbert says, "Most people eating a balanced diet don't really need any food supplements at all. Vitamins and minerals provide a nutritional insurance policy for some people: very young children, pregnant women, the elderly, and those on weight-reducing and other special diets. But there's no reason, unless your doctor advises it, to consume more than 100% of the RDA (the US government's Recommended Daily Allowance) specified for each vitamin and mineral."

VITAMIN AND MINERAL ANALYSIS

Natural Health Outreach, 6821 East Thomas Rd., Scottsdale, AZ 85251; (602) 994-9786. Computerized dietary analysis assessing your diet for the following: protein, fat, carbohydrates, calories, fiber, vitamins (A, B_1, B_2, B_3, B_5, B_6, B_{12}, folic acid, and C) and minerals (calcium, iron, phosphorus, potassium and sodium). You fill out a questionnaire, and the Outreach analyzes your diet; the cost is $15.00. Mineral hair analysis: Send 3 tablespoons of hair, and they use a spectromatograph to check 22 minerals, including toxic heavy metals. Cost: $30.00. The Outreach has a service they call a Metabolism Type Report which will determine if your metabolism is truly

that of a meat eater, a vegetarian, or someone who should be balanced in between. This analysis includes a complete description of recommended food and supplements to bring you into nutritional balance. Cost: $15.00.

Optimum Health Labs, West Valley Medical Center, 5363 Balboa Blvd., Suite 536, Encino, CA 91316; (213) 990-4442. Vitaminalysis (promoted as an accurate and inexpensive blood test for vitamin levels), digestive analysis, sports nutrition, and cytotoxic food allergy testing (171 foods tested). Nutritional supplements available as well.

Personalized Nutrition, 510 South Pacific Coast Highway, Redondo Beach, CA 90277; (213) 540-3325. Will formulate an advanced, up-to-date program designed to fit your own personal needs and life style. Supplements tailored to personal need.

VITAMIN AND MINERAL SUPPLY HOUSES

Choice Metabolics, American Biologics, 111 Ellis St., Ste. 300, San Francisco, CA 94102; (415) 981-8384 or (800) 227-4473. Vitamins (including injectables), enzymes, and minerals. Other specialty items, including the anti-aging drug, GH3. Research testing.

Freeda Vitamins, Dept. 26, 36 East 41 St., New York, NY 10017; (212) 685-4980. Conscientiously manufactured product, free of starch, coal tar, dye, sulfates, sugar, and artificial flavorings and colors. Freeda calls their vitamins 100 percent vegetarian.

Golden West Health Products, 18261 C-Enterprise Lane, Huntington Beach, CA 92648; (714) 848-0443 or (800) 854-7605. Producers of vitamins, minerals, yeast products, digestive aids, and herbs.

Honey Bea Sales, Kenesaw, NB 68956; (800) 228-4253; in Nebraska (800) 742-7829. Daily vitamin and mineral formula, plus variety of other products, including natural whey concentrates. Offers sales opportunities.

L & H Vitamins, Inc., 38–01 35th Ave., Long Island City, NY 11101; (800) 221-1152 or (212)

937-7400. Discount vitamin clearinghouse. They
advertise 20 percent savings on a long list of
known industry name brands.

Neo-Life, 25000 Industrial Blvd., Hayward, CA
94545. Makers of nutritional supplements; vitamins for sports, stress, and executive nutritional
packs.

Neuro Nutrition, 322 1/2 West Washington St.,
Hillcrest, San Diego, CA 92103; (619) 295-5536.
Vitamins, food supplements, life extension. Counseling offered for optimum health, weight loss,
brain nutrition, and muscle development. Testing
is also available: cytotoxic allergy, $175.00; hair
analysis, $24.00. Their catalog is available for
$2.00.

Nova Nutritional Products, PO Box 7300, Calabasas, CA 91302. Local dealers distribute a variety of specially suited vitamins, minerals, and
herb supplements. Nova 6 is designed for vege-

tarians. The product contains no artificial color-
ings, flavorings, preservatives, waxes, shellacs,
sugar, starches, or salt. Absolutely no animal
products!

The Nutrition Store, 2778 Sweetwater Springs
Blvd., Spring Valley, CA 92077. Vitamins, minerals, supplements, energy packs. Twenty-five
percent off all retail sales; with purchases over
$200.00, 30 percent off retail price.

Perfect Health Products, Box 397, Fairfield, IA
52556; (515) 472-5984 or (800) 547-5995, ext. 177.
Time-released vitamins.

Shaklee Corporation, 444 Market St., San Francisco, CA 94111. Success-oriented home sales
distributorship presently listed on the New York
Stock Exchange. Products are not cheap. Everything from vitamins, minerals, and supplements,
to soil conditioner, laundry soap, industrial cleaner,
beauty products. Write for details or ask a local
Shaklee distributor.

M. T. Thompson Co., 23529 South Figuero St.,
Carson, CA 90749. Manufacturers of complete
line of vitamins and minerals.

The Vitamin Shoppe, 204 East 86 St., New York,
NY 10028; (800) 223-1216 or 17, (212) 734-9661.
They list 98 companies whose entire line they
carry. If the product you wish is not listed in
their catalog, they will track it down for you, if
possible. They advertise 20 percent off.

Vibrant Health, Inc., 607 Market St., Kirkland,
WA 98033; (206) 828-4480. Makers of food supplements and "superfoods," including Vegetarian
Plus, wheat-grass tablets, wheat-grass/bee pollen
chews, chlorella micro-algae, and digestive enzymes. Works through local distributor network.

ORTHOMOLECULAR MEDICINE

Two-time winner of the Nobel Prize, Linus
Pauling (see Chapter 3) coined the term *orthomolecular* in 1968. Orthomolecular medicine involves gauging the correct molecular balance for
the body, and then providing that very environment. According to the Orthomolecular Medical
Society, orthomolecular medicine is an advanced

form of nutritional treatment.

Doctors following its practice are concerned with the total functioning of the body, and rely on metabolic tests to indicate imbalances. Treatment involves re-creating metabolic balance, rather than just providing symptomatic relief. Individual needs will always be different from one another, and optimum stasis will vary according to the state of the individual, climate, environmental pollution, and so on.

ORGANIZATIONS

Huxley Institute for Biosocial Research, 1114 First Ave., New York, NY 10021; (212) 759-9554. Orthomolecular physician referral service.

Orthomolecular Medical Society, PO Box 7, Agoura, CA 91301. Computerized referral guide and directory to active and associate members of the society who wish to be listed. Addresses, phone numbers, and specialty interests included. Includes sports medicine, pediatrics, family practitioners, allergists, and more. The society publishes a newsletter containing interesting bits of information and summaries of medical journal articles, published scientific research, books, and conferences.

BOOKS

Orthomolecular Nutrition: New Lifestyle for Super Good Health by Abram Hoffer and Morton Walker, with an introduction by Linus Pauling. Keats Publishing, CT, 1978, 209 pp; $2.25. A description of the careful balance of nutrients in the body, and how through this balance we can promote absolute health and prevent sickness.

TESTING

Colorado Health Professionals, 2575 Spruce St., Boulder, CO 80302; 449-6002. Orthomolecular therapy (vitamin and mineral supplements, nutritional counseling).

Oslerwelch Laboratories, 488 McCormick St., San Leandro, CA 94577; (415) 635-0365. Call collect. Orthomolecular testing. Vitamin and mineral assays, complete stool analysis, hormone analysis.

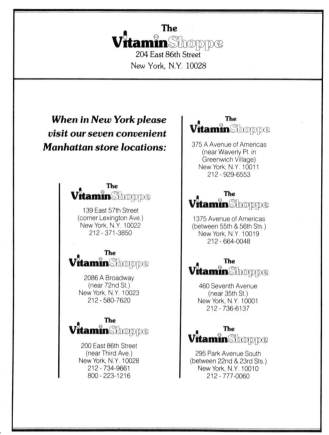

Fee schedule and further information by phone or mail.

SUPPLY HOUSES

Ortho-Molecular Labs, 2338 West Royal Palm Rd., Phoenix, AZ 85210; (603) 434-6254. Vitamin and mineral wholesaler.

Ortho Molecular Nutrition International, PO Box 5036, Manchester, NH 03108. "Vitamins and minerals are bound to soluble proteins which act as nutrient transporters that carry the vitamins and minerals through the intestinal walls into the blood stream to nourish all cells and organs in the body." Introductory offer for their daily vitamin is $8.50 for 45 tablets. They also make Alpha-Premium Supplement, fem-tabs, sports formula, un-stress, and a wide range of vitamins and minerals.

HAIR ANALYSIS

Advocates of hair analysis claim that careful study and testing of the human hair shaft can provide information as to deficiencies of many minerals in the body. Numerous articles have been published lately concerning the reliability of hair analysis for determining nutrient deficiencies. The studies have mostly said that too many outside factors influence the hair (environment, pollution, age of the hair shaft, hair coloring, hair conditioning, shampoo type, etc.). Scientists say the hair just is not an accurate enough barometer to supply the information we would like to have in formulating a maximum potential diet. Also, because the field is wide-open, there are many charlatans who will be glad to separate you from your money, reciprocating with a fabricated report. Hair analysis at best may be relevant for analyzing large groups of people to indicate trends or mineral affects on broad residential areas.

BOOKS

Understanding Body Chemistry and Hair Minerals Analysis by Catherine J. Frompovich, Frompov-ich Publications, RD 1, Chestnut Rd., Coopersburg, PA 18036; $4.95 plus $1.00 postage. Informative for both patient and health professional. Other self-published books available; request catalog.

LABORATORIES

Chiropractic Health Services, 1273 Westwood Blvd., Ste. 205, West Los Angeles, CA 90024; 473-1839. Hair mineral analysis and nutritional follow-up.

Life Resources, 32 Aqua View Dr., La Selva, CA; (408) 684-0811. Computerized hair analysis, blood analysis, nutritional counseling.

Trace Mineral Systems, 915 King St., Ste. B43, Alexandria, VA 22314. Hair mineral analysis, $36.95. Send one tablespoon of hair.

15
Power Foods

The perfect food—what is it? I've heard some people say it's brown rice; others will praise soybeans or tofu or spirulina. Wheat grass is often mentioned and so are sprouts. What's blue-green manna anyway, and why am I suspicious? Many of the foods advertised as fantastic may be so, but beware of marketing techniques that may induce you to spend your money excessively in the name of health, while simply enriching the coffers of others!

The absolutely *perfect* food does not exist, but the following are some of the best.

BEE POLLEN

Bee pollen is the male germ seed of flowers, plants, or the blossoms on blooming trees. An incredibly fine powderlike substance, pollen helps to form the ovules, the starting point for the production of fruits, vegetables, grains, and legumes. Pollen has a high vitamin and mineral content. It is a good protein source and contains a number of beneficial enzymes. Pollen can be eaten plain or in yogurt, fruit salad, or puddings.

C.C. Pollen, 7000 E. Camelback, Scottsdale, AZ 85251. Pollen products made by desert bees.

Honey Hollow, RT 4, Box 54G, Louisa, VA 23093. One ounce, $2.00; one pound, $14.00.

Huber Reeds, 28 Sussex St., Lindsay, Ontario K9V 3E8 Canada. Raw or dry. One pound, $8.00; three pounds, $21.00. Postpaid.

Joe Raiola, PO Box 181, Times Square Station, New York, NY 10108. Low-temperature-dried Austrian pollen.

BREWER'S AND NUTRITIONAL YEAST

Yeasts are a superior source of all B vitamins, minerals, and protein. Brewer's yeast is a by-product of brewing. Nutritional yeast is grown as a food. Most people mix their yeast with orange juice, but it can also be added to milk shakes, sprinkled in cereal, etc.

Nutritional Yeast, Farm Foods, 156 Drakes Lane, Summertown, TN 38483. Molasses is used as the base on which this yeast is grown. Contains all the B-vitamin complex, with vitamin B_{12} added, plus essential amino acids.

Fiber Yeast, Lewis Laboratories, 49 Richmondville Ave., Westport, CT 06880. Probably the best-tasting yeast, because it's grown on sugar beets, which are known to absorb nutrients from the soil faster than any other crop. The lab adds fruit, grain, and vegetable fiber. Fiber is that part of your diet that is not digested or metabolized, but stays in your intestine where it acts like a "train loaded with food moving at a steady pace through the intestines." Not only does fiber allow nutrients to get off and go into the bloodstream, but in exchange it picks up some new passengers, toxins and waste, and carries them out of your body.

GINSENG

"It is said that in order to test for true ginseng, two persons walk together, one with a piece of the root in his mouth and the other with his mouth empty. If at the end of five li *(two miles) the one with the ginseng in his mouth does not feel himself tired, while the other is out of breath, the plant is true."* (Chinese Materia Medica *by F. Porter Smith*)

Ginseng is a natural food, rich in germanium, calcium, magnesium, iron, and vitamins B_1 and B_2. Germanium is an element that has been found in the water of the fountain of Lourdes in France,

Ginseng

More precious than gold

where people have flocked for centuries for miracle cures. Ginseng is said to help the body to resist adverse physical, chemical, and emotional stress. In China it is known for its mental health benefits, as an anti-stress agent; a regulator of blood pressure, and anti-diabetic, a cure for impotence, and a preserver of health in old age.

Ginseng Special: Put some granular or concentrated ginseng in juice or sparkling water. Add a cinnamon stick or some fresh grated ginger.

BOOKS

About Ginseng by Stephen Fulder. Thorsons Publishers, 1984, 64 p.; $1.95.

The Complete Book of Ginseng by Sarah Harriman. Regent House, 1979, $4.95.

SUPPLIERS

Ginseng, Inc., 2836 Creek Lane, Birmingham, AL 35215; (205) 854-7236. Ginseng plants and seeds as well as dried ginseng roots, $8.95 per ounce; pure American ginseng powder, $9.50 per ounce. All items are postpaid in the United States.

Heise's Wausau Farms, Rte 3, Wausau, WI 54401; (715) 675-3862. Residents call Marathon County, Wisconsin, the "Ginseng Growers' Center of the World." "The climate's good, the soil's good, and the ginseng's been here a long time," writes Lyn O. Heise, president and general manager of the farm. They sell ginseng powder (1-ounce package, $5.25) and roots (1 ounce, $5.25), and will grade whole ginseng into smaller or larger roots, according to your desire. Wisconsin Cultivated Ginseng brings a premium price in the Far East market because of its recognized superior quality. Bee pollen and bee pollen–ginseng capsules are also available.

Il Hwa American Corporation, Empire State Building, 350 Fifth Ave, Ste 6103, New York, NY 10118; (212) 695-8416. Wholesaler of ginseng products made with fresh, fully matured organic six-year-old Korean roots. Il Hwa uses a low-temperature process to extract beneficial ingredients. They make ginseng tea, honeyed ginseng roots, powdered root capsules, and Ginseng-Up soft drink.

Il Hwa Korean Ginseng Center, 401 Fifth Ave, New York, NY 10016; (212) 686-3546. Retailer for the above corporation as well as a restaurant and natural food store. Occasionally runs discounts on ginseng products.

Korea Ginseng Center, 79 Fifth Ave, New York, NY 10003; (212) 242-0246; 65 East 59 St, New York, NY 10022; (212) 752-2525. Korean red and white ginseng. Red ginseng was thought to be more potent and was the exclusive domain of Korean royalty for thousands of years. Thirty grams of sliced Korean red ginseng is $16.30.

GRASSES

The two great proponents of eating live foods are Dr. Ann Wigmore and Victoras Kulvinskas (see Chapter 3). Wigmore claims to have cured herself of cancer with an inspiration from a passage in the biblical book of Daniel. This story tells of King Nebuchadnezzar, who was a wreck physically and mentally. He was advised by Heaven to "eat the grass as did the oxen." Wigmore took these words to heart, launched her research, and cured herself.

Victoras Kulvinskas claims, "The juice extracted from seven-day-old wheat grass is one of the most potent healers known to man. In the last decade I have researched all current alternative healing diets and I have never seen anything that offers more hope for mankind than wheat in the form of sprouts and grass juice, when done in conjunction with a rejuvenating living foods program.

The chlorophyll (70 percent) in wheat grass makes it a powerful blood detoxifier and rebuilder. Wheat grass is rich in vitamins C, A, D, E, K, and B complex. It contains the elements calcium, chlorine, cobalt, iron, magnesium, potassium, phosphorus, sodium, sulfur, and zinc.

Dr. Ann Wigmore warns: "Wheat grass is a powerful cleanser and may cause nausea shortly after ingesting, as an immediate reaction to the release of toxins within the system. Start with small amounts, 1 ounce or less, and gradually increase the daily intake to about 2 ounces."

Greenmagma, Green Foods Corp., 129 East Savarona Way, Carson, CA 90746; (213) 515-6856. The dried juice of young green barley plants. It is combined with brown rice to produce a powder which is meant to be dissolved in water, milk, or juice. It was discovered after ten years of research by a Japanese pharmacist/medical doctor, whose search led him to the most balanced concentration of vitamins, minerals, proteins, and enzymes, as well as the optimum taste. (The taste is said to be mildly sweet, and the powder dissolved in water resembles carrot juice.) It contains high concentrations of chlorophyll, proteins, vitamins,

PERFECT FOODS INC.

minerals, and enzymes, and is said to slow down the aging process, protects against carcinogens in food and the environment, and helps in the digestion and absorption of other nutrients.

Perfect Foods, Inc., 2656 East 29 St, Brooklyn, NY 11235; (212) 934-4735. Organically grown wheat grass. Retail and wholesale. Local deliveries. Wheat grass juicer sales and rentals. They sell sprouts, including sunflower and buckwheat. Perfect Foods produces and distributes fresh frozen wheat grass juice in 1-ounce cups. They'll ship fresh wheat grass, sprouts, and frozen juice anywhere in the United States.

Pines Distributors International, PO Box 1107, 1040 East 23 St, Lawrence, KS 66044; (913) 841-6016. Wheat grass grown in the fertile Kaw River Valley of eastern Kansas. Frozen wheat grass juice is available by UPS (8-ounce bottles for $11.95, but you must purchase in lots of 24 bottles). Also available are low-temperature-dried vegetables, instant wheat-grass juice (just add water), juicers, bee pollen, and wheat grass for pets. Also, barley grass, a concentrated source of chlorophyll, vitamins, minerals, protein, and enzymes. Made from organically grown young barley. Price: $15.95 for 350 tablets, postpaid.

SPIRULINA

Some people claim that it's best to eat at the bottom of the food chain before much of the pollution and poison are able to enter. Spirulina (found at the lowest end of the chain) is a form of blue-green algae or plankton. The Aztecs prized it, and the largest natural source in the world is Lake Texcoco, Mexico. Spirulina contains 18 of the 22 known amino acids, including all eight of the essential protein building blocks, thus making it a "complete protein." It is the best known natural source of vitamin B_{12}, richer even than liver. Spirulina contains high concentrations of vitamins A, B, B_2, B_6, D, E, H, and K. It also contains essential minerals, trace elements, cell salts, as well as enzymes necessary for body metabolism. Over 90 percent digestible, spirulina is a quick source of energy, and its naturally chelated vitamins are more thoroughly absorbed into the blood stream than manufactured vitamins.

(Chelation, which comes from the Greek word meaning *claw,* means that the vitamin or mineral is bonded with an organic compound, often an amino acid. This bonding step makes the body better able to absorb, through digestion, the mineral or vitamin, and use it in its systems.)

Blue-Green Manna, K. C. Labs, Klamath Lake, OR 97601. Algae products from a high mountain lake in Oregon. The algae is harvested then freeze-dried, which protects the high nutrient content of the fresh algae. This product is distributed by a network of private dealers. A list of the dealers in your area can be obtained by contacting the company.

Earthrise, PO Box 33, Boulder, CO 80306. They grow spirulina in specially made cultivation ponds under strictly controlled conditions, unlike algae grown in the "wild." Earthrise also manufactures a curious array of spirulina products, including diet spirulina formula, a spirulina granola bar, and pastalina and spirulina protein powders. They also publish a newsletter with lead stories such as: "The Art of Growing Premium Quality Spi-

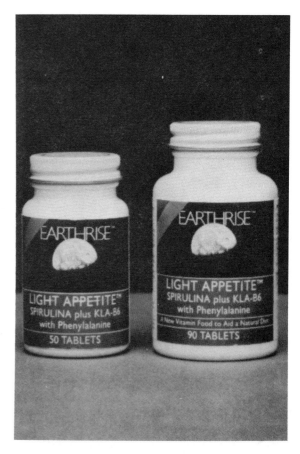

rulina," "Is Your Spirulina Pure?" and "Spirulina—The Perfect Food for Runners." A jar of one hundred 500-mg tablets is $7.75.

The Guadalupe Natural Products Spirulina Growing Kit, Rte 4, Box 522, Sequin, TX 78155; (512) 379-2148. 3004 Northeast Dr, Austin, TX 78723; (512) 928-2027. The kit contains a two and a half gallon growing tank (fish tank really), nutrients to make the water alkaline and provide food for the algae, a thermostat, an air pump, a thermometer, and a net for harvesting. A book of instructions is provided, as is a live strain of spirulina to start your farm. If the plants die, a new batch of spirulina will be provided without additional cost. Price: $44.95 postpaid.

Light Force, Box N, Boulder Creek, CA 95006. A multimillion-dollar spirulina company whose aims, as expressed by founder Christopher Hills, are to provide a "means to make people successful and feed the hungry at the same time." Light Force "started with a single, unknown product—spirulina—and has grown into a glistening monument to the power of men's dreams." Now they sell Power Packs (starting at $19.99); Life Enhancement formulas ($22.49), slenderizers, stress fighters, natural spirulina beauty products, environmental products, and the books of Dr. Hills, including *Nuclear Evoltuion* ($14.95), *You Are a Rainbow* ($2.95), and *The Joy of Slimming* ($3.95). Interested in starting a career? Life Force offers *Find Your Pot of Gold—The Course to Success* for $45.00. Their Product Presentation Kit costs $35.00.

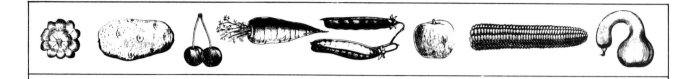

16

Personal Hygiene and Beauty Care

Most hygiene and beauty care products on the market today either contain animal ingredients (hooves, internal organs, etc., secured from the slaughterhouses), or have been tested on animals, or both. The infamous Draize test, in which several drops of a cosmetic or household product are put in the eyes of rabbits, is but one horrible example.

Three frequently used compounds, *elastin, glycerin,* and *stearate,* may be derived from either plant or animal matter. If these or the whole product are not specified on the label as vegetarian, the product probably includes slaughterhouse ingredients.

Chemical ingredients are frequently used in health and beauty products and tested on laboratory animals: sodium lauryl sulfate, methylparaben, propylparaben, and triethanolamine (TEA) should be looked for on labels.

MANUFACTURERS AND DISTRIBUTORS OF COSMETICS AND PERSONAL HYGIENE PRODUCTS

On the market today there are beauty and health care products containing all-natural, animal-test-free ingredients. The following companies are all cruelty-free, that is, they do not test their products on animals. In most every case, the companies use no slaughterhouse by-products, but derive cosmetic and personal hygiene formulas exclusively from plants. This list has been derived in large part from listings and information provided by Beauty Without Cruelty.

Aditi, 799 Broadway, New York, 10003; (212) 533-6962. Make-up, skin and hair care products, masks, colognes, after shave, bath oils, sun-tan lotion. No animal ingredients, no harmful perservative chemicals.

Aloe Vera, PO Box 3248, Simi Valley, CA 93063; (805) 522-5310. Aloe Vera juice is clear, yet thick enough to be used as a gel. It can be used as a shampoo, or as a salve for many different skin burns. Aloe vera is good for its muscle-relaxing qualities in massage, and it can be used as an aid to digestion and for its laxative qualities when diluted. This company manufactures and distributes sun-tan lotion, sun-burn ointment, shampoo, conditioner, skin cleanser, gel, scrub, mask, and toner.

Aloe Vera Gardens, 2916 North 35th Ave, Ste 3, Phoenix, AZ 85017; (602) 269-7160. Hydroponic indoor gardens, ripe for viewing. Manufacturers of aloe vera juice.

Almond Sun, PO Box 68, Trumbull, CT 06611.

They produce a facial mask that triples as a cleanser and moisturizer. Made from sesame meal, almond meal, white clay, corn meal, honey, calcium lactate, and aloe vera gel.

Amberwood, 125 Shoal Creek Rd, Fayetteville, GA 30214; (404) 461-8576. Wide variety of products, including skin care products, hair care, deodorants, toothpaste, shaving cream, cosmetics, fragrances, books, vitamins, household cleaners, notecards, postcards, rubber stamps (e.g.: IT'S 1985—ARE YOU STILL EATING AND WEARING DEAD ANIMALS?, $7.50 postpaid; BE KIND TO ANIMALS, DON'T EAT THEM, $5.50; VEGETARIANISM . . . THE HUMANE ALTERNATIVE $5.50).

Angel Eyes, Ltd, PO Box 3153, Madison, WI 53704. Cruelty-free cosmetics and toiletries, and they contribute a portion of their profits to animal rights organizations.

Aubrey Organics, Attn Mr. Aubrey Hampton, 4419 North Manhattan Ave, Tampa, FL 33614; (813) 877-4186. Avoids chemical ingredients known to have been recently tested on animals, including sodium lauryl sulfate, methylparaben, propylparaben, and TEA. Some of their many products may contain animal products. Read the label.

Auromere, Attn Dakshina, 1291 Weber St, Pomona, CA 91768; (714) 628-8255. Incense packets, sachets, essential oils, sandalwood soaps, and Vicco herbal toothpaste.

Autumn Harp, Box 49, Ripton, VT 05766; (802) 388-7690. Comfrey products including salve, lip balm, hand and body lotion, face cream, and three vegan baby products: oil, lotion, and powder.

Avacare, 9200 Carpenter Freeway, Dallas, TX 75247. Aloe vera products, including aloe brite toothpaste and Cello gel, an aloe vera juice recommended for tooth and gum care.

Barths, 270 West Merrick Rd, Valley Stream, NY 11580; (516) 561-8800. Make-up, skin cream, body cream. Although some items contain no animal products, others do. Check the labels. If stearates and glycerines are not designated vegetarian, they probably include slaughterhouse ingredients.

Beauty Naturally, 57 Bosque Rd, PO Box 426, Fairfax, CA 94930; (415) 459-1976. Nineteen shades of hair color, hair lightener, shampoos, conditioners, lash life, sunless bronze, and mouthwash. Some of these items may include slaughterhouse ingredients, others do not. Read the labels.

Beauty Without Cruelty, 175 West 12 St, #16G, New York, NY 10011. BWC is the champion of laboratory animals. This organization informs consumers and asks them to use only products that employ non-animal testing methods. BWC makes clear that cosmetics and household cleaners can be marketed "without confining, harming or killing animals in their manufacture and testing." BWC will supply current information and listings for many manufacturers with regard to natural, animal-free products and testing. BWC is a not-for-profit charitable organization, and they market their own line of cruelty-free health care and beauty products to help finance their animal rights, public awareness work.

Beauty Without Cruelty Ltd., PO Box 07437, Milwaukee, WI 53207; (414) 744-4022. Not presently affiliated with any other group of this name. Make-up, skin and hair care.

Beauty Without Cruelty, South Pacific, Attn Mrs. Lucille Healther, PO Box 1373, Auckland, New Zealand; tel: (9) 735-675. Owned by the Beauty Without Cruelty charity in New Zealand. Will ship wholesale or retail to the United States by air freight. Lipstick, perfume, skin and hair care. Information available through BWC New York.

Biokosma, Caswell Massey, 111 Eighth Ave, New York, NY 10011. Eleven Swiss skin care preparations, made with natural plant ingredients for dry, sensitive, exhausted, or aging skin. Free of all animal products and minerals.

Body Love, PO Box 2711, Petaluma, CA 94952; (707) 795-8174. Skin care, including herbal facial steams, and a soap alternative called Amazing Grains made from oatmeal, cornmeal, clay, and bentonite.

Börlind of Germany, Börlind Gesellschaft, 7260 Calw-Altburg, Schwartzwald (Black Forest) West Germany. U.S. distributor: PO Box 307, Grantham, NH 03753. Seven types of skin care combinations, including masks, tinted day creams, sun creams, and sunless bronze.

The Community Soap Factory, PO Box 32057, Washington, D.C. 20009; Liquid soaps for hands and body.

Con-Stan Nutrimetics, 19501 Walnut Dr, Box 1286, City of Industry, CA 91749; (714) 598-1381. A large catalog including make-up, nail polish, skin and hair care.

The Dodge Chemical Company, 165 Rindge Avenue Extension, Cambridge, MA 02140; (617) 661-0500. Animal-free make-up products for the funeral profession.

Dehohoba, The Four-D Marketing Company, 1305 West 21 St, Tempe, AZ 85282; (602) 894-9241. Hair care, sun-tan lotion, Teen Skin, all with jojoba oil.

Earth Science, PO Box 1925, Corona, CA 91720. Shampoo and conditioner, facial scrub, vitamin E complexion oil, almond aloe moisturizer, and jojoba oil. No animal products, except for wool derivatives.

Eve, PO Box 1261, Hurricane, UT 84737; (801) 635-2103. Shampoo and conditioner.

Everybody Ltd., Box 951, Boulder, CO 80306. Skin and lip items. Contain no animal or slaughterhouse ingredients.

Golden Lotus, 2800A South Shoshone, Englewood, CO 80110; (303) 761-0174. Four biodegradable household care products in 32-oz or one-gallon sizes: All-purpose cleaner, dishwashing soap, laundry soap, fabric softener. Also bottle pumps, skin and hair care products.

Herbalife, PO Box 12079, Boulder, CO 80303; (303) 443-5029. Herbal formulas to promote good health. Herbal weight control program. Herbal aloe juice, aloe skin care, herbal shampoo, plus herbal formulas for cardiovascular health, mental alertness and energy, women's health care, more.

Humane Alternative Products
NH Highway Hotel
Fort Eddy Road
Concord, NH 03301
Tel. 603-224-1361

Humane Alternatives Products, NH Highway Hotel, Fort Eddy Rd, Concord, NH 03301; (603) 224-1361. Distributes products of the some of the largest natural, animal-test-free manufacturers, including Golden Lotus, Weleda, Beauty Without Cruelty, Nutri-Metics, and Aubrey Organics.

Humphreys, 63 Meadow Rd, Rutherford, NJ 07070; (201) 933-7744. Humphreys Products are also available at: John A. Borneman, 1208 Amosland Rd, Norwood, PA 19074. Witch hazel, ointments and homeopathic combinations. Almost all of their products are free of slaughterhouse ingredients, save a few, which include sponge, extract of cuttlefish, bee venom, or serpent venom.

Ilona Of Hungary, 3201 East Second Ave, Denver, CO 80206; (303) 322-4212 or 333-3941. Skin care salons in Denver and New York (629 Park Ave,

New York, NY 10021; (212) 288-5155). Make-up, skin peeling, sun blocks, and other skin care.

Janca Jojoba Oil, 20 East Southern, Mesa, AZ 85202; (602) 833-4940. Jojoba oil is a substitute for sperm whale oil, and is cold-pressed from jojoba seeds. It can be used as after-shave, skin night treatment, bath oil, hair conditioner, or a skin protection from sun or wind. It softens and moisturizes and will not spoil, oxidize, or become rancid. Tom Janca buys quality jojoba seeds for current market price (presently $2.00 per pound). Contact him for information about laws regulating jojoba picking.

Naturade, 7100 East Jackson St, Paramount, CA 90723; (213) 531-8120. Make-up and skin and hair care items.

Nature Cosmetics Inc, 226 South Beverly Dr, Ste 100, Beverly Hills, CA 90212; (213) 278-3316. Twenty-seven nail polish shades, some including silk fiber protein "made from silk worm excrements." Their collagen is derived from sea plankton, their other proteins from plants. They avoid suppliers that do animal testing.

Nature de France, 100 Varick St, New York, NY 10013; (212) 925-2670. Skin and health care prod-

Janca's Jojoba Oil & Seed Co., Inc.
20 E. Southern, Mesa, Az. 85202
(602) 833-4940

Jericho Bath Salts, 527 Madison Ave, Ste 1211, New York, NY 10022. Dead Sea mineral bath salts and black mud masks for face and body imported from Israel. Also mineral and clay soap and shampoos.

Kiss My Face, PO Box 804, New Paltz, NY 12561; (914) 246-5011. Skin and hair care.

Loanda Products (formerly Beyond Soap), 114 Hamilton Dr, Novato, CA 94947; (415) 883-1235. Herbal soaps including lemon camomile, mint–comfrey, eucalyptus–sage, lavender, wheat germ-E. Gift packs available.

Mirror, Mirror on the Wall, CEASE, 247 Everett St, Middleboro, MA 02346. Large catalog of baby care, oral hygiene, pet products. Gift certificates (a portion of this money is donated to animal protection societies).

ucts made with green rose or white clay as developed by Raymond Dextreit in France. Poultices, masks, body packs, plasters, soap, and talcum. Although French law specifies that all cosmetics made and sold in France be tested on animals, Nature de France products sold in the United States are made here and not tested on animals.

Nyaanza Naturals, 4419 North Manhattan Ave, Tampa, FL 33614. Skin and hair care products designed for blacks and people of color. Nyaanza Naturals does not test on animals. Facial cleanser, oils, herbal mask, herbal astringent, moisturizing mist, make-up powder for black and dark-brown skin tones, ebony wood and jasmine shampoo, hair and scalp rinse, hair conditioner.

Orjene, 5–43 48th Ave, Long Island City, NY 11101; (212) 937-2666. Twenty-seven make-up products, skin and hair care, including suntan lotions and joggers' foot rub.

Paul Penders, 159 West 78 St, New York, NY 10024; (212) 595-6161. Skin care, after-shave cream, deodorant, bath oil, sun screen, and hair care products from Holland. Ads and labels state that their products are not tested on animals.

Rainbow Research Corp, 170 Wilbur Pl, Bohemia, NY 11716; (516) 589-5563. Hair coloring, and hair and skin care products. Only their soaps contain slaughterhouse ingredients.

Rokeach & Sons, 560 Sylvan Ave, Englewood Cliffs, NJ 07632. Coconut oil soap.

Schiff, Moonachie Ave, Moonachie, NJ 07074. Vegetarian vitamins (including children's) and cosmetics. Some are excellent, but others may contain slaughterhouse ingredients. Check the labels.

Shikai, PO Box 2866, Santa Rosa, CA 95405. Henna and other hair care products. One shampoo is made from the fruit pod of the acacia tree, found only in India and Burma. The pod is dried and ground into a powder, *shikakai* ("fruit for the head"). Used for centuries for thick, healthy hair.

Sombra, C & S Laboratories, 5600G McLeod N.E., Albuquerque, NM 87109; (505) 884-1417. Six clay make-up foundations and six clay blushers which contain no solvents, evaporating agents, or preservatives.

Sturdee, Island Park, NY 11558; (516) 889-6400. Many acceptable products, but some with slaughterhouse ingredients.

Sunshine Scented Oils, 3616 West Jefferson Blvd, Los Angeles, CA 90016. Fragrant oils for body and feet.

Toms, Railroad Ave, Kennebunk, ME 04042; (207) 985-2944. Toothpaste, mouthwash, soaps, and skin and hair care products, widely distributed in health food stores and groceries both here and overseas.

Touch of Beauty, 599 4th St, San Fernando, CA 91340; (213) 873-3862. Make-up, skin and hair care products.

Trans-India Products, 9261 West 3rd St, Beverly Hills, CA 90210. Two shampoos, one with acacia, traditionally used in India for thick, luxuriant hair.

Velvet, PO Box 5459, Beverly Hills, CA 90210; (213) 472-6431. All-in-one day and night moisturizer and shaving formula. Dealer inquiries invited.

Weleda, 841 South Main St, Spring Valley, NY 10977. Toothpaste, mouthwash, hair conditioners, lotion and oil, baby care products, bath essences and colognes. The ingredients in Weleda products come primarily from plants grown without pesticides or artifical fertilizers and from herbs grown in their natural habitats. No synthetic preservatives. All ingredients come from the mineral, plant, and animal kingdoms: chalk, quartz, cinnabar, rosemary leaves, myrrh gum, lavender flowers, beeswax, and lanolin. *Weleda News* is the Swiss parent company's quarterly review of articles by physicians, pharmacists, and others about medicine and hygiene. The first three issues focus on Health and Hygiene (no. 1), Body Care (no. 2), Mother and Child (no. 3), and have been translated into English. They are available free upon request. There is also a Weleda pharmacy at the corner of Hungry Hollow Road and Route 45 approaching Spring Valley.

West Coast Mineral Corp, 7338 Varna Ave #6, North Hollywood, CA 91605; (213) 982-9878. Masada Dead Sea mineral bath salt.

Yes Soap Shop, 1015 Wisconsin Ave NW, Washington, D.C. 20007; (202) 338-0910. Bath and hair care products.

Dry skin: Not only do wind, sun, alcohol, and smoking promote dry and wrinkled skin, but a daily bath does also. As one grows older, oil glands become less productive, resulting in dry, itchy skin. After 35 one should not bathe daily—the drying effects are too severe. Washing the genital area and underarms will suffice. It's not good to soak in hot water, but if you must, use an after-bath oil or moisturizer. Do not use bath powders, since they also promote the drying process. —Vegetarian Times

17

Grow Your Own

Ten acres of pastureland will produce ten times the amount of vegetable protein as it will meat protein. Ten times! An animal will eat 16 pounds of grain to produce only a single pound of meat. America's agricultural priorities must change, but in this era of huge factory farms, will they? More and more people are taking their nutritional life into their own hands, growing their own food in their own gardens, rooftops, even fire escapes. People are finding that raising some or all of what you eat is not only good for your body, but also for your mind.

ORGANIZATIONS

The Cornucopia Project, c/o the Cornucopia Project Information Service, 33 East Minor St, Emmaus, PA 18049. Sponsored by Rodale Press, this research project is exploring the steps necessary to sustain America's food supply in the twenty-first century. Cornucopia hopes to develop a better, more natural, more sustainable food system that will be far more productive and efficient than our present system. Proposed areas of study include soil, erosion, potential water shortages, nutrient recycling, the effects of plant combinations on pest control, and the ability of certain plants to repel or attract insects. The Project has issued a report, *Research Agenda for the Transition to a Regenerative Food System,* which proposes a more in-depth study of organic farms, which tend to maintain lower input and energy costs. In addition, the project strongly recommends the necessity to educate the public with regard to local food systems and develop better urban food production and distribution techniques. The Project publishes a quarterly newsletter. Six issues, $3.00

Federated Organic Clubs of Michigan, 4401 Maple Lane, Rives Junction, MI 49277. FOCM is a nonprofit, educational organization of health, gardening, and farming clubs throughout Michigan. The organization is made up of persons interested in pursuing the knowledge and methods of preparing the soil to produce food without chemicals, and learning various techniques in maintaining a healthy body. Organized under their auspices are the Battle Creek Organic Farming and Gardening Club, Esse Organic Health Club of Jackson, Genesee County Organic Farm and Garden Club, Nature Center Organic Club, Organic Soil and Health Builders of Southwest Michigan, Thornapple Valley Organic Growers, Towne & Country Organic Garden Club, Wayne County Organic Farm and Garden Club, and Tri-County Organic Farm and Garden Club (Ingham, Eaton, Clinton). For further information on any of these clubs contact the Federated Organic Clubs of Michigan.

Institute for Alternative Agriculture, 9200 Edmonston Rd, Ste 117, Greenbelt, MD 20770. I. Garth

Youngberg, executive director. A lobby group set up by the former United States Department of Agriculture Organic Farming Coordinator. The institute's aim is to provide a policy voice in Washington, D.C. for the biological, organic, and eco-farming constituency. Their monthly newsletter facilitates information exchanges between state and regional farming groups and organizations, reports on relevant legislation, reports on research and educational advances in alternative agriculture, reviews books of interest to farmers, and more. Annual membership is $15.00 and includes a monthly newsletter.

The Land Institute, Rte 3, Salina, KS 67401; (913) 823-8967. A nonprofit organization on the bank of the Smoky Hill River, southeast of Salina. In its education and research programs, the institute examines technology and ideas that could sustain the long-term capacity of the earth to support a variety of life and culture. The education program is open to ten agricultural interns (graduate or upper-level undergraduate students), who spend a 43-week "growing season" learning in the classroom and from physical work related to agriculture research (a 90-acre prairie pasture serves as the outdoor classroom). Students also participate in construction and maintenance of buildings, grounds, and equipment. Visitors are welcome and the institute periodically sponsors public lectures. The institute's publication, *The Land Report,* contains articles about student projects, special events, and agricultural research efforts at the institute. It is published three times per year; a subscription is $5.00

Maine Tree Crop Alliance, c/o Jack Kertesz, Environmental Science Center, Unity College, Unity, ME 04988. An attempt to coordinate tree publications, tree crop literature, and local projects. Newsletter includes information on fruit, nut and multipurpose trees (published three times per year; subscription, $2 per year).

Natural Food Associates, PO Box 210, Atlanta, TX 75551. A nonprofit, educational organization. Publishers of *Natural Food & Farming Magazine* and *Natural Food News.* NFA has a four-point objective: (1) To teach all who will listen the values of natural, poison-free food grown in rich, fertile soil. (2) To expose the dangers of chemical

contamination of our food, water, and land. (3) To show the interrelationship of soil, water, and human health. (4) To convince the American people that the prevention of environmentally caused degenerative diseases is necessary to save our civilization. The NFA has one national convention and several state and regional meetings each year in many major cities throughout the country. Their bookstore carries books on organic farming, nutrition, and natural living. A membership and one-year subscription to their magazine is $12.

NFA Demonstration Farm, US Highway 59, Atlanta, Texas (six miles west of Atlanta). An opportunity to visit a farm producing on a "fertile, living soil using the natural method of agriculture." Learn how to prepare your garden for growing fruits and vegetables the natural way.

The National Association for Gardening, 180 Flynn Ave, Burlington, VT 05401. The National Association for Gardening believes gardening adds joy and health to life while improving the environment. NAG encourages food gardening by people at home, in community groups and in institutions. Toward this end they: (1) Serve as a home and community garden center clearinghouse. (2)

Sponsor community garden programs for neighborhoods, landless groups, the disabled, the elderly, youth, schools, churches, clubs, prisons, hospitals, and housing projects. (3) Test garden products, techniques, and systems. (4) Produce the *Gardening For All/Gallup National Gardening Survey,* an annual report on home and community food gardening information for the country. A one-year membership, which includes a subscription to their magazine, *Gardening for All,* is $12.00.

Seed Savers Exchange, c/o Kent Whealy, Rural Route 2, Box 111, Princeton, MO 64673. Gardeners working together to save heirloom and endangered vegetable varieties from extinction. Seed Savers networks gardeners to this end. A year's subscription is $6.00 and gets you a copy of the 224-page "Winter Yearbook," a copy of the "Fall Harvest Edition," free membership listings, free plant finder service listings, and free seeds from the growers network.

Tilth, 4649 Sunnyside North, Seattle, WA 98103; (206) 633-0451. Tilth, which means the cultivation of the earth, focuses on the exchange of ideas and information for new approaches to agriculture in the Pacific Northwest. Membership numbers more than 1400. They are active in growing food, saving farmland, developing local markets, improving forest practices, and more. Regional Tilth membership is $10.00 per year and includes their newsletter. Tilth maintains a library, and has quite a few local chapters:

Good Earth Tilth, Scott McManus, Rte 1, Box 372, Cashmere, WA 98815; (509) 782-3325.

Methow Tilth, Bob Elk, PO Box 512, Methow, WA 98834; (509) 923-2411.

Nooksack Tilth, Gretchen Hoyt, 3550 Alm Rd, Everson, WA 98247; (206) 966-4157.

Northern Idaho Tilth, Stephen Bishop, PO Box 509, Sagle, ID 83860; (208) 263-8627.

Okanogan Tilth, Michael Pilarski, PO Box 1050, Tonasket, WA; (509) 485-3169.

Palouse Tilth, Nathan Jacobsen, S.E. 320 High St, Pullman, WA 99163.

Rogue Tilth, Judy Weiner, 348 Hussey Lane, Grants Pass, OR 97526; (503) 476-8979.

Santa Tilth, Janice Masterjohn, Rte 4, Box 152, St. Maries, ID 83861; (208) 245-3685.

Seattle Tilth, Regina Hugo, 4649 Sunnyside North, Seattle, WA 98103; (206) 633-0451.

Siskiyou Tilth, Tom Ward, c/o 100 Eagle Mill Rd, Ashland, OR 97520; (503) 482-0320.

South Humboldt Tilth, Ram Fishman, 3010 Ettersburg Rd, Garberville, CA 95440; (707) 986-7504.

Southwest Washington Tilth, Gary Kline, 820 North Puget, Olympia, WA 98506; (206) 357-6236.

South Whidbey Tilth, Michael Seraphinoff, 3830 So. 530 E., Greenbank, WA 98253.

Spokane Tilth, Tom Tuffin, No. 225 Division St #30, Spokane, WA 99202; (509) 236-2353.

Willamette Valley Tilth, Tom Forster, 3586 Willamette, Eugene, OR 97405; (503) 345-1218.

MAGAZINES AND NEWSLETTERS

The Family Food Garden, 464 Commonwealth Ave, Boston, MA 02115; (617) 262-7170. Reader-interactive magazine with advice, tips, and how to's that will be invaluable for the neophyte and interesting for the seasoned gardening veteran. *The Family Food Garden* has a terrific "Between Neighbors" feature where readers are able to trade seeds, plants, recipes, unusual food items, and gardening hints. The subscription rate is $12.00 for eight issues (1 year). The single-issue price is $1.95. Send subscriptions to 1818 Garden Ct., Marion, OH 43306.

Michigan Organic News, 4401 Maple Lane, Rives Junction, MI 49277. Uses a lot of reader-contributed articles. Helpful and earnest, with a lot of information and addresses to follow up on. A one year subscription costs $5.00. Published by the Federated Organic Clubs of Michigan.

Organic Gardening Magazine, 33 Minor St, Emmaus, PA 18049; (215) 967-5171. This magazine has been one of the cornerstones of Rodale Press publishing. Good selection of up-beat articles in a traditional style. A one-year subscription is $12.00.

BOOKS

The Acres U.S.A. Primer. The ACRES U.S.A., Box 9547, Raytown, MO 64133; $20.00. A knowledge-packed book about you and the land, and the adjustments you must make to benefit both of you. They also produce the monthly magazine *ACRES U.S.A.*, which bills itself as a voice for eco-agriculture and keeps abreast of developments in biological and organic farming and gardening. Deals editorially with health topics, national economics. Twelve issues for $9.00.

The Complete Book of Edible Landscaping, by Rosalind Creasy. Sierra Books, 1983, New York, NY, 339 pp; $25.00. Information-packed, detailed, instructive. A reference volume that will help you have a fruitful yield at the same time you beautify your environment. Paying close attention to various regions, Creasy helps you plant edibles by the back door and along the driveway whether you live in Boise or Miami.

Gardening for All Seasons: The Complete Guide to Producing Food at Home, 12 Months a Year, by Gary Hirshberg and Tracy Calvan. Brickhouse Publishing, Andover, MA; $12.95. Gardening outdoors, indoors, and in the greenhouse. Includes a useful bibliography, a section on community gardens, food preservation, aquaculture, and food-producing trees.

The Herb Gardener's Resource Guide. Northwind Farm, Rte 2, Box 75A, Shevlin, MN 56676; $6.50 postpaid. More than 250 sources of foreign and domestic plants, seeds, greenhouses, tools, accessories, books, kitchenware, spices, and teas.

Home Soyfood Equipment edited by Ray Wolf. Rodale Press, 33 Minor St, Emmaus, PA 18049; $15.95. How to make tempeh, tofu, and soymilk at home. Tells how to make a soymilk/tofu press, a variable-size tofu box, and a tempeh incubator. Recipes, suggestions, and even tear-out patterns.

Gem Cultures, 30301 Sherwood Rd, Fort Bragg, CA 95437; (707) 964-2922. Tempeh starter using culture grown on medium containing vegetable ingredients only (powdered: $2.25 for enough to make three 1-pound batches). Also products for professional tempeh shops such as: sweet white rice koji starter, red rice miso koji starter, barley (mugi) miso koji starter, soybean (hatcho) miso koji starter, shoyu koji starter. Besides this, Gem Cultures is working with kefir, grains, *sufu* culture, which ferments tofu to a cheese consistency, and *natto,* the "limburger" of soybean food. Fresh sourdough starter as well.

Home Gardening Wisdom by Dick and Jan Raymond. Gardening Way, Charlotte, VT 05445; $9.95. A reference book thoroughly covering the gardening cycle from soil to seed to table. Well indexed.

Maritime Northwest Vegetable Gardening Almanac. Order from Binda Colebrook, 6906 Goodwin Rd, Everson, WA 98247; $3.00. A guide to year-round gardening in the Pacific Northwest.

Your Apple Orchard by A.P. Thomson. Vita Press, PO Box 331, Atlanta, TX 75551; $3.95 plus $1 postage and handling. The lifetime experiences of an apple grower. Includes helpful information for organic growers.

Guide to (almost) Foolproof Gardening. *Mother Earth News,* Mother's Bookshelf, 105 Stoney Mountain Rd, Hendersonville, NC 28791; $3.95. Compilation of articles from the magazine *Mother Earth News* for both beginners and experts, including up-to-date information on organic gardening.

WORKSHOPS

Permaculture Workshop, ALCYONE, PO Box 225, Ashland, OR 97520; (503) 482-0552. *Permaculture* is a term originated by Australian environmental scientist Bill Mollison. It refers to a self-perpetuating agriculture design organized so that food production, livestock, and human living arrangement interact, stabilize, and nurture one another. The system is self-reliant, and makes use of what is available on one's land to benefit all living things maintained thereon.

ALCYONE is a small residential farm community maintaining permaculture balance. They offer an in-depth course for a small group of people (30 maximum), with attention to personal situations, including hands-on practice and demonstration. A bioregional focus is stressed, with techniques and resources appropriate and available to northern California and Oregon. Two-weekend course, $175.

PLANT AND SEED COMPANIES

Bear Creek Farms, PO Box 411, Northport, WA 99157. Bear Creek Farms offers cold-hardy and draught-resistant fruits, nuts, shrubs, and grafted trees for northern growers, home gardeners, and commercial farmers. Grafted apples, grafted pears, and nut trees, including black walnut, butternut, hearnut, Carpathian walnut, Manchurian chestnut, Chinese chestnut, American chestnut, and hazelnut. Hard Manchurian apricots good for northern areas. Bear Creek is interested in tree and shrub seeds, and encourages seed collectors and amateurs to offer their seeds for purchase or barter. They also sell root stock for grafting and budding, and tools such as Victorinox budding/grafting folding knives ($8.50) and Felco no. 8 pruning shears ($24.00)

Bima Industries, PO Box 88007, Seattle, WA 98188. Untreated, high-germination, whole, natural seeds for sprouting. Five varieties: alfalfa, mung bean, radish, clover, cabbage, lentil, and wheat. Sprouting utensils and kits. Prices: 70 grams of seeds, $1.25; 170 grams, $2.50. Send for free catalog.

How to sprout according to the Hippocrates Health Institute. *What you need: a quart or larger wide-mouth glass jar or a sprout bag (an 8" × 12" nylon mesh bag). A rubber band should be used to secure a piece of mesh on the top (so water can be poured off without losing the sprouts). All seeds, grains, and legumes can be sprouted. Make sure your jar has enough room for the seeds to expand at least eight times their original size. For example, three tablespoons of alfalfa will fill a quart jar.*

Put the seeds to soak in lukewarm (preferably filtered) *water. Seeds soak according to their size. Small seeds, five hours; medium, eight; beans and grains, ten to fifteen hours.*

After the seeds have soaked, drain off the water. Rinse the sprouts twice daily with fresh water, then pour the water off. Keep this water. It is called rejuvelac *at Hippocrates and is full of vitamins and minerals. It has a slightly sour taste. Allow the sprouts to rest by tilting the jar upside down at a 40° angle so that fresh air can still enter through the mesh.*

Continue rinsing and draining twice a day for three to seven days. Make sure they are well drained and have plenty of air or they will mold and spoil. You rinse to give the sprouts moisture, not to clean them.

Removing the seeds is called harvesting. Alfalfa, radish, red clover, and mung beans should be harvested, but fenugreek, sunflower, peas, grains, and lentils should not. To harvest, dump the sprouts in a dishpan full of water. Heavy hulls sink to the bottom and the light ones float to the surface, where they can be skimmed off.

Replace the sprouts in the jar and expose them to indirect light for two more days. This is to "green" them up: they will develop chlorophyll.

Eat or refrigerate. They can be kept for about a week.

W. Atlee Burpee Company, Warminster, PA 18974. Huge selection of seeds and supplies.

Cross Seed Company, PO Box 125, Bunker Hill, KS 67626; (913) 483-3416. Cross carries organic seeds for sprouting and milling. Their supplies include Chinese red cowpeas (domestic adzuki), soybeans, striped variety whole raw or roasted sunflower seeds, pumpkin seeds, sesame seeds, whole oats, whole barley, whole rye, lentils, yellow popcorn, fenugreek, and quite a bit more; and if they don't stock it, they'll try to get it for you. Cross Seed will also stone-grind your flour needs on request. Very good selection of sprouting seeds as well. Send for catalog.

Ginseng, Inc., 2836 Creek Lane, Birmingham, AL 35215; (205) 854-7236. Ginseng is native to the eastern half of the United States. It is an herb and grows great in well-shaded, well-drained hardwood forests. Wild ginseng is preferred to cultivated and fetches three times the price. For those who are interested in growing ginseng commercially, if you order $1800.00 or more, Ginseng Inc. will come to your farm. They'll help you locate the best growing site, provide you with information and literature on the best types of shade and material available, take a soil test sample and inform you of your soil's requirements, advise you on proper preparation of soil using equipment you already have, and make suggestions for any additional necessary equipment. They will discuss applications of different types of fertilizers (organic or chemical), recommend harvesting at various stages of growth, and provide you with marketing information for selling your ginseng plants and seeds.

If you don't have an $1800 order, president Steve Ward will send you a booklet, *How to Grow Ginseng*, for free. This will tell you about the possibilities, *whys*, and *wherefores* of growing native American ginseng, both wild and cultivated. Everything is simple and clear, and easy to understand. Spring plant deliveries start February 1 and continue till the beginning of the growing season, in the middle of March. If you order after that, you will be scheduled with the fall delivery, which begins the first of August and continues through December 15. First-year ginseng plants start at $9.00 for 25 plants and move right up to $1200.00 for 10,000. Ward also sells second-, third-, and fourth-year plants.

Gurney's Seed and Nursery Company, Yankton, SD 57079. Lots of corn, pumpkin, and melons. Very complete overall selection.

Hartmann's Blueberry Plantation, Rte 1, Grand Junction, MI 49056; (616) 253-4281. All varieties of northern and southern blueberry plants.

Johnny's Selected Seeds, Albion, ME 04910; (207) 437-9294. A very strong (but not exclusive) commitment to organic farming methods. ''While we strive to supply seed grown with minimal chemicals it should be made clear that top quality, high germination, vigor, and trueness-to-type is our primary emphasis.'' For commercial growers and home gardeners. If you would like to know the source of Johnny's seeds, they have prepared a leaflet which they'll mail you free of charge upon request. Beside excellent seeds, Johnny's also sells watering and greenhouse supplies, weather

equipment, LaMotte soil-testing kits, biological and botanical insecticides, rectangular-blade Japanese vegetable knife, corn shellers, and a small but well-chosen selection of books.

Kelly Brothers Nurseries, Dansville, NY 14437. Berries and good selection of fruit trees, nut trees, grapes, asparagus, figs.

Makielski Berry Farm and Nursery, 7130 Platt Rd, Ypsilanti, MI 48197; (313) 434-3673 or 429-9355. Raspberry specialists, red, black and purple. Also blackberries, rhubarb, currants, gooseberries, asparagus, blueberries, and strawberries.

Mariposa Foundation, 415 Residence St, Moscow, ID 83843. Propagates native food plants and is willing to trade bulbs for seeds. For more information send a SASE.

Nichols Garden Nursery, 1190 North Pacific Highway, Albany, OR 97321. Herbs and rare seeds, including vegetables, garlic, flowers, and ornamental gourds, and yogurt culture. Nichols also sells gardening books and how-to manuals con-

cerned with turning the backyard into a little extra cash with profitable garden projects (five ideas; manuals are $3.35).

George W. Park Seed Company, PO Box 31, Greenwood, SC 29646. Large flower and vegetable mail-order seed company.

Peace Seeds, 1130 Tetherow Rd, Williams, OR 97544; (503) 846-7173. A seed company devoted to *ahimsa,* or, the practice of harmlessness. They have a collection of 3000–3500 different kinds of plant seeds representing 147 of the 360 plant families known to grow on Earth. Their seeds are 50 cents per pack.

Saginaw Valley Nut Nursery, 8285 Dixie Highway, Birch Run, MI 48415. Black walnuts. Twenty seeds plus planting information costs $5.00.

Stokes Seeds, 737 Main St, Box 548, Buffalo, NY 14240. Besides 141 pages of vegetable and flower seeds, Stokes carries all kinds of gardening accessories, canning and preserving equipment, novelty items (T-shirts, caps, and aprons), and books.

Territorial Seed Company, PO Box 27, Lorane, OR 97451. Set up to serve gardeners west of the Cascade Mountains, they feature seeds for year-round gardening. Customers receive a free magazine, *The Gardener's Journal,* which contains specialty and regional information, including planting calendars and descriptions of vegetable varieties especially hearty to the region.

West Wind Farm, Bob Cooperrider, Rte 1, Box 308, Sheridan, OR 97378; (503) 843-3492. Sprout seeds are grown with organic fertilizers, stored, cleaned, and bagged on the farm. Certified organically grown by Oregon Tilth-Provender Certification. Radish, red clover, mustard, Alaska pea, rye, and white wheat. Sample pack available for $4.75. Free catalog.

BEES AND HONEY

If you live in the country near some succulent fields and you have the space, beekeeping can be a satisfying as well as interesting and money-making pastime.

The Walter T. Kelley Company, Clarkson, KY 42726; (502) 242-2012. Bee supermarket complete with a beehive factory. Everything you can imagine for the beekeeper, including three-banded Italian queens by airmail ($6.00 each April 1 to June 1, $3.50 each June 1 to November 10), observation hives, protective clothing, veils, and jumbo capping melter to separate the wax from the honey ($950).

Sunstream Bee Supply, PO Box 484, Pittsburgh, PA 15230. Starlight, Midnight, Italian Queens, package bees. Equipment catalog is 50 cents.

FARM AND GARDEN TOOLS

Earthway, PO Box 547, Bristol, IN 46507; (219) 848-7491. Precision garden seeders ($55.95) and additional seed plates for cucumbers, lima beans, broccoli and more; cultivators ($59.95); spade potato planters ($26.95); and garden tractor mount seeder/fertilizer ($238.95).

Garden Way Manufacturing Company, 102 St and Ninth Ave, Troy, NY 12180. Well-known maker of Troy-Bilt roto tiller–power composter.

Kemp Company, 160 Koser Rd, Lititz (Lancaster County), PA 17543; (717) 627-7979. Shredders and shredder-chippers. These tools will provide you with a total organic waste processing system. Shredders shred, grind, and pulverize almost any common waste matter, including compost, weeds, leaves, vines, corn, sunflower stalks, brush trimmings, sticks, sludge, phosphate rock, sod, soil, manure. Chippers will dispose of branches up to 3″ diameter, yielding uniform dime-size chips that can be used as decorative mulch. Prices begin at $482 for a two-wheel, 3 horsepower engine with 16 shredding teeth.

The Kinsman Company, River Road, Point Pleasant, PA 18950; (215) 297-5613. Steinmax electric shredders ($199.95), newspaper shredder for making mulch ($49.95), compost bins, and rotosieves to make your own blend of potting soil ($39.95).

HYDROPONIC GARDENING

Hydroponics is gardening without soil. Often hydroponics is carried on indoors with the benefit of artificial light. Plant food is mixed with water and washed over the gravel-anchored plant roots several times a day. The concentrated food and continuous light produces large, beautiful plants, but often people complain that the fruit and vegetables are not as tasty as their counterparts grown outside in natural soil.

SUPPLIES

Agrilite, 93829 River Rd, Junction City, OR 97448. All kinds of grow lights, halides, sodiums, systems. Brochure is $2.00.

Aqua-Ponics, 1920 Estes Rd, Los Angeles, CA 90041; (213) 254-1920. Variety of hydroponic gardens, ranging in price from $349 to $799. (Smaller, less expensive systems are available.) Everything you need for hydroponic gardening, including books.

The Light Machine, 8474 Commerce Ave, Ste A, San Diego, CA 92121. Supernova Light systems ($209); reflectors; meters to measure pH, light, and moisture; and fertility testers ($9.95).

BOOKS
All books available from Aqua-Ponics, 1920 Estes Rd, Los Angeles, CA 90041.

Grow More Nutritious Vegetables Without Soil by James D. Taylor. $24.00. This book contains a section on organic hydroponics.

Hydroponic Food Production by Howard M. Resh. $19.95. Commercial hydroponic farming methods.

Hydroponic Gardening by Raymond Bridwell. $6.95. A hydroponic gardener recounts his personal experiences.

Hydroponic Greenhouse Gardening by Joel Hudson. $5.95. Principals, planning, troubleshooting.

ORGANIC FERTILIZER

Canton Mills, Inc., Box 97, Minnesota City, MN 55959; (507) 689-2131. Natural-base fertilizers.

J. Francis Co., Rte 3, Atlanta, TX 75551; (214) 796-5364. Biodynamic compost and compost starter.

Growing Crazy, 2460 South Beyer Rd, Box MN, Saginaw, MI 48601. Organic plant sprays, biological soil supplements, preventions for milky spore disease, seaweed and fish matter fertilizer, compost starter, mineral nutrients, foliage sprays, soil testing. Send $1.25 for catalog.

Memphis Worm Farms, 650-N Compress, Memphis, TN 38106. Red worms for soil improvement and composting. Prices: 2 lbs, $18.00; 3 lbs or more, $8.25 per lb.

Natural Farm Products, Spencer Rd, Kalkaska, MI 49646. Natural fertilizers, feed supplements, fish emulsion, seaweed products. Free catalog.

Ohio Earth Food, Inc, 13737 Dunquete Ave N.E., Hartville, OH 44632; (216) 877-9456. Maxicrop liquid seaweed, kelp meal, rock phosphate, more.

Joe Scrimger, 4550 Barnes Rd, Clifford, MI 48727; (313) 688-2019. Biological fertilizers.

Thompson Sales Co, Box 246, Montgomery, AL 36101; (205) 263-6696. Commercial supplier of fertilizer and soil supplements.

ORGANIC PEST CONTROL

In order to control pests organically, you have to have predators around. Some predators that are beneficial to your garden are garter snakes, toads, insect-eating birds, ladybugs, and preying mantises. Ladybugs control aphids and other microscopic insects. Trichogramma wasps are stingless and lay their eggs on the larvae of pesky members of the fly family. When the eggs hatch, they make short shrift of the fly from the inside out. Predatory insects are no more expensive then

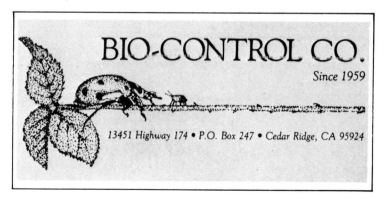

chemical solutions, and in many cases can be had for less. Order from:

Bio-Control Company, 13451 Highway 174, PO Box 247, Cedar Ridge, CA 95924; (916) 272-1997. Ladybugs, lacewings, and other beneficial insects. Books, free information, and catalog.

Fountains Sierra Bug Company, PO Box 114, Rough and Ready, CA 95975. Ladybugs, lacewings, more.

King's Natural Pest Control, PO Box 695, Cimerick, PA 19468. A selection of bugs.

Rincon-Vitova Insectiaries, PO Box 95, Oak View, CA 93002. Good selection of beneficial insects.

BOOKS

Organic Plant Protection by Rodale Press. 33 East Minor St, Emmaus, PA 18049; $18.95.

ORGANIZATIONS

Citizens Against Chemical Contamination, 11463 Bringold Ave, Lake, MI 48632; (517) 588-9845, 588-9871, 588-9751. Five-dollar yearly membership includes four issues of the newsletter. The organization focuses on the use and problems created by pesticides. Articles deal with specific chemicals and offer organic alternatives. Book reviews and conference dates.

18
Cookbooks

Vegetarian cooking once meant brown rice and soggy vegetables, but today, thanks to creative chefs and cookbooks like the *Moosewood* (see below), meatless cooking is haute cuisine. Scrumptious meals, not only for daily life, but also for parties and special occasions, can be found in the pages of the following books. These are really just a smattering of the hundreds of volumes that are on the shelf today. If you have a favorite, please drop a line and let me know, and it'll be included in the update of the *Vegetarian Connection*.

Bread Winners by Mel London. Rodale Press, Emmaus, PA, 384 pp; $17.95. Two hundred and forty-one different bread recipes.

The Carob Way to Health by Frances Sheridan Goulart. Warner Books, 160 pp; $5.95. Alternatives to chocolate in the diet.

Carrot Cookbook. Williams Printing, 417 Commerce, Nashville, TN 37219; $5.95 postpaid. Two hundred and twenty-seven recipes for breakfast, lunch, and dinner. Snacks as well.

The Complete Dairy Foods Cookbook by E. Annie Proulx and Lew Nichols. Rodale Press, Emmaus, PA, 304 pp; $15.95. How to make everything from cheese to custard in your kitchen.

Cooking with Fruit by Marion Gorman. Rodale Press, Emmaus, PA, 352 pp; $14.95. Hundreds of recipes, including breads, salads, drinks, desserts, and snacks, that lend themselves to enhancement by the addition of fruit. Not all are vegetarian.

Creative Cooking With Grains and Pasta by Sheryl and Mel London. Rodale Press, Emmaus, PA, 320 pp; $16.95. Complete explanation of grains and their uses. Three hundred recipes. One section devoted to whole-grain pastas.

The Delicious World of Raw Foods by Mary Louise Lau. Rawson Associates Publishing, New York; $5.95.

The Do of Cooking by Cornelia Aihara. GOMF (George Ohsawa Macrobiotic Foundation) Press, 902 14th St, Oroville, CA 95965, 230 pp; $13.95. Best recipes organized by the seasons of the year.

The Farm Vegetarian Cookbook. Edited by Louis Hagler. The Book Publishing Company, 156 Drakes Lane, Summertown, TN 38483; $6.95. A creative cookbook from the Tennessee commune, The Farm. Teaches you how to pump out some unusual soybean fare like barbeque glutton ribs and pizza. More modest stuff too, like tips on canning, how to make soymilk and yogurt.

The Festive Vegetarian: Recipes and Menus for Every Occasion by Rose Elliot. Pantheon; $6.95.

French Vegetarian Cooking. Simple Recipes by Bernadette. Perigee/Putnam, New York, 192 pp; $6.95. French model tells how to prepare food the vegetarian way.

Good Cooking from India by Shahnaz Mehta and Joan Korenblit. Rodale Press, Emmaus, PA, 288 pp; $14.95. More than 200 traditional Indian recipes.

The Good Grains. Edited by Charles Gerras. Rodale Press, Emmaus, PA, 96 pp; $5.95. How to prepare interesting grain dishes at a moderate price.

The Green Thumb Cookbook. Edited by Anne Moyer and the editors of *Organic Gardening* magazine. Rodale Press, Emmaus, PA, 384 pp; $16.95. How to make the best use and prepare what you grow in your garden.

The International Macrobiotic Cuisine Whole World Cookbook by the editors of the *East–West Journal*. PO Box 1200, 17 Station St, Brookline, MA 02147; $6.95. Complete macrobiotic meals compiled by a dozen chefs. Meals from France, Italy, China, Mexico, the Middle East, and the United States. Includes detailed instructions for using pressure cooker, and preparing basics such as whole-wheat pie crust and sourdough starter. Unusual stuff, too, like *seitan* and *amesake*.

Kathy's Kitchen by Kathy Hoshijo. c/o Self Sufficiency Foundation, PO Box 1122, Glendale, CA 91209; $12.95. A companion volume to Kathy Hoshijo's progressive, ''new cooking and eating'' nationally syndicated television program of the same name. Also: *Kathy Cooks Naturally* (Bantam, New York; $4.50). An extensive handbook of kitchen intelligence.

Kids Are Natural Cooking. Prepared by the Parents Nursery School. Houghton Mifflin, Boston, MA; $6.95. Colorful book of child-tested recipes using good foods for home and school. Superlative gift for a kid with too many trucks or dolls.

Laurel's Kitchen by Laurel Robertson, Carol Flin-ders, and Bronwen Godfrey. Bantam, New York; $4.95. A complete reference center for the vegetarian kitchen. Four hundred recipes.

Let's Cook It Right by Adele Davis. Signet, New York; $3.95. How to protect your health and well-being by preparing foods properly. A classic by a pioneer in the field of good health.

Light Eating For Survival by Marcia Acciardo. 112 pp. Omangod Press, Woodstock, CT. Order from 21st Century Publishing, 401 North Fourth St, PO Box 702, Fairfield, IA 52556, 112 pp; $5.95. Raw-food recipes as prepared by Viktoras Kulvinskas and the Survival Foundation (see Chapter 3).

Low-Cost Natural Foods. Edited by Charles Gerras. Rodale Press, Emmaus, PA, 96 pp; $5.95. Designed to provide the consumer with the information to get the most out of his food dollar. Shopping, storage, and preparation tips.

Mexican Vegetarian Cooking by Edith Metcalfe de Plata. Thorsons Publishing, Wellingburough, Northhampshire, England, 128 pp; $6.95.

Milk-Free Diet Cookbook, by Jane Zukin. Sterling Publishing, New York, 155 pp; $6.95. Cooking for the lactose-intolerant.

The Moosewood Cookbook by Mollie Katzen. Ten Speed Press, PO Box 7123, Berkeley, CA 94707, 220 pp; $8.95. An exceptional vegetarian cookbook, full of one terrific recipe after another, many with an international flavor passed from one generation to the next. By the author of *The Enchanted Broccoli Forest*.

Mother Earth's Vegetarian Feasts by Joel Rapp. William Morrow, 105 Madison Ave, New York, NY 10016, 1984, 204 pp; $8.95. Sophisticated vegetarian recipes presented with humor. By the author of *Mother Earth's Hassle-Free Vegetable Cooking*.

The Natural Foods Cookbook by Beatrice Trum Hunter. Jove Press, New York, 1961; $2.75. The basis for many a kitchen, and has been for more than 30 years. Covers the basics, and hasn't aged badly. Two thousand recipes.

The New French Gourmet Vegetarian Cookbook by Rosine Claire. Celestial Arts Publishing, Millbrae, CA $5.95.

The New Healthy Trail Food Book by Dorcas S. Miller. East Woods Press, Charlotte, NC; $4.95. Natural eating outdoors.

No Oil–No Fat Vegetarian Cookbook by Trudie Hoffman. Professional Press Publishing Company, 13115 Hunza Hill Terrace, Valley Center, CA 92082; (619) 749-1134; $6.75 ppd. Incorporates what Trudie Hoffman and her husband, Jay, learned from studying the Hunza people, who are known for living a long time in vigorous health.

No Salt Needed Cookbook. Edited by Charles Gerras. Rodale Press, Emmaus, PA, 96 pp; $5.95. How to bring out natural flavors of food without using salt. Teaches about other herbs and spices, and makes frequent use of sauces.

Oats, Peas, Beans and Barley Cookbook by Edyth Young Cottrell. Woodbridge Press, Santa Barbara, CA, 283 pp; $7.95. The author is a research nutritionist at Loma Linda University.

Putting It Up With Honey by Susan Geiskopf. Quicksilver Press, PO Box 340, Ashland, OR 97520; $6.95. Ideas and recipes for storing foods.

Rodale's Basic Natural Foods Cookbook. Edited by Charles Gerras. Rodale Press, Emmaus, PA, 800 pp; $21.95. Massive volume with more than 1500 recipes. Includes shopping tips, glossary of cooking terms, how to get the most nutrition out of your food. Excellent reference work for both beginner and expert.

Rodale's Naturally Delicious Desserts and Snacks by Faye Martin. Rodale Press, Emmaus, PA, 416 pp; $19.95. More than 300 recipes.

Rodale's Soups and Salads Cookbook and Kitchen Album. Edited by Charles Gerras. Rodale Press, Emmaus, PA, 288 pp; $15.95. Three hundred recipes.

Spirulina Cookbook by Sonia Beasley. University of the Trees Press, PO Box 644, Boulder Creek, CA 95006; $6.95. Over 100 recipes on how to prepare algae.

The Tao of Cooking: An International Vegetarian Cookbook by Sally Passley. Ten Speed Press; $7.95. Authentic ethnic recipes following the tenets of Tao philosophy as adapted by the Tao Restaurant in Bloomington, Indiana.

Tassajara Cooking by Edward Espe Brown. Shambhala Publications, Boulder, CO 1973; $8.95. A starting place for those ready for vegetarian cooking and philosophy. More guidance than recipes, but in an attractive way.

Ten Talents by Frank J. Hurd and Rosalie Hurd. Box 86 A, Rte 1, Chisholm, MN 55719; (218) 254-5357; $9.95. A cookbook that sprang from the kitchen of a talented vegetarian cook. Proven home recipes. "The one who understands the art of properly preparing food, and who uses this knowledge is worthy of higher commendation than those engaged in any other line of work. This talent should be regarded as equal in value to Ten" (from E.G. White, *Diet and Food*).

The Throw Out Your Stove & Greasy Dishes No Cook Cookbook: For Living on 25 Cents a Day! by Joseph de Nolfo, Jr. Order from: Vegetarian Society, Box 5688, Santa Monica, CA 90405; 96 pp; $3.95. A layperson's guide to self-sufficiency with living foods and indoor gardening. Nolfo is the founder/director of The Greenhouse, a learn-by-doing Living Foods Education Center in Portland, Oregon.

The 20-Minute Natural Foods Cookbook by Sharon Claessens. Rodale Press, Emmaus, PA, 256 pp; $14.95. Fresh, nutritious food without spending much time in the kitchen.

The UNcook Book by Elie and Dr. Elton Baker. Communication Creativity, PO Box 213, Saguache, CO 81149; $5.95. What to do with raw foods.

The Vegan Kitchen by Freya Dinshah. American Vegan Society, Malaga, NJ, 1974. Cooking without animal products.

The Vegetable Spaghetti Cookbook by Derek Fell and Phyllis Shaudys. Pine Row Publications, Box 428, Washington Crossing, PA 18977; 96 pp; $4.95. How to grow and cook spaghetti squash, with plenty of recipes for vegetarians.

Vegetariana by Nava Atlas. Doubleday, New York, NY; 224 pp; $12.95. Interweaving of beautiful illustrations, with creative recipes and "literary anecdotes on the delights of vegetarian cookery from Mark Twain's thoughts on cauliflower to Pliny the Elder's advice on leeks." Good gift material.

Vegetarian Dishes from Around the World by Rose Elliot. Pantheon, New York, NY; $7.95.

The Vegetarian Epicure, Volume I and Volume II by Anne Thomas. Vintage/Random House, New York; $7.95. Handsome books of elegant cuisine, long-standing classics in the vegetarian world. Thoughtful array and selection of recipes.

The Vegetarian Weight Loss Cookbook by Frances Sheridan Goulart. Simon and Schuster, New York, NY; 176 pp; $7.95.

Vegetarianism for the Working Person—Quick and Easy Vegetarian Recipes. Baltimore Vegetarians, Box 1463, Baltimore, MD 21203; (301) 752-8348; $3.00. Fifty easy-to-follow vegetarian recipes using commonly found supermarket ingredients. In most cases recipes take no more than 20 minutes to prepare. Each copy of the book also includes a poster highlighting cooking tips found inside.

The Versatile Vegetable Cookbook by Delores Riccio and Joan Bingham. Van Nostrand Reinhold, New York, 1983; $15.50. A book that focuses on the "new" vegetable, rather than that old soggy, overcooked thing people used to push around their plate distractedly. Good information on how to select vegetables, prepare them, and present them nicely on a plate.

The Wild Gourmet: A Forager's Guide to the Finding and Cooking of Wild Food by Babette Brachett and Maryann Lash. David R. Godine Publisher, Boston, MA 1975. Interesting, fun book for campers and those who love the outdoors.

The Wok: A Chinese Cookbook by Gary Lee. Nitty Gritty Books, Concord, CA 176 pp; $3.95. A simple how-to of Chinese cooking. Well illustrated. Nice gift book.

Wokcraft by Charles and Violet Schafer. Yerba Buena Press, San Francisco, CA 108 pp; $4.95. Good introduction to the wok.

The Yoga Way Cookbook: Natural Vegetarian Recipes. Himalayan International Institute of Yoga Science and Philosophy, Honesdale, PA, 1982; $6.95. More simple, traditional vegetarian fare.

Zen Macrobiotic Cooking by Michel Abehsera. Citadel Press/Lyle Stuart, 120 Enterprise Ave, Seacaucus, NJ 07094; $7.95. Engaging introduction to the Zen macrobiotic way of life.

A few of Abehsera's do's and don't's of cooking:
Do learn to cook rice and cook it well.
For the best tea, do previously warm the teapot with boiled water before brewing.
Don't cook foods over a high flame.
Don't throw away the green parts of vegetables, such as carrot or raddish tops. Use them for soup.
Don't boil vegetables. Sauteeing preserves vitamins and minerals.
Add salt just before the end of cooking. Don't add salt at the table.

Do do your stirring with a wooden spoon or chopsticks. Metal spoons may damage pots and "break" vegetables.
Use spring or well water.
Don't use aluminum utensils. Clay, glass, and cast-iron pots are preferable. Clay especially heightens the taste (watch for lead in the glazes). Stainless steel is recommended.
Don't peel vegetables, brush them
Do eat the slightly scorched rice at the bottom of the pot. It is very rich in minerals.
Don't eat and cook. It spoils your ability to create. An empty stomach is one of the secrets of any creative activity.
Do use a Japanese knife, wide and heavy, for cutting vegetables. Work on a clean cutting board, which should be washed as often as possible.

19

Cooking Schools

The following list of cooking schools is but a sample of what can be found throughout the country. Many classes are offered through local vegetarian societies (see listings in Chapter 1, What is Vegetarianism). Also look in the newspapers and magazines mentioned in Chapter 30, Vegetarian Networking; many cooking course offerings are mentioned in these periodicals.

Cuisine Naturelle, 16a Madrona, Mill Valley, CA 94941; (415) 381-0776. Natural foods cooking school run by Mary Carroll Dremann.

The Himalayan Institute of New York, 78 Fifth Ave, New York, NY 10011; (212) 243-5995. A branch of the Himalayan International Institute in Honesdale, Pennsylvania (founded by Swami Rama). Classes include vegetarian cooking, diet, and nutrition.

The Natural Gourmet Cookery School, 365 West End Ave, New York, NY 10024; (212) 580-7121. Annemarie Colbin, director. Using all fresh and wholesome foods, learn to put together delicious, well-balanced meals. Learn the healing properties of food as well. Class choice is varied, instructive, and interesting, and designed for the novice chef, the novice vegetarian, the old hand, kids, and even professional chefs who want to add a more up-to-date style of cuisine to their menus. Some

the natural gourmet cookery school

365
west end avenue
suite 1E
new york city
10024

(212) 580-7121

of the things that captivated me were the blueberry couscous cake (which was mentioned in the description of the course, *Kids Can Cook, Too*), the *Oriental-style "clay pot" meal*, and Japanese *Nabe-Mono* of the *Easy and Elegant Meal* course. Other courses are *Cooking that Heals; Health-Supportive Cooking for Cold Weather, Warm Weather* (changing according to the season); *International Natural Cuisine; Sugarless Desserts*; and an in-depth study course *Food and Healing, East and West*. Annemarie Colbin and her school enjoy an excellent reputation. Tuitition varies. Write for brochure. The school also caters large and small parties, and on Saturday evening if you call ahead you can have a "night out and a fine meal'' prepared by the school's professional students. The meal is buffet, the price $10.00 Class courses differ slightly according to season.

The Sprout House, 210 Riverside Dr, New York, NY 10025; (212) 864-3233. Steve Meyerowitz, alias the ''Sproutman,'' runs the Sprout House out of his home. His classes focus on vegetarian diets, sprouting, fasting and food combining. The ''Sproutman'' will teach you how to make gourmet sprout fare, including sprout bagels, sprout pizza, and sprout ice cream. A series of four classes costs $80.

Yoga Meditation Society of New Jersey, 29 Washington St, Morristown, NJ; (201) 540-1677. Lots of classes including vegetarian cooking.

Vita Village, 7121 West Broward Blvd, Plantation, FL, (305) 792-0026. Natural foods cookery classes held at a health foods store. Classes deal with meal planning, grains, desserts, soups, complete family meals, and vegetarian, macrobiotic, and Oriental philosophies.

20

Government Information and Services

There is a vast storehouse of government information waiting to be tapped. The American Statistics Index (ASI) indexes many of these government documents containing numerical information. The publishers reproduce government documents on microfiche, which they file according to their own numbering system. Virtually every major city and many universities have a library equipped to help you track down this information.

GOVERNMENT AGENCIES

Bureau of Nutrition, Department of Health, 93 Worth St, Room 714, New York, New York 10013. They publish a small booklet entitled the *Vegetarian,* focusing on combining different elements to create a well-rounded diet. Includes recipes. The bureau also sponsors a service, "Phone a Nutritionist": (212) 925-7315, 566-6022, 566-6023. They also have a daily nutrition message in English (431-4540) and Spanish (431-4558).

The Consumer Product Safety Commission, 1111 Eighteenth St NW, Washington, D.C. 20207. Attn Nancy Harvey Steorts, Chairwoman.

The Environmental Protection Agency, 401 M St SW, Washington, D.C. 20460.

Environmental Protection Agency Toxicology and **Microbiology Division,** 26 West St. Clair, Cincinnati, OH 45268; (513) 684-7401.

Food and Drug Administration, 5600 Fishers Lane, Rockville, MD 20857. Attn Arthur H. Hayes Jr, Administrator.

LOBBIES AND RELATED GROUPS

American Fund for Alternatives to Animal Research (AFAAR), c/o Thurston, 175 West 12 St, New York, NY 10011; (212) 989-8073.

Animal Welfare Institute, PO Box 3650, Washington, D.C. 20007; (202) 337-2333.

Association for Creative Change, The Alban Institute, Mount St. Albans, Washington, D.C.; (202) 244-3588.

Audubon Naturist Society, 8940 Jones Mill Rd, Chevy Chase, Md 20815; (301) 652-9188.

Bioenergy Council, 1625 I St NW, Washington, D.C. 20006; (202) 833-5656.

Center for Community Organizations, 1214 16th St NW, Washington, D.C. 20007; (202) 467-5560.

Center for Environmental Education, 624 9th St NW, Washington, D.C. 2000 ; (202) 737-3600.

Center for Renewable Resources, 1001 Connecticut Ave NW, Washington, D.C. 20036; (202) 466-6880.

Center for Science in the Public Interest, 1755 S St NW, Washington, D.C. 20009; (202) 332-9110.

Citizen's Energy Project, 1110 6th St NW, #300, Washington, D.C. 20001; (202) 387-8998.

Clear Water Action Project, 1341 G St NW, Washington, D.C. 20005; (202) 638-1196.

Coalition for a Non-Nuclear World, 236 Massachusetts Ave NE, Washington, D.C. 20002; (202) 483-4284.

Congressional Clearing House on the Future, 3564 House Annex Number 2, Washington, D.C. 20515; (202) 225-3153.

Council on Environmental Quality, 722 Jackson Pl NW, Washington, D.C. 20006; (202) 633-7027.

Defenders of Wildlife, 1244 19th St NW, Washington, D.C. 20036; (202) 659-9510.

Environment Policy Center, 317 Pennsylvania Ave SE, Washington, D.C. 20003; (202) 547-6500.

Environment Protection Agency, U.S. EPA, Washington, D.C. 20036; (202) 655-4000.

Environmental Action Foundation, Dupont Circle Building, Ste 724, Washington, D.C. 20036; (202) 659-9682.

Environmental Action, Inc, 1346 Connecticut Ave NW, Washington, D.C. 20036; (202) 833-1845.

The Environmental Defense Fund, 1525 18th St NW, Washington, D.C. 20036; (202) 833-1484.

Environmental Information Center, 325 Pennsylvania Ave SE, Washington, D.C. 20003; (202) 547-0110.

Environmentalists for Full Employment, 1536 16th St NW, Washington, D.C. 20036; (202) 347-5590.

Friends of the Earth, 530 7th St SE, Washington, D.C. 20003; (202) 543-4313.

Greenpeace, USA, 2007 R St NW, Washington, D.C. 20009; (202) 462-1177.

Humane Society of the United States, 2100 L St NW, Washington, D.C. 20037; (202) 452-1100.

Infant Formula Action (INFACT), 1201 16th St NW, Washington, D.C. 20036; (202) 331-1751.

Institute for Ecological Policies, 9208 Christopher St, Fairfax, VA 22031; (703) 691-1271.

Institute for Food and Development Policy, 2588 Mission St, San Francisco, CA 94110.

League for Urban Land Conservation, 1150 Connecticut Ave NW, Washington, D.C. 20036; (202) 457-1039.

National Audubon Society, 1511 K St NW, Washington, D.C. 20005; (202) 466-6600.

National Information Center for Quiet, PO Box 57171, Washington, D.C. 20037; (202) 524-5600.

National Wildlife Federation, 1412 16th St NW, Washington, D.C. 20036; (202) 797-6800.

Nation Response Center for Water Pollution, U.S. Coast Guard G-TGC-2, 2100 2nd St SW, Washington, D.C. 20593; (202) 426-2675.

Natural Resources Defense Council, 1725 I St NW, Ste 600, Washington, D.C. 20006; (202) 223-8210.

Sierra Club, 330 Pennsylvania Ave SE, Washington, D.C. 20003; (202) 547-1144.

Spiral Feedback, PO Box 80323, Lincoln, NE 68051. Society for the Protection of Individual Rights and Liberties.

Urban Environment Conference, 666 11th St NW, Washington, D.C. 20001; (202) 638-3385.

World Future Society, 4916 St. Elmo Ave NW, Washington, D.C. 20014; (202) 656-8274.

World Information Service on Energy, 1536 16th St NW, Washington, D.C. 20036; (202) 387-0818.

World Peace Movement, PO Box 2, Ojai, CA 93023.

Worldwatch Institute, 1776 Massachusetts Ave NW, Washington, D.C. 20036; (202) 452-1999.

GOVERNMENT PUBLICATIONS

Consumer Information Catalog, Consumer Information Center, Department J, Pueblo, CO 81009. Free. Published four times a year, the catalog lists booklets from approximately 30 government agencies. Many of the publications are free. Pamphlets of interest to vegetarians include:

The Confusing World of Health Foods. Discusses health, organic and natural foods, comparing them with conventional foods with regard to cost and nutritional value.

Roughage. Focuses on high-fiber diets and their effect on health.

Vegetarian Diets. Weighs the benefits and possible risks of vegetarianism.

Other titles, for which there is a fee, include: *Dwarf Fruit Trees* ($2.00); *Growing Tomatoes in the Home Garden* ($2.00); *Growing Vegetables in the Home Garden* ($3.25); *Mini-Gardens for Vegetables* ($2.25); and *Storing Vegetables and Fruits* ($2.25).

NOTE: There is a $1.00 user fee for processing an order for two or more free booklets.

United States Government Printing Office, Washington, D.C. 20402. Publishes *Dietary Goals for the United States, Ideas for Better Eating, Home Canning of Fruits and Vegetables, Nutrition and Your Health,* more.

21

University Courses, Study, Growth and Training Centers

Our culture is thinking differently about diet and nutrition in recent years. As our thinking changes, our educational institutions must also try to offer relevant curricula to their students. More and more universities are offering courses in progressive nutrition. No longer does one have to attend a small fringe workshop group to find the information he or she demands. Local vegetarian groups and regional networking newspapers can put you in touch with the courses you would like to take. What follows is a partial list of available offerings.

Aletheia, 515 N.E. 8th, Grants Pass, OR 97526; (503) 479-4855. Some nutrition workshops.

American College of Nutripathy, 6821 East Thomas, Scottsdale, AZ 85251; (602) 946-5515.

American College of Nutrition, 1704-E Eleventh Ave South, Birmingham, AL 35205. Degree programs in nutrition leading to bachelors, masters, or doctorate. "Learn how to develop your own nutrition consultant practice."

Antioch University, San Francisco, 650 Pine St, San Francisco, CA 94108; (415) 956-1688. Bachelor of arts program in holistic health and master of arts in holistic studies.

Antioch University, Seattle, 1165 Eastlake Avenue East, Seattle, WA 98109; (206) 343-9150. Progressive whole-system education, undergraduate and graduate.

Aromatherapy Institute, 123 Davenport Rd, Toronto, Ontario M5R 1H8 Canada; (416) 964-6803. A diploma course in a specialized massage treatment incorporating the use of natural essential oils to promote personal well-being. Taught by Anne Roebuck. In the United States: Aromatherapy Institute, Box 77, Norwood, NJ 07648.

Association for Human Resources, PO Box 727, Concord, MA 01742; (617) 259-9624. Master's program in humanistic psychology, in conjunction with Vermont College and Beacon College, led by a group of therapists who work closely with the individual, offering a dialogue that encompasses emotional, behavioral, social, intellectual, and spiritual aspects of the person and the learning experience.

Association for Research and Enlightenment, PO Box 595, Virginia Beach, VA 23451; (804) 428-3588. Study centered on the work of the famous psychic and healer, Edgar Cayce.

Asunaro Institute, PO Box 2546, Escondido, CA 92025; (714) 749-5678, 743-6890. Author of *Heal-*

ing Ourselves, Noboru Muramoto teaches a learn-as-you-take-part course in the preparation of miso, tamari, tekka, and mochi. Lectures on salt, umeboshi, natto, and more. Macrobiotic courses, including cooking. Rural environment.

Dr. Edward Bach Centre, Mount Vernon, Sotwell, Wallingford, Oson, OX10 OPZ England; tel: Wallingford (0491) 39489. Bach Flower Remedy training and certification program for beginning and advanced counselors. In United States contact: The National Association of Certified Bach Remedy Counselors (NACBRC), 271 Fifth Ave, Ste 3, New York, NY 10016; (212) 683-4793. (See Chapter 6.)

Best of Health, 60 East 13th St, 4th floor, New York, NY 10003; (212) 674-2813. One-day intensive course on dynamic nutrition. Price: $75.00.

Burlington College, 95 North Ave, Burlington, VT 65401; (802) 862-9616. Associated with the Institute for Social Ecology (ISE) to make an education and research program that addresses critical ecologic and social questions.

California School of Herbal Studies, PO Box 350, Guerneville, CA 95446; (707) 869-0972. Good selection of herbal classes and doings, including herbal hot spring retreats, natural cosmetics, wild herb cooking classes, and field identification.

Clayton University, PO Box 16150, St. Louis, MO 63120; (800) 325-6100. Bachelors, masters and doctorate in nutrition.

College of the Atlantic, Bar Harbor, ME 04609; (207) 288-5015. Fantastically situated, accredited school offering a four-year program awarding the bachelor of arts degree in human ecology.

Druid College, PO Box 1352, Philadelphia, PA 19105; (215) 288-5700. Eight-week night course on herbalism and health ($265). Each segment of the course can be taken individually: herbalism ($165) or health ($135).

Esalen Institute, Big Sur, CA 93920. The center, situated in a stirring locale, provides seminars, workshops, residential programs, consulting, and research on a variety of subjects, including massage and nutritional awareness.

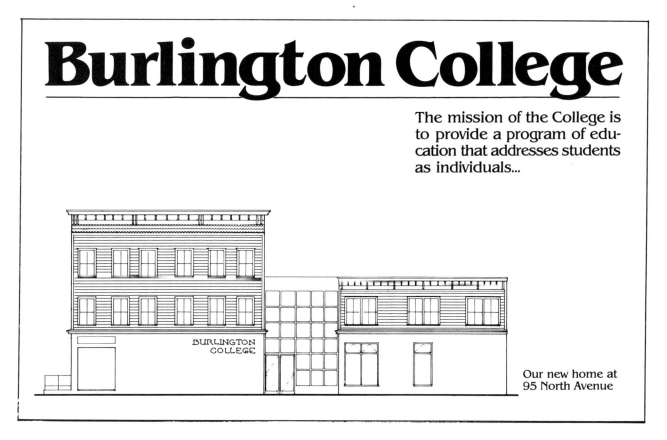

California School of Herbal Studies

Goddard College, Plainfield, VT 05667; (802) 445-8311. Bachelor of arts in nutritional studies.

Heartwood, California College of the Natural Healing Arts, 220 Harmony Lane, Garberville, CA 95440; (707) 923-2021. Multifaceted program. Offers associate degree, bachelor of science, and master's degrees, but also individual interesting offerings and workshops, summer sessions.

Himalayan Institute of New York, East–West Books, 78 Fifth Ave, New York, NY 10011; (212) 243-5995. Courses in vegetarian cooking, homeopathic first aid, breathing, yoga therapy, more.

Hippocrates World Health Organization, 25 Exeter St, Boston, MA 02116; (617) 267-9525. Run by

GODDARD COLLEGE

Dr. Ann Wigmore (see Chapter 3, Vegetarian Authorities). Her staples are: Live foods, sprouts, and wheat grass. A two-week ''learn by doing'' program begins each Sunday. Learn all the skills needed to continue the program at home. Ten-week ''health ministers'' program prepares you for a career in holistic health. Ten-session, five-week, night school program. Free open house every Sunday at 4:00 P.M. Free book and equipment list.

Interweave Center, 31 Woodland Ave, Summit, NJ 07901; (201) 763-8312. Variety of classes and social functions, some with a vegetarian bent.

John F. Kennedy University, 12 Altarinda Rd, Orinda, CA 94563; (415) 254-0200. Study of nutrition counseling, clinical holistic health education, health counseling. Accredited by Western Association of Schools and Colleges. Study leads to M.P.A. or M.B.P.A.

Kushi Institute, PO Box 1100, Brookline Village, MA 02147; (617) 731-0564. Macrobiotic studies on both a full- and part-time basis.

Lawrence/Harrison Institute, 1990 Broadway, Ste 1206, New York, NY 10023; (212) 307-1399. Holistic practitioner training programs.

Mandala Holistic Health, Box 1233, Del Mar, CA 92014; (619) 481-7751. Holistic studies.

Michigan State University, College of Agriculture and Natural Resources, Room 104, Agriculture Hall, East Lansing, MI 48824. Attn Dean James H. Anderson. Program in organic *biological ag-*

KUSHI INSTITUTE
MACROBIOTIC EDUCATION FOR A HEALTHY AND PEACEFUL WORLD

A great challenge faces us all in the next decade. Issues involving the quality of life on this planet will be explored and directions set which could well decide the future of humanity. The Kushi Institute offers you an opportunity to make a positive contribution to this process.

Studies at the Institute are directed toward the total development of the individual, providing a well-balanced program of physical, mental and spiritual development. The program is designed to adapt to the needs of the individual whether they are seeking to establish a more healthy way of life, discover a sense of direction for their future or acquire specific professional skills.

For students interested in career development, the program of the Institute is unique. The theory and practical application of Oriental Medicine and traditional healing techniques are thoroughly covered by a teaching staff with extensive professional experience both as instructors and practitioners. In the field of Cooking and Food Processing, our program offers practical "hands-on" experience in all of the traditional techniques of preparation for foods such as tempeh, seitan, tofu and a wide range of condiments and specialty food items.

Past graduates of the Kushi Institute have been active all over the world in the establishment of educational activities, research projects or the creation of health counselling services. Together with our European affiliates in London, Amsterdam and Antwerp and a world-wide network of over 300 East West Centers, we are able to offer countless opportunities for rewarding work to those who complete our program.

Graduates of the Kushi Institute are uniquely prepared to make a positive contribution to the transformation of world society in areas as diverse as healing, world hunger, institutional catering, community service projects or education.

EXTENSION SERVICES AND SPECIAL EVENTS

The courses at the Kushi Institute are offered on both a full and part-time basis. This allows students the opportunity to build up credits over a period of time. Completion of all three levels of study is one of the criteria for certification by the Kushi Institute Review Board, which certifies Macrobiotic Teachers and Counsellors.

After completion of studies, participants are requested to establish one year's work in an approved apprenticeship program or field work prior to certification as a Graduate Advisor.

Each session the Institute offers special courses and workshops in a variety of subjects for both full and part-time students. These events include classes with visiting teachers as well as programs offered by the resident teaching staff. A full schedule of these events can be obtained from the office three weeks prior to the beginning of each new session.

THE SUMMER INTENSIVE
July 11-August 19

Each year the Kushi Institute offers a special intensive course for students who wish to study in a more condensed program. Last year over 70 men & women from all parts of the world came to Boston to participate. In addition to the resident teaching staff, last year's students had the opportunity to study with Yogi Amrit Desai, Vincent Harding, Rev. Jomyo Tanaka, Murray Snyder, Bill Spear and others.

The classes in the Intensive program are all offered during the day with the exception of occasional special lectures and social events.

One indication of the success of our program is that a great percentage of the students participating in the summer intensive enroll for the next year's course. Applications for the 1983 Intensive are now being accepted. Send $2.00 for a complete course outline and details.

The Challenge of Leadership

SESSION DATES AND TIMES

Basic courses are scheduled Monday through Friday; occasional weekend meetings are required. Workshops and electives are scheduled before and after regular class hours, including weekends.

Special social events and field trips are planned from time to time.

The present Full-Time course of studies consists of three sessions of approximately 12 weeks each.

Spring .... April 11-July 1
Summer Intensive ... July 11-August 19
Fall 1983 .... Sept. 12-December 9

A calendar with a list of instructors, schedule of meetings, course times and room numbers will be available upon request one month prior to each session.

STUDIES IN LEVEL I CONSIST OF:

Michio Kushi Seminars
Macrobiotic Philosophy
Nutrition & Human Needs
Shiatsu Massage & Corrective Exercise
The Principles of Health Assessment & Oriental Diagnosis
Macrobiotic Cooking
Anatomy & Physiology I
Meditation & Spiritual Practices
Principles of Macrobiotic Medicine
Community Service

STUDIES IN LEVEL II CONSIST OF:

Michio Kushi Seminars
Macrobiotic Philosophy & World Religions
Nutrition and Social Needs
Anatomy & Physiology II
Shiatsu Massage & Corrective Exercise II
Oriental Diagnosis
Macrobiotic Cooking for Special Needs
Meditation & Spiritual Practice
Macrobiotic Medicine II
Community Service

STUDIES IN LEVEL III CONSIST OF:

Macrobiotic Philosophy & Social Issues
Oriental Diagnosis & Human Behavior
Advanced Macrobiotic Cooking
Meditation & Spiritual Practice
Shiatsu Massage Workshop
Macrobiotic Medicine III
Joint Studies
Community Service

DIRECTORS AND STAFF

Michio Kushi, *President*
Aveline Kushi, *Vice President*
Dr. Marc Van Cauwenberghe, *Director*
Olivia Oredson, *Cooking School*
Judith Clinton, *Administrative Asst.*
Phillip Kushi, *Business Manager*

KUSHI INSTITUTE TEACHING STAFF

Michio Kushi
Aveline Kushi
Shizuko Yamamoto
Dr. Marc Van Cauwenberghe
Bill Tara
Ed Esko
Wendy Esko
Olivia Oredson
Lenny Jacobs
John Mann
Judy Waxman
Tonia Gagne
and special guests and visiting teachers.

To register use the form on the reverse side or a facsimile. For a catalog of more detailed course descriptions, send $2 in cash, traveler's check, money order or certified check to:
Kushi Institute
P.O. Box 1100
Brookline Village, MA 02147
(617) 731-0564

Schedule A. Notice of non-discriminatory policy as to students. The Kushi Foundation, Inc. admits students of any race, color, nationality and ethnic origin to all the rights, privileges, programs and activities generally accorded or made available to students at the school. It does not discriminate on the basis of race, color, nationality and ethnic origin in the administration of its educational policies, scholarship and loan programs and athletic and other school administered programs.

---

riculture, the term used at Michigan State University for organic farming. The university does not use the term *organic farming* because they feel it has become synonymous with non-chemical farming, and the scientists at the university feel that knowledge of chemistry can only benefit a farmer.

National College of Naturopathic Medicine, 11231 SE Market St, Portland, OR 97216; (503) 255-4860. Continuing education classes in nutrition and health topics, including Oriental medicine, dance massage.

Natural Foods Now Training Programs, Joel Rauch, director, 5650 Kirby, South 229 (south of Bissonnet), Houston, TX 77005; (713) 790-1176. Interested in a career in natural foods? They offer training to help you enter the health food industry. Courses in health food store management, res-

taurants, vitamins, cosmetics, herbs, direct distributorships, sales, public speaking, classes, workshops, open universities, and more. The school of nutrition is the main branch of the training program. It offers courses in all aspects of natural foods, including family utilization, buying and saving, preparation. A diploma is issued upon completion of the course, along with a special "starter kit."

New England Nutrition Association, Goddard College, 468 Commonwealth Ave, Boston, MA 02215; (617) 247-0896. Nutritional studies covering areas such as interpretation of allergy testing, megavitamin therapy, fasting, and detoxification diets. Career programs in nutrition.

Natural Health Center, South Route, Box 10, Lavina, MT 59046; (406) 575-4487. Holistic approach featuring, among other things, nutritional counseling.

Omega Institute for Holistic Studies, PO Box 571, Lebanon Springs, NY 12114; (518) 794-8850. Summer campus: Lake Drive, RD2, Box 377, Rhinebeck, NY 12572; (914) 266-4301. Seminars and intensives in an adult summer camp environment.

Polarity Wellness Center, 38 West 28 St, New York, NY 10001; (212) 889-3555. 34 Gurney St, Cambridge, MA 02138; (617) 497-4172. Very interesting sessions on nutrition include geriatric nutrition, analysis of diet types, different types of fasting, nutrition in pregnancy and for adolescents. One course (ten sessions) costs $200. Courses can be undertaken on an individual basis. Each session is $25.

Platonic Academy of Herbal Studies, Box 409, Santa Cruz, CA 95061; (408) 423-7923. A professional training program for herbalists resulting in a license in the practice of herbal medicine. Tuition is $700 per semester. Tutorial classes by mail are $150 for a set of ten lessons.

Religious School of Natural Hygiene, 6344 Pacheco Pass Highway, Hollister, CA 95023; (408) 637-1920. Natural Hygiene's California Health Sanctuary, where one may learn the philosophy of natural hygiene. Membership costs $25.00/year and includes a subscription to *Naturally, The Hygienic Way*, the school's newsletter. You can't go to the sanctuary unless you're a member of the religious school. A stay at the sanctuary costs $250 per week; minimum stay, two weeks. Extensive mail-order book service.

Rudolf Steiner College, 9200 Fair Oaks Blvd, Fair Oaks, CA 95628; (916) 961-8727. The German educator and thinker, Rudolf Steiner, believed in the wholeness and integration of all systems. Educational facilities dedicated to his teachings exist all over the world. The college in California offers a variety of courses, including biodynamic gardening.

Ryokan College, 12581 Venice Blvd, Los Angeles, CA 90066; (213) 390-7560. Masters and doctoral programs in nutrition.

(801) 489-4254

School of Natural Healing, PO Box 412, Springville, UT 84663; (801) 489-4254 or (800) 453-1406. The late Dr. John Christopher's program of herbalist training seminars (see Chapter 3: Vegetarian Authorities). Nine-day master herbalist course runs $795.00.

Society for Nutrition Education, 1736 Franklin St, Oakland, CA 94612; (415) 444-7133. Excellent educational material for the health professional and low-cost information for consumers including *First Food* ($1.50), a guide for new parents, with practical information about baby's first solid foods. *A Guide for Food and Nutrition in Later Years* ($1.50) tells the best diet for an older person and includes a fold-out chart showing the best sources

of major nutrients and a resource list of publications and organizations with special emphasis on the elderly. Also available is a *Brief Guide to Becoming a Nutrition Advocate*, which tells how to influence public policy on nutrition ($3.75).

Soycrafters Apprenticeship Program, PO Box 747, Vashon Island, WA 98070; (206) 622-6448. Offers instruction in all aspects of soyfoods production, marketing, research, and development. The term of the program is 21 days. Key topics covered

The Soycrafters
Apprenticeship Program

are sanitation and safety; bean selection; curding, ladling, and packaging of tofu; the use of inoculate; incubating, packaging, and trouble-shooting in tempeh manufacturing; soyfreeze; soyloaf; steamed tofu; soymilk; plans for business, including marketing survey and strategies; start-up costs; capitalization; accounting; shop layout, maintenance; by-product use; and developing new products. The course costs $2500.00 per individual or $2000.00 per group member from the same business.

Survival Foundation, PO Box 77, Woodstock Valley, CT 06282; (203) 974-2511. Workshops, lectures, seminars, and weekend retreats pertaining to raw food nutrition, natural healing, body ecology, and new age spirituality. Supervised by Viktoras Kulvinskas (see Chapter 3, Vegetarian Authorities).

University for Humanistic Studies, 2445 San Diego Ave, San Diego, CA 92110; (619) 452-7792, 296-7204. Undergraduate and graduate courses in nutritional studies.

Vega Institute, 1544 Oak St, Oroville, CA 95965; (916) 533-9900. Herman and Cornelia Aihara teach macrobiotic theory and practice (including cooking) in monthly three-week sessions.

Wainwright House, 260 Stuyvesant Ave, Rye, NY 10580; (914) 967-6080. Cross-cultural center for development of human resources, with an interesting array of courses, including some dealing with diet, exercise, and the pressures of daily life. Residential options. Services include *The Listening Post*: "If you'd like to have an hour's confidential talk with a trained listener, call weekdays between 9 and 5 for an appointment." This service is free of charge.

Wild Rose College of Natural Healing, PO Box 253, Station M, Calgary, Alberta T2B 2H9 Canada; (403) 266-1199. Courses offered on campus or as tape and cassette correspondence classes in herbology and nutrition including *Nutrition for the Householder, Vitamins and Minerals for Health*, and *Health, Pregnancy and Childbirth*.

Wise Woman Center, Susun B. Weed, PO Box 64, Woodstock, NY 12498. Herbalist, gardener, feminist, artist, witch, Susun Weed teaches and lectures on what she knows; herbs and wild foods. Program includes Weed Walks. She also publishes an herbal source of minerals which she sells for 50 cents.

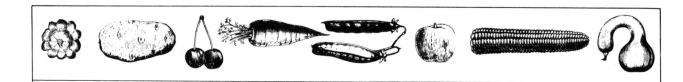

22

Home Study

If you're too busy or can't attend courses outside the house, home study might be the perfect solution. Progress at your own pace, at your leisure; but beware—those seeking courses leading to a degree should be sure the home study program does in fact have accreditation.

Be Healthy Education Company, 4 Lauren Lane, Norwich, CT 06360. Author Sylvia Klein Olkin (*Positive Pregnancy Through Yoga* and *Successful Parenting Through Yoga*) offers fairly priced programs (most are $9.95) for positive pregnancies and birthing, stretching, insomnia.

Better Health and Nutrition Center, Rte 2, PO Box 960, Richmond, VA 23233; (804) 747-8837. Iola Gifford has been a naturalist for 25 years and she brings you her knowledge in 20 lessons, paperbound and put together for easy reading. The lessons focus on: organic farming, indoor organic gardening, the value of sprouts and greens, reasons to be a vegetarian, junk food, cooking, enzymes and enzyme power, food combining, Hippocrates, reducing and fasting, detoxification, elimination, colon care, and more. Iola's particular expertise is in raw foodism ($20.00). Her cookbook, *The Natural Cookbook for the 20th Century,* is $5.00.

College of Life Science, 6600-D Burleson Rd, Box 17128, Austin, TX 78760; (512) 385-2781. Studies in nutritional and health principles and their practical application for achieving high energy. One course costs $50.00 for seven lessons. More classes available, including *Careers in Health* segment. The *Health Reporter* is the college's newspaper. Published 18 times annually, it is available for $12.00 for six issues. *Healthful Living,* a second publication, is a monthly; a year's subscription is $12.00.

Creative Audio, 8751 Osborne, Highland, IN 46322; (219) 838-2770. Free catalog of tapes of Dr. Jeffrey Bland, Devaki Berkson, Arthur Kaslow, Michael Cessna, Harry Rein, Joel Grossman, and many other health professionals. Also includes convention tapes, such as the 1981 American Holistic Medical Association Conference in La Crosse, Wisconsin.

Donsbach University, 7422 Mountjoy, Huntington Beach, CA 92648. The school of nutrition offers bachelors, masters, and doctoral degrees through a mail-order, home-study program. Thorough, far-reaching course. Tuition and fees: bachelor of science, $2495.00; M.S. $3195.00 and Ph.D., $3495.00. Some electives are: *Pediatric Nutrition I–V,* three sections taught by Dr. Lendon H. Smith (see Chapter 12, Vegetarianism and Children); *Psycho-Nutrition* taught by Carlton Fredericks; *Geriatric Nutrition* by Cheraskin and Ringsdorf; eight courses on *General Nutrition* by Richard Passwater (see Chapter 3, Vegetarian

Authorities); Dr. Donsbach himself teaches a course on *Superhealth*. A mini-course in nutrition (12 cassettes and equipment, including a filmstrip projector) is $495.00.

East–West Master Course in Herbology, Box 712, Santa Cruz, CA 95061. Taught by master herbalist, Michael Tierra, author of *Way of Herbs*. Thirty-six lessons, $250; introductory lesson, $10.

Health Unlimited, PO Box 49215 A, Los Angeles, CA 90049. Susan Smith Jones, *Vegetarian Times* fitness columnist, devised this audio cassette "pep" course: *The Main Ingredients: Positive Thinking, Exercise and Nutrition* ($12.50). The thrust of Ms. Smith Jones' work is, "Anything you can do, you can do better."

Institute of Human Development, PO Box 41165, Cincinnati, OH 45241. Metaphysical and self-development tapes. New age music offerings.

International Holistic Center, PO Box 15103, Phoenix, AZ 85060. HELP educational cassette tapes include "Allergies and Daily Life" ($6.95), "Introduction to Live Foods and Transition Diet"

($6.95), "Minerals (also Vitamins) and their Roles in Body Balance" ($6.95 each), "Vegetarian Transition Diet" ($6.95), "Sprouts, Live Food Meal Preparation" ($6.95), "Indoor Gardening for Survival" ($6.95), more.

National Center for Homeopathy, 1500 Massachusetts Ave NW, Ste 41, Washington, D.C. 20005. At-home course for the licensed health professional and the layperson.

Nutritionists Institute of America, 312 West 8 St, PO Box 19481, Kansas City, MO 64141; (800) 821-5234 or (816) 842-2942. Certified nutritionist home study program. A three-month course leading to an assistant nutritionist certification, sug-

gested for health-food store clerks and managers, mothers, fathers, householders, is $395. Associate nutritionist, a six-month course, advised for health care facility personnel, food service managers and staff, school, and child care staff, is $600. The professional nutritionist course is a year long ($1125), and is recommended for health care facility staff, school and government food programs, community health programs, health centers, cooking school staff, and private practitioners.

Nutricise, Computer Resource Technologies, 13 West 36 St, New York, NY 10018; (212) 563-2293. A computer program that tells you the number of calories you burned in exercise, rates the aerobic quality of your workout, determines the degree to which the foods you ate provided you with 12 essential nutrients, and reports your total caloric intake for the day and the source of those calories. The program will recommend an ideal body weight for you, exercise to increase caloric output, food sources rich in the nutrients found to be low in your diet, and ways to cut back on or redistribute your calorie intake. The cost is $79.95.

Other home computer nutritional analysis programs:

Eat, Penn State University, Nutrition Department, 202 Human Development Building, University Park, PA 16802. Apple Computers. Cost: $125.

Eat Smart, Eat Smart Kit, Consumer Public Relations, The Pillsbury Company, Pillsbury Center, Minneapolis, MN 55402. Apple. Cost: $19.75.

InShape, DEG Software, 11999 Katy Freeway, Houston, TX 77079. IBM-PC. Cost: $95.

Nutri-Bytes, Center for Science in the Public Interest, 1755 S St NW, Washington, D.C. 20009. Kaypro, IBM-PC. Cost: $30.

Nutri-Calc, Patient Care Data Systems, PO Box 143, Penn Yan, NY 14527. TRS 80, Apple, IBM-PC, Altos. Cost: $129.

Nutrient Analysis System, DDA, PO Box 26, Hamburg, NJ 07419. Apple. Cost: $199. Also, *You Are What You Eat;* cost: $79.95.

Nutritionist N Squared Computing, 5318 Forest Ridge Rd, Silverton, OR 97381. Apple, IBM-PC. Cost: $145.

The Seven Essentials Of Health by Philip J. Welsh and Blanche Leonardo. One installment per month for 12 months. No theory, but practical health principles discovered and used by Dr. Welsh in his own life. How to maintain or regain one's health with nature's help. Available from Vegetarian Society, Inc, Box 5688, Santa Monica, CA 90405; (213) 396-5164. Complete course, $25.00.

Mindbody, PO Box 1038, Manhasset, NY 11030; (516) 365-7722. Training tapes, books (including their own cookbook), appliances (including wheatgrass juicer, Champion juicer, Aqua Clean water distiller).

Source, PO Box W, Stanford, CA 94305; (415) 328-7171 or (800) 227-1617, Ext 514. Cassette learning systems made by Emmett E. Miller. "Software for the mind." Sampler available for $2.00.

Unlimited Potentials Institute, 9390 Whitneyville Rd, Alto, MI 49302; (616) 891-9213. Self-hypnosis tapes dealing with a wide variety of topics, including weight loss and gain, gaining control of habits, self-healing, and more.

23

Health Food Stores

TRADE ORGANIZATIONS

National Nutritional Foods Association (NINFA), PO Box 2089, Carlsbad, CA 92008. This nonprofit corporation serves the health/nutritional/natural foods industry. Members include retailers, wholesalers, jobbers, brokers, manufacturers, distributors, publishers, and bulk suppliers. They stage an annual convention and trade show. They have a code of ethics and goals which includes an exchange of ideas while increasing trade.

Northwest Provender Alliance, PO Box 3588, Portland, OR 97208; (503) 344-1930. Trade association for natural food businesses located mainly in the Pacific Northwest. Publishes the quarterly *Provender Journal.*

TRADE MAGAZINES:

Health Foods Business. Howmark Publishing Corporation, 567 Morris Ave, Elizabeth, NJ 07208; (201) 353-7373. Trade magazine for owners and managers of health food stores.

Nutrition News, 837 West Holt Ave, Pomona, CA 91768; (714) 629-1557. Handout for health food stores designed to educate customers, promote the store, and sell products. A quantity of 100 would cost $29.00 per month; 2000 cost $202.00.

Whole Foods Magazine, PO Box 19531, Irvine, CA 92713 (714) 549-4834. "The voice of the natural foods industry," published in the interest of the health and natural foods industry, and is, therefore, distributed free.

HEALTH FOOD STORES

The information included for the health food stores and co-ops listed below is a sample listing. Phone numbers have been included wherever possible.

Food co-ops are stores owned by their members. Most offer a wide variety of natural, bulk, and organic produce. Membership requires buying a share, typically $10 to $25 at joining, which is refundable upon leaving. Members are also expected to pay a small monthly charge or help work in the store. Food cost savings are typically 10 to 20 percent or more, not to mention the benefits of community participation, social events, and helping to build an alternative food system.

ALABAMA

Dayspring Natural Foods, 223 Opelika Rd, Auburn 36830; (205) 821-1965. Sells food in bulk, as well as locally produced honey, yogurt, fruit juices.

Foods for Life, 2007-L Memorial Parkway NW, Huntsville 35820; (205) 859-0790.

Katie's Health Food Store, 6464 Highway 90 West, Mobile 36661; (205) 661-3065. Mail and phone orders.

Valley Health Foods, 117 South Cherry, Florence 35630; (205) 764-5340. Also 1601 Woodward Ave, Muscle Shoals 35660; 381-4260.

ALASKA

The Natural Pantry, 101 East Northern Light Blvd, Anchorage 99521; (907) 277-5455. One hundred fifty-six bulk items, delicatessen, snack bar, cooking classes, produce. COD and mail orders okay.

Pacific Rim Natural Foods, 4001 Sixth Ave South, Seattle, WA 98108; (800) 426-3511 or (206) 624-1681. Wholesale distributor for Alaska: produce, dairy, natural foods.

Whole Earth Exchange, 2600 College Rd, PO Box 80228, Fairbanks 99708; (907) 479-2052. Bulk foods, mail order.

ARKANSAS

Health Food Center, 1321 State Line Ave, Texarkana 75502; (501) 792-5921.

Mary's Natural Foods, 220 Highway 71 South, Springdale 72764; (501) 751-4224.

Mountain Ark Trading Company, 109 South East St, Fayetteville 72701; (501) 442--7191. Mail order macrobiotics. Free catalogue. Phone 24 hours.

The Old Country Store, 655 Broadway, Hot Springs 71909; (501) 624-1172. Vegetarian sandwiches to go.

Waye's Health and Light Store, 444 North Grand, Hot Springs 71909; (501) 623-3038.

ARIZONA

Cinema Park Health Foods, 5515 North 7th St (at Missouri), Phoenix 85014; (602) 274-2402. Fully stocked natural foods and vitamins.

Gentle Strength Co-op Natural Foods, 40 East 5th St, Tempe 85281; (602) 968-4831. Member-owned, not-for-profit co-op, requiring members to work each month in exchange for a 20 percent discount on products sold. The co-op has a full line of produce, both organic and non-organic, grains, seeds, nuts, dairy products, herbs, vitamins, and so on. Books, a deli with fresh sandwiches daily, and a variety of workshops, outings, lectures and demonstrations are also featured.

New Age Health Center, 4821 North Central Ave, Phoenix 85012; (602) 265-1983. Macrobiotic foods, herbs, produce and perishables, books, a nutritional consultant on staff, and a community networking bulletin board.

CALIFORNIA

Carmel Valley Natural Foods, Village Center, Carmel Valley 93924; (805) 659-2811.

Community Market, 860 First St at H St, Encinitas. Main Store, (619) 753-4632; produce, 753-9172. Large selection of organically grown produce and bulk items.

Co-opportunity Consumers Cooperative, 1530 Broadway, Santa Monica 90404; (213) 451-8902.

Cornucopia Natural Food Store, 3690 The Barnyard, Carmel 93923; (408) 625-1454. Organic produce, raw dairy, herbs, bulk grains.

Erewhon Natural Food Market, 8001 Beverly Blvd, between Crescent Heights and Fairfax, Los Angeles 90048; (213) 655-5441. Certified California-grown organic produce plus all essentials. "Healthycatessen" features hot soup, fresh sandwiches, salads, desserts. Take out.

Fresh Apple Health Foods, 3121 Harrison Ave South, Lake Tahoe 95705; (916) 541-7677.

Good Earth Natural Foods, 123 Bolinas Rd, Fairfax 94930; (415) 454-4633. Strong organic produce. Flour stone-ground on premises. Bulk grains, beans, herbs, nut butters, unrefined oils, miso, spring water, whole-grain baked goods, food supplements, natural cosmetics, cookware, and books.

Grain Country, 3448 30th St, San Diego 92102; (619) 298-1052. Macrobiotic food store, organic food, bulk food, books.

The Grainary, Pacific Grove 93950; (408) 372-2533. Grains, raw dairy, produce.

Hearthstone, 7235 Owensmouth, Canoga Park 91303; (818) 704-1344. Whole-grain bakery, plus natural foods delicatessan and book section. Workshops are planned on premises. They specialize in wedding and birthday cakes, using honey as a sweetener.

Mountain View Briarpatch Cooperative Market, 333 Bryant St, Mountain View 94041. Bulk items, grains, nuts, dried fruits, spices, teas, organic produce, raw dairy products, and low-sodium items, plus a full range of grocery and household items found at a regular grocery store. Because it is a cooperative there is a slight surcharge for guest shoppers.

Natural Food Center, 950 Del Monte Shopping Center, Monterey 93940; (408) 375-2188.

Nutrition Store, (two locations) 2778 Sweetwater Springs Blvd, Spring Valley 92077; (714) 698-3566. 7432 University Ave, La Mesa; (619) 697-3386. Includes a juice and sandwich bar. Staff nutritionist on the premises.

Organic Grocery, one block north of El Cajon Blvd at 47th and Monroe, San Diego 92116; (619) 284-9524. Organic produce, bulk grains. Natural foods lunch counter, juices, soups, salads, sandwiches.

Rainbow Grocery and Rainbow General Store, 1899 Mission St, San Francisco 94103; (415) 863-0620 or (415) 626-1511. Worker-controlled collectives. The general store discounts vitamins, natural cosmetics, juicers, and the like. The grocery sells produce, natural foods, and frozen, packaged, and bulk foods. There is also a deli serving salads, sandwiches, soups, and juices.

Rainbow Wholesale, 1485 Egbert St, San Francisco; (415) 822-6000. Part of the same collectively managed, nonprofit corporation as Rainbow Grocery, they sell basic food products in bulk. They stock 1000 different items including grains, beans, nuts, seeds, oils, condiments, sweeteners, crackers, rice cakes, juices, pasta, nut butters, sea vegetables, macrobiotics. Bulk generally translates to a minimum of 25-lb sacks, 5 gallons, or cases of 12 of any one item.

Real Food Company, 1023 Stanyan St, San Francisco 94117; (415) 564-2800, 3939 24th St, San Francisco 94112; (415) 282-9500. 2140 Polk St, San Francisco 94109; (415) 673-7420. 200 Calendonia, Sausalito 94965; 332-9640. 770 W Francisco Blvd, San Rafael 94974; 459-8966. Organic produce, bulk foods, herbs, vitamins, cosmetics, appliances.

Seacoast Natural Foods, 3352 Adams Ave, San Diego 92116; (619) 283-9442. A complete line of natural cosmetics, and all major brand name vitamins.

Southern California Cooperative Warehouse, 2022 Sacramento St, Los Angeles 90021; (213) 622-3303. A supplier of groceries and natural bulk foods. They also have a directory service to local co-ops. SCCW says they "support a system in which control over the means of production, distribution and consumption of goods and services is vested directly with the people who use, need and work in them." The food system is a place where people can begin to regain control over what kinds of food they eat.

T & T Natural Foods, 506 4th Ave, San Rafael 94974. 60 Red Hill Avenue, San Anselmo 94960. Full-line natural food stores, produce, bulk, herbs, spices, dairy, vitamins, cosmetics.

Tri-City Co-op, 11320 Mona Blvd, Los Angeles 90059; (213) 569-9194.

Venice–Ocean Park Food Co-op, 839 Lincoln Blvd, Venice 90291; (714) 399-5623.

COLORADO

Alfalfa's Market, 1825 Pearl St, Boulder 80302; (303) 447-2700. 1651 Broadway, Boulder 80302; (303) 442-0082.

Cooking Naturally, 1001 Grand Ave, Glenwood Springs 81601; (303) 945-7180. Restaurant and store.

Cottonwood Health Cottage, 2408 17th, Greeley 80631; (303) 353-2939.

Grain Mill Natural Foods, 116 9th, Steamboat Springs 80477; (303) 879-5731.

CONNECTICUT

Country Gardens 777 East Main St, Danielson 06239.

Darien Health Mart, 15 Tokeneke Road, Darien 06820.

Earth & Sea Natural Foods, 892 Bridgeport Ave, Shelton 06484.

Edge of the Woods, 275 Edgewood Ave, New Haven.

Four Seasons Health Foods, 91 South St, Danbury 06810.

Greenwich Health Mart, 30 Greenwich Ave, Greenwich 06830.

Health Well Natural Food Store, 356 Greenwich Ave, Greenwich 06830.

Mother Nature's Nutrition Center and Restaurant, 320 Kings Highway, Fairfield 06430. 1275 Post Road, Fairfield 06430.

Natural Living Center, 33 Danbury Road, Wilton 06897.

Nature's Cupboard, 145 Main St, Danbury 06810.

Nature's Way Health Foods, 922 Barnum Ave Cutoff, Stratford 06497.

Norwalk Natural Foods, 36 Main St, Norwalk 06860.

The Organic Market, 285 Post Road East, Westport 06880.

A Shift in the Wind, 183 R. Montowese St, Branford 06405.

Sprout's Natural Foods, 67 South Main St, Newton 06470.

Stamford Health Mart, 19 Cedar Heights Rd, Stamford 06977.

Sweetwater Natural Foods, 1591 Post Rd, Fairfield 06430.

DELAWARE

Jud Ryons Health Food Store, 912 Orange, Wilmington 19879; (302) 658-1900.

Nature's Way Old-Fashioned Natural Food, 2400 Kirkwood Highway, Wilmington 19879.

DISTRICT OF COLUMBIA

Home Rule Natural Foods, 1825 Columbia Road NW 20009; (202) 462-5150. Organic and tropical produce. Deli with juices, salads, sandwiches.

FLORIDA

A & C Natural Foods, 201 SW Monterey Road, Stuart 33490.

Granny Feelgood's Natural Foods, Restaurant and Health Products, 190 SE First Avenue, Miami 33131; (305) 358-6233. Large natural foods grocery and supply store incorporated with one of the best of natural food restaurants.

Gulf Coast Nutrition Center, 6281 McGregor Blvd, Fort Myers; (813) 482-2466. Natural juice and sandwich bar, whole foods, wheat-grass juice.

Healthfully Yours Nutrition Center, 2300 SE Ocean Blvd, Stuart 33494. Supplements, foods, mail orders, health bar.

Lantana Diet and Nutrition Shoppe, 416 North Dixie Highway, Lantana 33439; (305) 588-0040.

Morning Sun Health Foods, 120 Bridge Rd, Tequesta 33458; (305) 747-0037. Vitamins, herbs, natural foods, books. Bulk honey.

Mother Nature Natural Foods, 131 SE 17 St in the Southport shopping center, Fort Lauderdale 33301; (305) 463-0657. Bulk buying of nuts, seeds, grains, fruits, snack beans, organic flours, yeast, cereals, protein powder, peanut butter. Cosmetics, books, vitamins, oriental foodstuffs.

Namaste Baked Goods, 723 Broward Blvd, Fort Lauderdale 33301; (305) 462-4463. "A sugarless and honeyless pastry shop" featuring cakes, cookies, pies, and so on, but without sugar, honey, fructose, or saccharine. Safe for diabetics and hypoglycemics. Low in calories and carbohydrates.

Natural Food Barn, 2832 Stirling Rd (one block west of 1-95), Hollywood 33022; (305) 922-7496. Vitamins, minerals, books, bulk herbs, health foods, cosmetics, juice and sandwich bar.

Nature's Garden Bakery, 600 Collins Ave, Miami Beach 33139; (305) 534-1877. One of the main sources for health food stores throughout the state of Florida. Features wheat-free, yeast-free breads, salt- and sugar-free products, breads for all diets including the Scarsdale and Pritikin, sourdough gluten rolls and high-protein and low-calorie breads.

Nautical Foods, 1235 Commercial St NE, Jensen Beach 33457; (305) 334-1129. Complete selection of natural foods, vitamins, and herbs. Sandwich bar.

Peggy's Natural Foods, 8819 Bridge Rd, Hobe Sound 33455; (305) 546-4458. Natural foods and vitamins.

Touch of Nature, 2829 Bird Ave, Coconut Grove 33131; (305) 448-0065. Complete natural food market. Organic produce, macrobiotic supplements, herbs, more.

Village Health Food Store, 13236 North Dale Mabry, Tampa 33618; (813) 961-7972. Vitamins, minerals, homeopathics, colloids, specialties, allergy, skin and hair care, books, and nutritional counseling.

Vita Village, (two locations) 3369 Sheridan St, Hollywood 33021; (305) 961-1687. 7121 West Broward Blvd, Plantation 33317; (305) 792-0026. Macrobiotic food, hair analysis, whole food products, discount club membership. The Plantation store, located in the Plantation Center Shopping Center, also contains the Village Cafe, a natural foods restaurant feauturing macrobiotic cuisine.

Waterside Nutrition, Lake Worth 33460; (305) 439-7551.

Wholly Harvest Natural Foods, 4616 South Dixie Highway, West Palm Beach; (305) 659-3332. Complete macrobiotic section, book department, vitamins, organic produce, bulk herbs, fresh-baked breads, bottled juices, dried fruit, dairy section, bulk grains, seeds and nuts, herb teas. Juice and salad bar, skin-care salon, and nutritional counseling by appointment. Hair analysis.

GEORGIA

Annapurna Natural Foods, 605 Poplar St, Macon 31201; (912) 745-6310..

Brighter Day Natural Foods Market, 1102 Bull St, Savannah 31401; (912) 236-4703. Juice bar, full produce, portion organic.

Earth Household, 364 North Thomas St, Athens 30614; (404) 543-1956.

Unity Natural Foods Market, 2915 Peachtree Rd, Atlanta 30305; (404) 261-0110.

HAWAII

Homestead Natural Foods Market and Cafe, Honohaa, Hawaii 96727; (808) 775-0960.

Lahaina Foods 1295 Front, Maui (808) 667-2251.

IDAHO

Boise Consumer Co-op, 1515 North 13th 83703; (208) 342-6652.

Frank's Natural Foods, 3655 North Government Way, Coeur d'Alene 83814; (208) 664-8882. Mail and phone orders.

Health Nut Health Foods, 10370 Overland Rd, Boise 83709; (208) 376-8484.

ILLINOIS

Autumn Harvest Natural Foods, 1029 Davis St, Evanston 60201; (312) 475-1121. Organic produce, books, magazines, macrobiotics.

Chip and Dale's Natural Market, 109 North Oak Park Ave, Oak Park 60301; (312) 524-0406.

Fruitful Yield Stores, 606 West Cermak Rd, Berwyn 60402; (312) 788-9103
   1326 West Ogden Ave, Downers Grove 60527; (312) 969-7614.
   214 North York Rd, Elmhurst 60126; (312) 530-1445.
   1811 West Irving Park Rd, Hanover Park 60103; (312) 830-1140.
   704 South Main St, Lombard 60148; (312) 629-9242.
   4950 West Oakton St, Skokie 60077; (312) 679-8975.
These stores carry a full range of health food products, cosmetics, and vitamins. Their newsletter, the *Fruitful Yield* (721 North Yale, Villa Park, IL 60181), announces sales, promotes mail order service, and provides short articles about vitamins, supplements, and products sold in their stores.

New City Market, 1810 North Halsted St, Chicago 60614; (312) 280-7600. Complete natural grocery store.

INDIANA

Ecology Health Foods, 2213 South Michigan, South Bend 46624; (219) 289-1112.

Hoosier Health House, RR1, Box 369, Alexandria (State Road 28 at Interstate 69) 46001; (317) 358-4069.

Rainbow Days Health Store, 5888 East 82 St, Indianapolis 46278; (317) 849-3362. A complete line health food store, plus a resident nutritionist for consultation by appointment. Also classes in

nutrition, cleansing, detoxification, and food preparation.

Yesterday's Tomorrow, 2102 West Columbia, Evansville 47712; (812) 426-0523.

IOWA

Good New General Store Co-op, 801 Eighth Ave SE, Cedar Rapids 52401; (319) 363-1574.

Greens and Grains Natural Groceries, 5705 Hickman, Des Moines 50310; (515) 255-7380.

Paul's Grains, Rte 1, Box 76, Laurel, IA 50141; (515) 476-3373. Organically grown grains, winter and summer wheat, rye, barley, buckwheat, millet, corn, oats, soybeans, popcorn, stone-ground flour, homemade sorghum, fruits, vegetables.

Whole Earth Natural Foods, 706 South Dubuque, Iowa City 52240; (319) 354-4600.

KANSAS

Lytle Young Life Foods 5907 Woodson, Mission 66202; (913) 432-9222. Accommodates mail orders.

Manhattan Health Foods, 300 North 3rd, Manhattan 66502; (913) 776-6201.

Topeka Health Foods, 514 West 10, Topeka 67203; (316) 233-7591.

User Friendly Health and Nutrition Products, 824 Massachusetts, Lawrence 66044; (913) 842-5235.

KENTUCKY

Everybody's Natural Foods, 503 Euclid Ave, Lexington 40502; (606) 255-4162.

Good Foods Co-op, 2350 Woodhill Dr (lower level), Lexington 40509; (606) 266-3601.

Living Naturally, 1413 Diedrich Blvd, Russell 41169; (606) 836-2526.

Mother Nature's, US 60 Bypass, Versailles 40383; (606) 873-8482.

LOUISIANA

Beautiful Day Natural Food Stores, 428 East Boston, Covington 70433; (504) 892-7670.

Another Beautiful Day, 1709 Causeway Blvd, Mandeville 70448; (504) 626-3460.

Vitality Food Shoppe, 750 Oak Villa Blvd, Baton Rouge 70815; (504) 925-5780.

MAINE

Axis Natural Foods, Promenade Mall, Lewiston 04240; (207) 782-3348.

Barney's Health and Survival, 24-A Green, Augusta 04330; (207) 622-5723.

General Nutrition Center, 550 Center, Auburn 04210; (207) 782-9172.

Hanna Hill Circle of Health, Rte 41, Mount Vernon 04352; (207) 293-2201.

New Morning Natural Foods, 33 Main St, Biddeford 04005; (207) 282-9600.

Way of Life Center, Friendship St, Waldoboro 04572; (207) 832-4979.

MARYLAND

Day's Delight, Kent Plaza Shopping Center, Chestertown 21620; (301) 778-3292.

Down to Earth Bulk Natural Foods, Rte 50 west of Ocean City 21842.

Sun and Earth Natural Foods, 1923 West St, Annapolis 21404; (301) 266-6862. Also, 4701 Sangamore Rd, Bethesda 20816; 229-7876.

MASSACHUSETTS

La Commonplace Natural Foods, 57 Pleasant, Newburyport 01950; (617) 462-3521. State-line store, in addition to vegetarian/macrobiotic restaurant.

Earthfood Store, 24 Park St, Andover 01810, (617) 475-1234. Natural and organic foods, fertile eggs, bulk foods.

MICHIGAN

Betty's Grocery Store, 877 Hunter Blvd, Birmingham 48011; (313) 644-2323.

The Fruit Cellar, 23822 Ford Rd, Dearborn Heights, 48127; (313) 561-6610. Organic produce, macrobiotics, herbs, nuts, seeds, grains, books.

Good-n-Plenty Food Co-op, 22185 Van Dyke, Detroit 48234; (313) 759-6040. "Food for people, not profit."

NatuReal Foods, 23140 Woodward, Ferndale 48220; (313) 544-3289. Prepacked and bulk, dry foods, juices and herbs.

The Sprout House, 15309 Mack Ave, Detroit 48224; (313) 885-1048. Soy products in bulk, macrobiotic and natural foods, cooking classes.

Zerbo's Health Foods, 34164 Plymouth, Livonia 48150; (313) 427-3144. Very complete health food store, including hard-to-find macrobiotic specialty foods. Mail orders welcome.

MINNESOTA

Down Home Foods, 209 South Jefferson, Wavena 55390; (218) 631-2323.

Health Food Store, 20½ NW 4 St, Grand Rapids 55744; (218) 326-3993.

The Market Basket, 119 Washington Ave, Detroit Lakes 56501; (218) 847-7513.

The Miller's Harvest, 606 1st St, Princeton 55371; (612) 389-5125.

MISSISSIPPI

For Health's Sake, Highland Village, I-55 North, Jackson 39211; (601) 981-2838.

Good Earth Health Foods, 2505 14th, Gulfport 39501; (601) 863-7750.

Russeli's Energy Center, 1302 Government, Ocean Springs 39564; (601) 875-8882. Bulk foods; tea room.

Sunshine Health Foods, 406 Downtown Mall, Tupelo 38801; (601) 844-1560

Totally Organic Health Foods, Vieux Marche Mall, Biloxi 39514; (601) 374-5526. Tea room.

MISSOURI

Columbia Community Grocery Co-op, 1100 Locust, Columbia 65201; (314) 442-2116.

Earth Wonder Natural Foods, 2703 South Campbell, Springfield 65807; (417) 887-5985.

Hunt Health Food, 526 Joplin, Joplin 64801; (417) 624-3040.

Kay's Health and Nutrition Center, St. Louis 63114.

Skinny Minny's, 3600 South Noland Rd, Independence 64055; (816) 833-4054.

MONTANA

Bonanza Health Foods, 923 Grand Ave, Billings 59102; (406) 252-4923. Phone and mail orders accepted.

Brownie's Basics, 1803 Brooks Missoula 59801; (406) 728-3244.

Great Divide Exchange, 903 South First St West, Missoula 59405; (406) 543-6480. Mainly wholesale, but call.

The Healthy I, 25 South Idaho, Dillon 59725; (406) 683-4688.

Ma and Pa's Good Food Store, Exerdance Building, 75 East Park Plaza, Butte 59701; (406) 723-3223.

Natural Food Warehouse, 903 South 1st West, Missoula 59405.

NEBRASKA

Open Harvest Co-op, 2637 Randolph, Lincoln 68510; (402) 475-9069.

Peanut Hill Market and Bakery, 3845 South 48 St, Lincoln 68506; (402) 488-3167.

Tamarak's Foods of the Earth, 1613 First Ave, Scotts Bluff 69361; (307) 635-1514.

NEVADA

Du Bois' Health Center, 1907 North Carson, Carson City 89701; (702) 882-2451. Phone and mail orders accepted.

Mrs. Keough's Natural Foods, 215 West Bridge, Yerington 89447; (702) 463-3292.

Washoe Health Food, 1313 South Virginia at Arroyo, Reno 89502; (702) 323-3433. Mail orders accepted.

NEW HAMPSHIRE

Bonne Sante Natural Foods, 425 Mast Rd, Manchester 03104, (603) 623-1613.

The Common Market, 44 Main St, Durham 03824; (603) 868-7508.

Country Co-op, Rte 4, Epsom 03234; (603) 736-4592.

Earth Grown, 114 West Pearl, Nashua 03060; (603) 883-5402.

Granite State Natural Foods, 22 Pleasant, Concord 03301; (603) 668-2650.

Sterling Farms Health Food, 79 Old Post Road, Kettery; (603) 439-5360. Mail orders accepted.

NEW JERSEY

Aquarius Health Foods, 408 Cedar Lane, Teaneck

07666; (201) 836-0601. Full-range grocery with fresh produce and an organic food snack bar.

BE-VI Natural Foods, 6302 Bergenline Ave, West New York 07093; (201) 868-6596. Natural food store with snack bar featuring sandwiches and salads.

Clairmont Health Foods, 515 Bloomfield Ave, Montclair 07042; (201) 744-7122. Full-scale grocery plus a small lunch counter.

Diamond Springs Health Foods, 41 Diamond Springs Rd, Denville 07834.

Earth Things, 106 Rte 46, Rockaway 07866.

Fountain of Vitality, 372 Springfield Ave, Berkley Heights 07922.

Gandhi's Grocery, Rte 206 North, Ramsey 07446.

Healthfair, 625 Branch Ave, Little Silver 07739.

Lakewood Health Foods, 222 Clifton Ave & Third St, Lakewood 08701.

Margate Natural Foods, 7807 Ventnor Ave, Margate 08402.

Natural Foods General Store, 675 Batchelor, Toms River 08753.

New Age Natural Foods, 87 East Main St, Chester 07930; (201) 879-6210. Fresh organic produce. Book section with more than 1000 titles.

Organica Natural Foods, 246 Livingston St, Northvale 07647.

Pyramid Vitamin and Health Food Center, 449 Main St, Metuchen 08840.

Red Bank Health Foods, 25 Monmouth St, Red Bank 07701.

Sun Valley Health Foods, Pleasant Run Mini Mall, Warren 07060.

Taste of Dawn Natural Foods, 110 Main St, Butler 07405.

Vitacare Health Foods, Wayne Hills Mall, Hamburg Turnpike, Wayne 07470.

Whole Earth Center, 360 Nassau St, Princeton 08540; (609) 924-7421. Health food store with a take-out delicatessen.

Wild Oats Natural Foods, 1300 Richmond Ave, Point Pleasant Beach 08742; (201) 899-2272. Includes a lunch counter featuring soups, salads, and sandwiches.

NEW MEXICO

Health Food Shop, 1320 17th, Los Alamos 87544; (505) 662-4900.

Health Food Store, 816 Spruce, Las Cruces 88001; (505) 523-5275.

The Natural Cafe and Great Eastern Sun Food Store, 1494 Cerrillos Rd, Sante Fe 87501; (505) 983-1411.

New Life Co-op, 623 Aqua Fria, Sante Fe 87501; (505) 988-2443. Warehouse, 530 South Guadalupe; (505) 983-1090.

Organic Mountain Food Co-op, 1405 West Picacho Ave, Las Cruces 88005; (505) 523-0436.

Sattvic Foods, 321 Osuna NE, Albuquerque 87107; (505) 344-4686. Wholesale distributor of sprouts, yogurt, more.

Southwest Soy Foods, 2889 Trades Road West, Sante Fe 87501; (505) 471-8979.

NEW YORK

A-Bree Health Foods, 33 East Main St, Bayshore 11361.

Amber Waves of Grain, 69 Bleneida Ave, Carmel 10512.

Ayurveda Nutrition Center, 44–07 Kissena Blvd, Flushing 11358.

Back to the Land Natural Foods, 144 Seventh Ave, Brooklyn 11215.

Capitol Health Nutrition Center, 357 New York Ave, Huntington 11746.

Cauldron, 306–8 E 6 St, New York 10003.

Chappaqua Health Foods, 95 King St, Chappaqua 10514.

Colonial Health Foods, 43 North Front, Kingston 12401.

Commodities, 117 Hudson St, New York 10013. Enormous macrobiotic store with a lecture area.

East Village Baker's Dozen, 130 St. Mark's Place, New York 10009. Great whole-grained breads with lots of special baked treats daily, including vegetarian pizza.

Family Health Food Store, 181 New Dorp Lane, Staten Island 10306.

Four Corners Diet and Health Food Center, 1752 Victory Blvd at Manor Road, Staten Island; (212) 442-9383. Not only a health food store, but you can also call up and order lunches and dinner to take out.

Good Food Store, 316 Waverly Ave, Syracuse 13210; (315) 423-3594. Macrobiotic foods and cooking classes. Books, nutritional information.

Health Shoppe, 10–12 Fort Salonga Rd, Fort Salonga.

House of Nutrition, 49 Raymond Ave, Poughkeepsie 12603.

The Incredible Bulk, 829 Franklin Ave, Thornwood 10594.

Integral Yoga Natural Foods, 250 West 14 St, New York, 10011.

Monsey Health Center, 42 Main St, Monsey 10952.

Mung Bean, 6522 Jericho Tpke, Commack 11725.

Natural Market, 44 Rte 303, Tappan 10983.

New York Health Emporium, 159–01 Horace Harding Expwy, Flushing 11365; (718) 358-6500. Wholesale and retail, one of the largest selections of organically grown fruits and vegetables in the metropolitan area. Open seven days a week, the emporium stocks an extensive selection of books, magazines, and natural hygiene–related pamphlets. Good array of juicers, seed and nut grinders, distillers, etc. Bulk grains and herbs, nuts, raw rennetless cheeses, yogurts, legumes, much more. Also a fine juice bar.

Perelandra Natural Foods, 154 Montegue St, Brooklyn Heights 11201.

Ray Oriental Health Food Store, 2445 Broadway, New York 10024.

Real Food Store, 188 Main St, New Paltz 12561.

Rice Patch Basic Foods, 227 Sullivan St, New York 10012.

Rose Garden, 19 West Main St, Southampton 11946.

Solar Gardens, 1958 Madison Ave, New York 10035; (212) 427-1644. Vitamins, juices, herbs, health products, books.

Whole Foods, 117 Prince St, New York 10012; (212) 673-5388. Soho natural foods market with a delicatessen in the rear serving both hot and cold foods to go.

NORTH CAROLINA

Dinner for the Earth, 160 Broadway, Asheville 28801; (704) 253-7656. Senior citizen discount policy.

Friends of the Earth Natural Foods, 114 Reynolda Village, Winston-Salem 27106; (919) 725-6781.

Govinda Nutrition Center, 127 North Main St, Spring Lake 28390; (919) 497-2578.

Makers Market, Carr Mill Mall, Chapel Hill 27514; (919) 967-9334.

The Only Earth, 712 North Elm St, High Point 27262; (919) 886-4315. Includes a restaurant open for breakfast and lunch.

NORTH DAKOTA

Earth Pantry, North Brook Shopping Center, Bismarck 58501; (701) 258-7987.

Grand Forks Food Co-op, 1602 Ninth Ave N, Fargo 58102; (701) 775-4542.

Magic Mill and Natural Center, 20 West Central, Minot 58707; (701) 852-4818.

Northern Health Foods, 13 South 4 Moorhead, Fargo 58103; (701) 236-5999.

Tochi Products, 1111 Second Ave North, Fargo 58102. Wholesale distributors.

OHIO

Farmacy Natural Food Store, 28 West Stimson, Athens 45701; (614) 593-7007. They have a juice bar and lunch counter.

Li'l Sprout Natural Food, 2500 Shawnee Rd, Lima 45854 (419) 991-2236.

Raisin Rack Natural Food Emporium, 3919 Cleveland Avenue NW at 40th, Canton; (216) 492-3360. Also, Belpar Square Mall, Jackson Township 43030; (216) 492-1800.

Schlarman Natural Foodstore, 2941 Fort Recovery-Minster Road, Fort Recovery 45846; (419) 375-2659.

Spatz Health Foods, 607 Main St, Cincinnati 45202; (513) 621-0347.

Toomey Natural Foods Market, 525 Baker Dr, Milford 45150; (513) 831-4771.

OKLAHOMA

Adventist Book Center, 4735 NW 63, Oklahoma City 73132; (405) 721-6114. Seventh-Day Adventist books and food.

The Earth Natural Food and Garden, 309 South Flood, Norman 73069; 364-3551.

God's Gift Real Food Grocery, 310 West Kenosha, Broken Arrow 74012; (918) 258-0871.

Nature's Sunshine Products, Rte 1 south of Broken Bow 74728; (405) 584-3808.

Pearson's Natural Food Center, 131 West Owen K Garriot, Enid 73701; (405) 234-5000.

West Side Store, 1510 North Rockwell, Oklahoma City 73127; (405) 789-3773.

OREGON

Ashland Community Food Store, 37 3rd St, Ashland 97520.

Farmers Market, 603 Rogue River Highway, Grants Pass 97526.

Food Front, 2675 NW Thurman St, Portland 97210; 222-5658. Cooperatively owned grocery with lots of bulk foods, dairy, fresh produce, groceries, vitamins, books. Discounts for working members and senior citizens.

Health Food and Pool Store, 141 North 3rd St, Springfield 97477; 747-1532. Fully stocked health food store plus vegetable, flower, and herb seeds.

Williams General Store, 20180 Williams Highway, Williams 97544.

PENNSYLVANIA

Avatar Golden Nectar and Golden Temple Kitchen, 321 Bridge, New Cumberland 17070; (717) 774-7215.

Earthlight Supply, Quaker Plaza, Stroudsburg 18360.

Food Naturally, 301 Main St, Emmaus 18049; (215) 967-3600. Restaurant, study center (cooking classes), wide selection of macrobiotic staples, books, etc. Fresh baked bread.

Great Pumpkin Health Foods, 304 South High, Westchester 19380; (215) 696-0741.

Marini Health Foods, 1736 Hawthorne Ave, Havertown 19083.

Mother's Hearth Natural Food Store, 33 West State St, Media 19063; (215) 566-3818.

Natural Goodness, 726 Market St, Philadelphia 19106; (215) 923-3280. Natural food store, vitamins, herbs, cosmetics, books, juice bar, and take-out vegetarian food. Catering and cooking classes as well.

Nature's Food and Restaurant, 48 Baltimore, Gettysburg 17325; (717) 334-7723.

RHODE ISLAND

Au Natural Natural Food Store, 21 Long Wharf Mall, Newport 02840; (401) 846-4146.

For the Health of It, 181 West Main St, Norton; (401) 285-4236.

Hartman's Back to Basics, 250 Main St, Greenwich 02818; (401) 885-2679. Full inventory. Breadbaking classes.

Tri-Natural Health Foods, 371 Putnam Pike, Smithfield; (401) 231-2288.

SOUTH CAROLINA

Books, Herbs and Pieces, 2034 Maybank Highway, Charleston 92412; (803) 795-2421.

Carolina Nutrition Corner, 2514-A East North St at Pelham Road, Greenville 29607; (803) 268-5542.

God's Green Acre Natural Foods, 130 West 3rd at North St, Summerville 29483; (803) 873-3953.

The New Leaf, 372 King St, Charleston 29401; (803) 577-0573.

Rosewood Natural Foods, 2737 Rosewood Dr, Columbia 29205; (803) 765-1083.

SOUTH DAKOTA

Black Hills Staple and Spice Company, 601 Mount Rushmore Rd, Rapid City 57701; (605) 343-3900.

General Nutrition Center, University Mall, Brookings 57006; (605) 692-6300.

Sprout House, 429 Kansas City, Rapid City 57701; (605) 348-9440. Wholesale distributor.

TENNESSEE

DeKalb Health Food, Highway 70, Smithville 37166; (615) 597-1284.

Eden Way Natural Foods, 4005 North Broadway, Knoxville 37917; (615) 688-6781.

Full Sun Grocery, 115 Frazier Ave, North Chattanooga 37405; (615) 267-5820.

Natural and Organic Foods, 6914 Kingston Pike, Knoxville 37919; (615) 584-8422.

TEXAS

Cowtown Natural Foods Store and Co-op, 3539 East Lancaster, Fort Worth 76103; (817) 535-9407. "Foods for people, not for profit."

Down to Earth Health Food Store, Houston 77001; (713) 358-1940.

Family Farm, 9111 Boudreaux, Tomball 77375; (713) 370-4054. Health food store and country kitchen. Organic produce, vitamins, herbs.

Harthomp and Moran Natural Foods, 9189 Forest Lane, Dallas; (214) 231-6083.

Horizon Natural Food Store, 9336 Westview, Houston 77055; (713) 461-0857. Organic produce, grocery department, macrobiotics.

Krause Acres Natural Food, 615 South Texas Blvd, Weslaco 78596; (512) 968-3241.

A Moveable Feast, 3827 Dunlavy at Alabama, Houston 77006; (713) 528-3585. A grocery with all the necessities for good eating, whole-wheat flour and corn meal ground on premises daily, cheeses, pasta, sauces, organic produce, natural and exotic jams and jellies, whole-grain breads, macrobiotic section, books, cosmetics, life extension section, cookware, kitchenware.

Real-Life Natural Food, 125 Ridgewood Village, Garland 75040; (214) 271-1595.

UTAH

The Bread Basket, 83 East Center, Provo 84601; (801) 377-6150. Restaurant on premises.

Child's Bakery and Health Food, 125 North Main, Spanish Fork 84660; (801) 798-7119.

Knitty Gritty Store, 128 South Main St, Hurricane 84737; (801) 635-4369.

Mother Nature's Restaurant, A-812 University Mall, Orem 84057; (801) 224-4900.

Sunshine Natural Foods, 650 South Maine St, Cedar City 84720; (801) 586-4889.

Zion's Wholesale Food and Mercantile Co-operative, 95 South 300 West, Provo 84601; (801) 374-1763. Open to public shopping.

VERMONT

Llama, Toucan and Crow, 130 Main St, Brattleboro 05301; (802) 254-5376.

Vermont Sprout House, 10 C North, Bristol 05443; (802) 453-3098.

VIRGINIA

Blue Mountain Trading Company, 923 Preston Ave, Charlottesville 22903; (804) 293-4111.

Heritage Store, PO Box 444, Virginia Beach 23458. Specializing in Edgar Cayce items including health foods.

Ledbetter Health Food, 1404 Planting Ct, Princess Anne 427-3779.

WASHINGTON

Good Earth Nutrition, 1340 Commercial, Bellingham 98225 (206) 733-3480.

Issaquah Natural Foods, 35 West Sunset Way, Bellevue 98225 (206) 392-7142.

Keil's Food Store, 2930 Ocean Beach Highway, Longview 98632; (206) 577-5857.

Lynden Nutrition Center, 444 West Front St, Lynden 98264; (206) 354-4884.

Pacific Rim Natural Foods, 4001 Sixth Ave South, Seattle 98108; (206) 624-1681.

Puget Consumers Co-op, 10718 NE 68 St, Kirkland 98033; (206) 828-4621.

WEST VIRGINIA

Doc Williams Country General Store, 1004 Main St, Wheeling 06003; (304) 233-4771.

Food for Life Nutrition Center, 120 Randolph St, Charleston 25302; (304) 346-2840.

Mother Earth Foods, 1638 19th St, Parkersburg 26101; (304) 428-1024.

Treddle's Health Foods, 1141 National Rd, Wheeling 06003 (304) 242-2080.

WISCONSIN

Bay Natural Foods, 722 Bodart St, Green Bay 54301; (414) 437-4750.

Bits and Peace's Food Co-op, 900 Arcadian, Waukesha 53186; (414) 544-9130.

Livin' Water Super Natural Foods Restaurant/ Livin' Bread Bakery, 318 State St, Madison 53703; (608) 251-2319. Macrobiotic restaurant, cooking classes, organic bakery with nationwide delivery to homes and stores. Free catalog.

Nature's Health Foods, 118 North Main St, Oconomowoc 53066; (414) 567-8320.

WYOMING

Here and Now Natural Foods, Teton Village Rd,
Jackson 83001; (307) 733-2742.

Mountain Source, 115 Yellowstone Ave, Yellowstone Mountain 82190; (406) 646-7553.

Noah's Ark Nutrition Center, 1906 Thomas Ave,
Cheyenne 82001; (307) 638-3229.

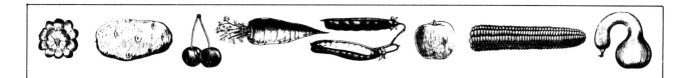

24

Bookstores and Libraries

To many people the vegetarian movement is only part of a larger movement to a "new age," where pollution and hatred have been eliminated, and humanity can flourish and realize its potential. Many of the following bookstores are described as stocking new age books. Many of these books are by authors with a vision, who feel that it is time the vision became reality.

This list is meant as a starting point in your quest for information. It does not include all the bookstores carrying vegetarian information, but it does encompass a representative group. If you know of a particularly good bookshop that you think would be useful to people, please write me, and the store will be listed in the next edition of this *Vegetarian Connection*.

BOOKSTORES AND LIBRARIES

ARIZONA

Book Spring, 8115–1 North 35 Ave, Phoenix 85021; (602) 973-2562. Bookstore specializing in knowledge of the higher worlds, but also, books about balanced living, whole health, etc. Gift shop, classes, and workshops. Monthly journal and free out-of-state catalog.

Changing Hands Bookstore, 414 South Mill Ave, Tempe 85281; (602) 966-0203. New and used bookshop. Nutrition section, alternative life styles, massage, children's books.

CALIFORNIA

Art & Harmony, 3780 Mission Blvd, San Diego 92109; (619) 488-2352. Gift and bookshop, natural fiber clothing, natural skin care products.

Bodhi Tree Bookstore, 8585 Melrose Ave, Los Angeles 90069; (213) 659-1733. Relaxed atmosphere. Large stock of books on new age philosophy. Mail-order service available. Used book branch next store: (213) 659-3227.

Cancer Book House, 2043 North Berendo St, Los Angeles 90027; (213) 663-7801. Long list of books and reprints on nutrition, cancer, and other nutritionally related diseases. Mail order.

Dawn Horse Bookstore, 923 C St, San Rafael 94901; (415) 457-4191. Spiritual and practical books whose subjects include diet, health, science, sexuality, religion, yoga. Large selection of new age musical tapes. Film series Friday, Saturday, Sunday evenings.

East–West Book Shop, 1170 El Camino Real, Menlo Park 94025; (415) 325-5709. Owned and operated by the Yoga Fellowship of Ananda Cooperative Village. New and used books, out-of-print and first editions. Will buy books, and encourages mail orders. Friday night lecture series.

Full Circle Bookstore, 3910 El Cajon Blvd, San Diego 92105; (619) 283-8663. Books on holistic health, metaphysics, consciousness growth, fiction, non-fiction, Eastern philosophies, records, tapes, plus yoga institute and samadhi floatation tank ($15 per session).

Gateways, 825 Pacific Ave, Santa Cruz 95060; (408) 429-9600. New and used books, special orders welcomed.

Ginko Leaf, 21109 Costanso St, Woodland Hills 91364; (213) 716-6332. Wide spectrum of books, both new and used, from nutrition to health to children's books to fiction. Offers include the Baker's Dozen book club, where you buy 12 books and get the thirteenth free. Nutrition classes available.

The Philosophical Library, 355 West Felicita & Center City Parkway, Safeway Center, Escondido 92025; (619) 745-2724. New age books and tapes, classes, lectures, lending library.

DISTRICT OF COLUMBIA

Yes Bookshop, 1035 31st St NW 20007; store phone: (202) 338-7874; mail orders: (202) 338-2727.

FLORIDA

Agartha Secret City Esoteric Bookstore, 1618 Ponce De Leon Blvd, Coral Gables 33134; (305) 441-1618. Write for mail-order catalogue: lots of unusual items, in addition to health, diet, yoga, healing, etc.

Books by the Park, 2713 SW Thirty-seventh Ave, Miami 33145; (305) 442-0468. Diet, alternative health, non-sexist children's books.

Ellie's Books, Snelling Plaza, 4000 South Tamiami Trail, Sarasota 33581; (813) 922-3693. New age books and tapes.

Gladstar Bookshop, 845 South Yong St (US 1), Ormond Beach 32074; (813) 673-4117.

New Age Books and Things, 4401 North Federal Highway, Fort Lauderdale 33308; (305) 771-0026.

New Age Centre Bookstore, 2500 East Curry Ford Rd, Orlando 32806; (305) 898-2500.

Rainbow New Age Bookstore, 6290 North Atlantic Ave, Cape Canaveral 32920; (305) 784-0930.

WHVH Bookshop, 1237 King St, Jacksonville 32204; (904) 387-2064. Wide range of books on health, yoga, and more, from beginners to advanced.

ILLINOIS

Olcott Library and Research Center, Box 270, 1926 North Main, Wheaton 60187; (312) 668-1571. Located at the national headquarters of the Theosophical Society, this library has a collection of over 20,000 volumes. There is a mailing service that loans books throughout the United States and Canada. (An annotated guide is available for purchase to help with selections.)

The Quest Book Shop, 306 West Geneva Rd, Wheaton 60189; (312) 665-0123. Located on the serene 40-acre grounds of the Theosophical Society of America, the bookshop has a wide selection, including a well-stocked vegetarian section.

MASSACHUSETTS

Horai-San Macrobiotic Book Shop, 242 Washington St, Brookline 02146; (617) 277-4321. Mailorder service. Free catalogue available. Discounts available.

MICHIGAN

New Beginning Book Shop, 4902 Highland Rd, Pontiac 48054; (313) 674-4277.

Mayflower Books, 23136 North Woodward, Ferndale 48220.

Middle Earth Bookshop, 2791 East 14th Mile, Sterling Heights 48077; (313) 979-7340.

NEW JERSEY

The Book Seer, 440 Boulevard, Hasbrouck Heights 07604; (201) 288-8655. Bookstore devoted to spirit, mind, and body. Uses available space for classes. Call or write for brochure.

New Age Bookstore, 29 Washington St, Morristown 08057; (201) 540-1677. Located with the

Yoga Meditation Society of New Jersey, an affiliate of the Himalayan International Institute. They have a full range of titles.

NEW YORK

Argus Archives, 228 East 49 St, New York 10022; (212) 355-6140. Small private library available for research, but requiring one day's notice. Animal welfare, vegetarianism.

East–West Books, 78 Fifth Ave (near 13 St), New York 10011; (212) 243-5994. Vast bookstore full of pleasant surprises. Cookbooks, nutrition, philosophy, exercise, religion.

Liberation Book Store, 421 Lenox Ave (at 131 St), New York 10037; (212) 281-4615.

Samuel Weiser's, 740 Broadway (near 8 St), New York 10003; (212) 777-6363. Large, well-stocked bookstore. Good vegetarian section; new age, occult, metaphysical, Eastern philosophies. New books, but also old, hard-to-find volumes.

OREGON

Center of Light Bookstore, 3815 SE Belmont #3, Portland 97215; (503) 238-1604. Health, nutrition, metaphysics, etc.

Peralandra, 790 E Eleventh Ave, Eugene 97401; (503) 485-4848. Personal and spiritual growth, psychology, healing, the occult. New age music.

Sunnyside Church, 3520 SE Yamhill St, Portland 97214. The basement of this church contains a library of over 1000 volumes pertaining to vegetarianism, nutrition, health, and spiritual growth.

TEXAS

Aquaroam Age Bookshelf, 4603 Chaucer, Houston 77005; (713) 526-7770. Near Rice University. New age books.

Grok Books, 503-B West 17th, Austin.

MAIL ORDER BOOKS AND PUBLISHERS

Association for Research and Enlightenment (ARE), PO Box 595, Atlantic Ave (at 67 St), Virginia Beach, VA 23451. Books, tapes, records, courses, many dealing with the philosophy of psychic healer, Edgar Cayce.

Aurora Book Companions, Terminal Box 5852, Denver, CO 80217. Health and nutrition related. Discount mail order catalogue available.

Bi-World Publishers and Woodland Books, PO Box 1144, Orem, UT 84057; (800) 453-1420. Mostly books dealing with herbs.

Center for Science in the Public Interest, 1755 S St NW, Washington, D.C. 20009. The center has an interesting book and poster catalogue, including a brand-name guidebook to additives in liquor, a *Sodium Scoreboard,* a *New American Eating Guide,* and *Creative Food Experiences for Children.*

Christopher Publications, PO Box 412, Springville, UT 84663. The works of the late Dr. John R. Christopher, herbologist.

Deep Roots Publications, 606 Market St, Lewisburg, PA 17837. Publishes inexpensive booklets like *Freebies and Cheapies for Healthful Living* ($1.00), a comprehensive list of addresses for free or inexpensive wholesome products and reading materials, and *Mail Order Catalogs of Natural Products* ($1.00); also a comprehensive list, this time of companies with free or inexpensive catalogues from which you may order natural items. Also: *Beginner's Guide to Meatless Casseroles, Whole Foods from A to Z,* and the *What to Do with Tofu Cookbooklet.*

Devorss & Co., PO Box 550, Marina Del Rey, CA 90291. One dollar for their catalogue; 3000 titles. Metaphysics, inspiration, health, new age, and self-improvement.

Garden Way Publishing, 1083 Schoolhouse Rd, Pownal, VT 05261. Illustrated, in-depth monograph booklets with step-by-step instruction from experts. Titles include: *Grow the Best Strawberries, Cold Storage for Fruits and Vegetables, Berries, Rasp & Black, Grafting Fruit Trees, 'Scat' Pest Proofing Your Garden, Improving Your Soil, Grow the Best Asparagus, Building* *and Using Cold Frames, Grow the Best Tomatoes, Great Green Tomato Recipes, Cover Crop Gardening, Jam, Jellies and Preserves, Planting Your Dwarf Fruit Orchard, Potatoes, Sweet and Irish, All the Onions and How to Grow Them, Great Grapes, Grow 15 Herbs for the Kitchen, Grow Super Salad Greens, How Safe is Your Water?, Drought Gardening, Build an Underground Root Cellar.* The booklets are $1.95 each, but if you buy five or more they're $1.50.

Keats Publishing, 27 Pine, PO Box 876, New Canaan, CT 06840; (203) 966-8721. *Good Health Guides* series, which includes Beatrice Trum Hunter's *Brewer's Yeast, Wheat Germ and other High Power Foods,* Richard A. Passwater's *Marine Lipids,* Jack Joseph Challem's *Spirulina,* and many others ($1.45 each). Basic books on preventive health care, Spanish language editions, cookbooks, and many more interesting titles.

Light Living Library, PO Box 190, Philomath, OR 97370. This library sells its short, unusual information packs by the page (10 cents). Everything is brief, to the point, cheap, and much of it useful. Interesting networking through their "Message Post," which functions as an information and people exchange.

National Health Federation, PO Box 688, Monrovia, CA 91016. Reprint list and many books from a variety of well-known health writers, including Paavo Airola (see Chapter 3, Vegetarian Authorities), Dr. Donsbach (see Chapter 25, Home Study), anti-nuclear activist, Dr. Helen Caldicott, and many more.

North American Vegetarian Society, PO Box 72, Dolgeville, NY 13329. Good list of books of interest to vegetarians. Available by mail.

Shiloh Medical Publications, Rte 1, Box 4070, Poland Spring, ME 04274. Seventh-Day Adventist publications, including *Get Well at Home* and *Favorite Wildwood Recipes.*

21st Century Publishing, 401 North Fourth St, PO Box 702, Fairfield, IA 52556; (515) 472-5105. Affiliated with Viktoras Kulvinskas' Survival Foundation (see Chapter 3, Vegetarian Authorities), their list includes many books about raw and live foods, sprouts, chlorophyll, natural healing, and radical vegetarianism. Many unusual and hard-to-find titles, including the work of Johnny Lovewisdom (see Chapter 2, The Different Types of Vegetarianism).

Wellington Books, Hillsboro, NH 03244. The books of Beatrice Trum Hunter, including the *Natural Foods Cookbook,* the *Natural Foods Primer, Whole Grain Baking Sampler, Food Additives and Your Health,* and more.

BOOK CLUBS

Rodale Press Self-Sufficiency Book Club, PO Box 10627, Des Moines, IA 50336. Good selection of broad range of subjects including, *Using Plants for Healing, Naturally Great Foods Cookbook, Seed Starter's Handbook, Square Foot Gardening.* Quite a bit about solar heating, energy, livestock, and more.

ENGLAND

Vegetarian Society of the United Kingdom Limited, Parkdale, Dunham Rd, Altrincham, Cheshire WA14 4QG. The Vegetarian Society of the United Kingdom Limited runs an excellent bookshop in London. The Vegetarian Centre and Bookshop (53 Marloes Road, Kensington, London W8 6LA) is open Monday to Friday 9:30 to 5:30. The bookshop deals in over-the-counter sales only. Books and publications available by mail are from the society itself. Vegetarian Society Publications available include: *Catering for Vegetarians,* which explains a vegetarian diet to conventional caterers; *Greenplan,* a vegetarian plan for English farming; *Dayplan Two,* a week's vegetarian and vegan recipes nutritionally assessed; Rose Elliot's *Vegetarian Baby Book; Vegetarianism and Infant Feeding, Well-Being for the Elderly, Vegetarian Ethics, Wholemeal Recipes,* and much, much more. There is a good list of books and pamphlets for children and baby care and a list of vegan books. In addition you can pick up some ballpoint pens with the inscription "Make no Bones About it—Go Vegetarian." They also sell bumperstickers, lapel buttons, car stickers, letter cards, envelope stickers, patches, carrier bags, posters, T-shirts, ties, and scarves with the international vegetarian symbol of a stylized V-shaped seedling.

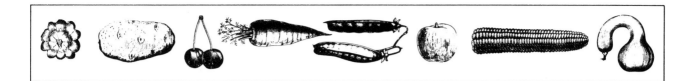

25

Restaurants

GUIDEBOOKS

Guide to Natural Food Restaurants by Loren Cronk. Daystar Publishing Company, 1983, 220 pages; $8.95. A guidebook, assembled through a questionnaire, listing 500 of the nation's health food and vegetarian restaurants.

Pritikin Guide to Restaurant Eating by Nathan and Ilene Pritikin. Bobbs Merrill, NY; 1984; 210 pp; $11.95. How to eat healthfully in restaurants.

The Vegetarian Times Guide to Dining in the U.S.A. compiled by Kathleen Moore and the editors of *Vegetarian Times*. Atheneum, New York, 1980, 314 pp; $8.95. A book made possible in large part by the readers of *Vegetarian Times* magazine, who contributed suggestions for over 500 of the nation's leading vegetarian and natural food restaurants.

Where the Vegetarians Eat by Nathaniel Altman. Keats Publishing, 1982, 208 pp; $4.95. Three hundred listings, many of them sampled first-hand

RESTAURANTS

ALABAMA

Country Life Vegetarian Restaurant, 1124 280 Bypass, Phenix City 36867; (205) 297-7696.

Golden Temple Emporium, 1901 Eleventh Avenue South, Birmingham 35205; (205) 933-6333.

Pearly Gates Natural Foods, 2308 Memorial Parkway SW, Huntsville 35801; (205) 534-6233.

ALASKA

The Bread Factory, 835 I St, Anchorage 99501; (907) 274-2882.

The Cauldron, 328 G St, Anchorage 99501; (907) 276-0592.

The Fiddlehead Restaurant and Bakery, 429 West Willoughby Ave, Juneau 99801; (907) 586-3150. Homemade baked goods and vegetarian dishes, but some meat on the menu.

ARIZONA

Homeward Bound Natural Foods Restaurant, 4 San Francisco St, Flagstaff 86001; (602) 779-0986.

Mosaic Cafe, 1065 North Silverbell Rd, Tucson 85705; (602) 624-4512.

New Morning Cafe, 2911 N 16 St, Phoenix 85016; (602) 279-6322.

ARKANSAS

The Health Barn, Highway 43 East, Harrison 72601; (501) 741-3627.

Robin's Restaurant, 103 South East St, Fayetteville 72701; (501) 442-3506. "New American cuisine" with vegetarian and macrobiotic entrees included. Take-out available.

CALIFORNIA

Comeback Inn, 1633 Western Washington Blvd, Venice 90291; (213) 396-7255. No processed foods, no animal or dairy products; fresh juices, herbal teas, natural wines, and beer. Saturday and Sunday night entertainment. Outdoor garden.

Curry Pot, 2837 Highland Ave, National City 92050; (619) 477-9009. Sri Lankan cuisine with vegetarian specialties.

Golden Temple Conscious Cookery, 7910 W 3 St, Los Angeles; (213) 655-1891. Exotic menu and fine homemade sugar-free pastries. All baked goods, including wedding cakes, can be specially ordered. Gourmet catering service is available.

Inaka, 131 South La Brea, Los Angeles 90036; (213) 936-9353 or 932-8869. Traditional Japanese-style country dining. Whole grains, vegetables; they also have seafood. Non-dairy, sugar-free desserts. Entertainment every second night.

Khatmandu Juice Bar, 1503 30th St (at Beech Street in Golden Hill), San Diego; 233-4271. Sandwiches, salad and sprout bar, whole-wheat croissants and pastry, smoothies, sugarless and soy ice cream, non-alcoholic beer and wine.

Kung Food, 2949 Fifth Ave (near Balboa Park), San Diego; 298-7302. A variety of vegetarian dishes in a smoke-free environment. Specials have included: tofu almondine, vegetable Neapolitan, mushroom–spinach lasagne, and tofu wellington.

L'Chaim Vegetarian Cafe, 134 West Douglas, El Cajon 92022; 442-1331.

Milly's Cafe, 1613 4th St, San Rafael 94901; (415) 459-1601. Traditional vegetarian fare in combination with ethnic choices and the inspiration of creative chefs. They will accommodate special dietary requests if at all possible.

Natural Fudge Company, 5224 Fountain Ave, Hollywood 90029; (213) 669-8003. Open for breakfast, lunch, and dinner, but not exclusively vegetarian. Entertainment.

1044 1st, Encinitas 92024; (619) 942-1249. A natural foods restaurant, but not exclusively vegetarian.

Paru's Indian Vegetarian Restaurant, 5140 Sunset Blvd, Hollywood 90029; (213) 661-7600. Southern Indian–style cooking. Family-owned. Patio for outdoor dining.

Peyton's Place, Carmel Crossroads Mall, Rio Road and Hwy 1, Carmel 93923; (408) 624-0544. Natural foods cafe.

The Prophet, 4461 University Ave, San Diego 92105; (619) 283-7448. International menu including French stuffed mushrooms, Creole gumbo, and African ground peanut soup. Live music.

Sleeping Lady Cafe, 58 Bolinas Rd, Fairfax 94930; (415) 456-2044. Vegetarian restaurant and nightclub (entertainment telephone line: 459-6778). Cooperatively owned, entertainment nightly.

COLORADO

Country Life Vegetarian Cafeteria, 149 North College, Fort Collins 80524; (303) 221-4666.

The Little Kitchen, 716 East Hyman St, Aspen 81611; (303) 925-1966.

Mishawaka Inn, 1500 Poudre Canyon, Bellevue 80512; (303) 482-4420.

Pachamama Restaurant, Pearl and 18th Sts, Boulder 80302; (303) 447-0580. Vegetarian food prepared in the traditional style of the Andes.

The Pantry Natural Foods and Granary, 1124 Yampa St, Steamboat Springs 80477; (303) 879-2552.

Zach's, 1480 Humboldt St, Denver 80218; (303) 831-0870.

CONNECTICUT

Bloodroot, 85 Ferris St, Bridgeport 06605; (203) 576-9168. Feminist restaurant and bookstore overlooking Long Island Sound.

La Boca, 526 Main St, Middletown 06457; (203) 346-4492. Mexican restaurant with quite a few vegetarian dishes.

Garden of Eating, 76 Jefferson St, Hartford 06106 (203) 525-8189. Vegetarian, but they also serve fish.

Good Harvest Restaurant, 686 Main St, Middletown 06457; (203) 346-5743. Natural foods restaurant plus health food store.

Love and Serve, 35 Amogerone Way, Greenwich 06830; (203) 661-8893.

The Mischievous Carrot Natural Foods Restaurant, 6 Holmes St, Mystic 06355; (203) 536-7126.

Sesame Seed, 68 West Wooster St, Danbury 06810; (203) 743-9850.

DELAWARE

The Vegetarian, 9 E 8 St, Wilmington 19801; (302) 571-8176.

DISTRICT OF COLUMBIA

Food for Thought, 1738 Connecticut Ave NW 20009; (202) 797-1095.

Health's A Poppin', 2020 K St NW 20006; (202) 466-6616.

Kalorama Cafe, 2228 18th St NW 20009; (202) 667-1022.

Naturally Yours Cafe, 3205 Prospect St, Georgetown 20007; (202) 338-4031.

FLORIDA

Alive and Well, 612 Lake Ave, Lake Worth 33460; (305) 586-VEGI. Natural foods restaurant.

Granny Feelgoods, 190 SE First Ave, Miami 33131; (305) 358-6233. Award-winning gourmet eating establishment since 1971. Top-quality products, top-quality preparation.

Spiral Restaurant, 1630 Ponce De Leon Blvd, Coral Gables 33134; (305) 446-1591. Natural and seafood cuisine, no meat or poultry. No sugar; only maple syrup or honey sweeteners.

Village Cafe, 7121 Broward Blvd, Plantation 33317, in the Plantation Center Shopping Center; (305) 792-0026. Part of the Vita Village Health Food Store, they serve macrobiotic cuisine, juices, salads, sandwiches, hot platters, and homemade soups.

Wealth of Health, 1208 South Pasadena Ave, St. Petersburg 33707; (813) 345-0163. Sandwiches, smoothies, soups, daily specials.

Wildflower Natural Food Restaurant, 5218 Ocean Blvd, Siesta Key; (813) 349-1758. Vegetarian cooking, open breakfast, lunch, and dinner. Closed Sundays.

GEORGIA

Country Life Vegetarian Restaurant, 1217 Eberhart Ave, Columbus 31904; (404) 323-9194. All-you-can-eat vegan buffet.

Nature's Last Stand, 1847 Peachtree Rd, Atlanta 30309; (404) 352-1100. Vegetarian fast foods by day, elegant dining by night.

Nature's Way, 6135 Peachtree Parkway, Norcross 30071; (404) 448-4675.

Soul Vegetarian Restaurant, 631 Peachtree St NE (at North Avenue) Atlanta 30309; (404) 873-1503. Run by the Hebrew Israelites of North East Africa. Lunch counter and full service restaurant.

HAWAII

Aricia's Beach-Inn Kitchen, 59–174 Kam Highway, Sunset Beach, Oahu 96712; (808) 638-8200.

Laulima Fine Vegetarian Foods, 2239 South King St, Honolulu; (808) 947-3844.

ILLINOIS

Blind Faith Cafe, 800 Dempster St, Evanston 60202; (312) 328-6875. A self-service, predominantly organic restaurant. Fresh baked breads daily.

Blue Gargoyle, 5655 South University Ave, Chicago 60637; (312) 955-4108.

Good Nature Deli, 810 Harrison St, Oak Park 60304; (312) 383-4663. Vegan restaurant, soyfood specials.

Heartland Cafe, 7000 North Glenwood Ave, Chicago 60626; (312) 465-8005.

INDIANA

Cornucopia, 303 South Michigan St, South Bend 46601; (219) 288-1911.

Still Water Restaurant, 929 East Westfield Blvd, Broad Ripple Village, Indianapolis 46220; (317) 259-1921. Whole foods restaurant offering vegetarian and macrobiotic foods.

KANSAS

Sister Kettle Cafe, 1347 Massachusetts Ave, Lawrence 66044; (913) 842-1126.

KENTUCKY

Sunshine Harvest Inn, 1769 Bardstown Rd, Louisville 40205; (502) 454-5561. Buffet-style, organic foods whenever possible.

LOUISIANA

Earthreal Living Store and Restaurant, 3309 Line Ave, Shreveport 71106; (318) 865-8947.

Eat No Evil, 405 Baronne St, New Orleans 70112; (504) 524-0906. Lunchroom, cafeteria-style.

MAINE

Corsican Pizza House, 76 Union St, Brunswick 04011; (207) 729-8117. Vegetarian pizza. Not everything served is vegetarian.

The Hollow Reed, 334 Fore St, Portland 04111; (207) 773-2531. Some vegetarian entrees on a predominantly fish menu.

Second Ceres, 21 Pleasant St, Portland 04101; (207) 774-5408. Macrobiotic.

MARYLAND

Berwyn Cafe, 5010 Berwyn Rd, College Park 20740; (301) 345-2121. Health food store, restaurant, and catering service.

Community Cafe and Bookstore, 4949 Bethesda Ave, Bethesda 20014; (301) 986-0848. Collectively run community center.

Green Earth Natural Foods, 823 N Charles St, Baltimore 21201; (301) 752-4465.

MASSACHUSETTS

Corn Mother Cafe, 92 Water St, Newburyport 01950; (617) 465-9051. Macrobiotic.

Emerald Garden, 29 Center St, Nantucket 02554; (617) 228-3947. Outdoor garden, strictly vegetarian.

Five Seasons Restaurant, 669A Centre St, Jamaica Plains 02130; (617) 524-9016.

Middle East Restaurant, 4 Brookline St, Cambridge 02139; (617) 354-8238.

Open Sesame, 48 Boylston St, Brookline 02146; (617) 277-9241.

L'Odeon, 166 Harvard Ave, Allston 02134; (617) 254-9786. International natural foods restaurant and macrobiotics.

Sanae, 272A Newbury St, Boston 02116; (617) 247-2475. Small macrobiotic restaurant.

Seventh Inn, 69–71 Providence St, Boston 02116; (617) 437-1568. Elegantly appointed and expensive natural foods and macrobiotic dining.

Something Natural Something Else, 50 Cliff Rd, Nantucket Island 02554; (617) 228-0507.

MICHIGAN

Down To Earth, 10025 Belding Rd NE, Rockford 49341; (616) 691-7288. Country farmhouse setting with some vegetarian entrees.

Healthy Jones, 29221 Northwestern Highway (at 12 Mile), Southfield 48034; (313) 353-7766. Huge menu.

Inn Season, 500 East Fourth St, Royal Oak; (313) 547-7916. Vegetarian specials, but not strictly vegetarian.

Merlin's Retreat Vegetarian Cafe, 801 Detroit St, Flint 48502; (313) 767-9050.

Sevá Gourmet Vegetarian Restaurant, 314 East Libert St, Ann Arbor 48104; (313) 662-2019.

The Sprout House, 15309 Mack Ave, Detroit 48224; (313) 885-1048. Natural food and macrobiotic specialties.

MINNESOTA

All Eclectic Kitchen, 26 Fifth Avenue South, St. Cloud 56301; (612) 253-5814.

Blue Heron Cafe, 1123 West Lake St, Minneapolis 55408; (612) 823-4743. Collectively run vegetarian restaurant.

Mud Pie Vegetarian Restaurant, 2549 Lyndale Avenue South, Minneapolis 55405; (612) 927-4416. Accommodating to all vegetarian diets, with an interesting array of international dishes.

New Riverside Cafe, Cedar and Riverside, Minneapolis 55443; (612) 332-9989. Serving vegetarian food since 1970.

Seward Cafe, 21–29 Franklin Ave, Minneapolis 55404; (612) 332-1011. Whole-food restaurant proud of their burritos and breakfasts.

MISSOURI

Earth Wonder, 2703 South Campbell, Springfield 65807; (417) 887-5985.

Golden Temple of Conscious Cookery, 4059 Broadway, Kansas City 64111; (816) 561-6440.

Govinda's, 3926 Lindell Blvd, St. Louis 63108; (314) 535-8085. Hare Krishna cafeteria. All you can eat.

MONTANA

Alice's Restaurant, 123 East Main St, Missoula 59801; (406) 728-2803.

Cup of Sun Cafe, 15 Meridian Rd, Kalispell 59901; (406) 755-1134.

The Gilded Lily Restaurant, 515 South Higgins, Missoula 59801; (406) 542-0002.

NEBRASKA

Marvin Gardens, 3229 Harney St, Omaha 68131; (402) 345-0820.

Open Harvest Snack Bar, 2631 Randolph St, Lincoln 68508; (402) 475-9069.

NEVADA

Alfalfa's, 1107 East Tropicana, Las Vegas 89109; (702) 736-6441.

Golden Temple Conscious Cookery, 902 South Virginia, Reno 89101; (702) 786-4110. Operated by disciple of Yogi Bhajan.

New Sprout Natural Foods Cafe, 4726 East Flamingo Rd, Las Vegas 89121; (702) 456-5656.

NEW HAMPSHIRE

Fiddlehead Cafe, Main St, Franconia 03580; (603) 823-9907.

The Folkway, 85 Grove St, Peterborough 03458; (603) 924-7484. Community-run restaurant.

Natural Selection, 44 South State St, Concord 03301; (603) 224-4757.

Suzanne's Kitchen, Main St, Ashland 03217; (603) 968-7614.

NEW JERSEY

Country Fare Cafe, 60 Diamond Spring Rd, Denville 07834; (201) 625-1055. An outdoor garden setting and a vegetarian menu.

Eatery Amulette, Olde English Sq, Rte 522 at Ridge Road, South Brunswick (201) 329-2777. Natural foods restaurant, international menu. Weekend entertainment.

Frog Pond Cafe, Morton Ave, R.D. #1, Milleville 07855 (609) 455-3796. Features a Thursday night $8.00 vegetarian smorgasbord.

Greenliner Diner, 179 Nassau St, Princeton 08540; (609) 683-0240. Vegetarian-oriented, but some fish and chicken offered.

Hackettstown Community Hospital Cafeteria, 651 Willow Grove St, Hackettstown 07840; (201) 852-5100. The hospital is run by the Seventh-Day Adventists, and they have opened their cafeteria to the public. Good prices, good food.

Health Emporium, 398 Broadway (at 18 St), Bayonne 07002 (201) 858-2260. Attractive food in a garden setting.

High Street Cafe, 5 High St, Morristown 07960; (201) 285-0821.

India House, 6–13 Fairlawn Ave, Fair Lawn 07410; (201) 791-8222. Strictly vegetarian Indian food.

Juice Factory, 55 Wayne Hills Mall, Wayne 07470; (201) 696-8866. Juice, salad, and snack bar.

Park and Orchard Natural Foods Restaurant, 227 Park Ave, East Rutherford 07450; (201) 939-9292. Home-baked bread and only natural ingredients, but not strictly vegetarian. Natural beer and wine containing no stabilizers or preservatives. Really fine reputation.

Richard's Natural Health, 10 White Horse Rd, Vorhees 08043; (609) 627-5057. A cafeteria-style restaurant in a health food store. The food is macrobiotic and well priced.

NEW MEXICO

Bakery Cafe, 118 Yale St SE, Albuquerque 87106; (505) 255-0749. Full-service vegetarian restaurant with excellent baked goods and homemade soups.

Mother Nature and Son, 3118 Central Ave SE, Albuquerque 87106; (505) 255-7640.

NEW YORK

American Pie, 68 W 70 St, New York 10021; (212) 787-5446. Whole-wheat pizza.

Angelica's Kitchen, 42 St. Mark's Pl, New York 10003; (212) 228-2909. A fine reputation for excellent food, large portions. Macrobiotic cooking.

Annam Brahma, 84–43 164th St, Jamaica, Queens (718) 523-2600. Whole natural foods, specializing in Indian cuisine.

Arnold's Turtle, 51 Bank St, New York 10014; (212) 242-5623. Vegetarian Greenwich Village haunt.

Cauldron, 306 E 6th St, New York 10003; (212) 473-9543. A kosher macrobiotic restaurant that's been around for years. Health food store next door.

Chandra Gardens, 310 E 86th St, New York 10028; (212) 628-2642. Combination Indian and Western vegetarian.

Country Life, 48 Trinity Pl, New York 10006; (212) 480-9142. Well known in lower Manhattan, this Seventh-Day Adventist cafeteria offers much for your money, and a lively atmosphere to boot. Health food store on premises.

Dojo, 24 St. Mark's Pl, New York 10003; (212) 674-9821. Popular East Village sidewalk cafe with vegetarian food served in a Japanese tradition.

East–West Restaurant, 105 E 9 St, New York 10011; (212) 260-1994. A restaurant of long-standing excellence. Serves fish.

Eat, 11 St. Mark's Pl, New York 10003; (212) 477-5155. Popular little East Village cafe.

Free as a Bird, 85 Jefferson St, Monticello 12701; (914) 794-5691.

Ital Safari, 617A Flatbush Ave (at Rutland), Brooklyn 11225; (718) 282-5187. Natural foods lunch counter.

King David's, 129 Marshall St, Syracuse 13210; (315) 478-9463.

Lois Lane's, 42 Street (at Ninth Ave), New York 10017; (212) 695-5055. Eat in, take out, free delivery. All baking done on premises. Homemade soups.

Lotus Light Cafe, 227 W 13 St, New York 10011; (212) 929-0586. Natural foods restaurant.

212·929·0586

227 West 13th Street
New York, N.Y 10011

Madras Woodland, 310 E 44 St, New York 10017 (212) 986-0620. Top-of-the-line vegetarian fare, expensively priced.

Monya's Natural Kitchen, 253 E 52 St, New York 10022; Monya runs it, does all the cooking, and waits on the tables, too. Open only for lunch weekdays.

Moosewood Restaurant, DeWitt Mall, Seneca and Cayuga Sts, Ithaca 14850; (607) 273-9610. Excel-

lent cooperatively run restaurant, one of whose members wrote the *Moosewood Cookbook.*

Morningstar Catering, 178 Hillturn Lane, Roslyn Heights 11577; (516) 484-6226. Healthy, delicious party food from wedding to intimate dinner party.

Ms. Juice, 135 Seventh Ave South, New York 10014; (212) 675-0864. Tiny, tiny juice and sandwich bar.

Nature's Kitchen, 150 Fulton St, New York 10038; (212) 233-6102. Vegetarian-style cafeteria.

Plum Tree, 150 First Ave, New York 10011; (212) 734-1412. Enticing combination of Japanese and Chinese vegetarian offerings, many tofu dishes.

Quantum Leap, 65–64 Fresh Meadow Lane, Fresh Meadows; (718) 461-1307. Also 88 W 3rd St, New York 10012; 677-8050. Natural foods restaurant, vegetarian and macrobiotic.

Souen, 2444 Broadway, New York 10025; (212) 787-1110. 210 Avenue of the Americas, New York 10014; (212) 807-7421. Japanese, traditional macrobiotic-style cooking excellently prepared. Rave reviews from all over.

The Vegetarian Hotel, PO Box 457, Woodridge 12789; (914) 434-4455. In business since 1920, this Catskill hotel has been a summer stopping place for many individuals and vegetarian groups. The food is classically kosher.

Vegetarian Paradise, 48 Bowery, New York 10013; (212) 571-1535. Chinatown's only strictly vegetarian restaurant.

Veggie U.G.B. (Universal Great Brotherhood), 235 W 14th St, New York 10011; (212) 620-8148. Lacto-vegetarian.

Whole Wheat and Wild Berries, 57 W 10th St, New York 10011; (212) 677-3410. Bustling Village natural food restaurant.

New World Food Center, 2035 Fifth Ave (between 125 and 126 Sts), New York 10035; (212) 722-9432. All types of vegetarian food, but the highlight might be traditional African foods.

NORTH CAROLINA

Irregardless Cafe, 240 Daniels St, Raleigh 27605; (919) 833-9920.

They Laughed at Edison, 3200 Monroe Rd, Charlotte 28205; (704) 372-4312.

OHIO

Bassett's Health Foods and Restaurant, 3301 West Central Ave (in the Westgate Village Shopping Center), Toledo 43606; (419) 531-2911. Natural foods cafeteria.

Earth by April, 2151 Lee Rd, Cleveland Heights 44118; (216) 371-1438. Award-winning vegetarian restaurant.

Genesis 1:29 Vegetarian Restaurant, 12200 Euclid Ave, Cleveland 44106; (216) 421-9359.

New World Food Shop, 347 Ludlow Ave, Cincinnati 45220; (513) 861-1101.

OKLAHOMA

The Golden Temple, 2504 North Military Rd, Oklahoma City 73115; (405) 521-1288.

Macrame Cafe, 29237 Paseo, Paseo Design Center, Oklahoma City 73103; (405) 521-9378.

Nature's Storehouse, 8201 South Harvard St, Tulsa 74136; (918) 481-0404. Lunch counter that's part of a health food store.

OREGON

The Clearwater Community Cafe, 631 Rose St, Roseburg 97470; (503) 673-1468.

The Food Goddess Restaurant, 1233 SW Morrison, Portland 97205; (503) 228-3536. International natural foods.

The Garden House, 155 SE Vista Ave, Gresham 97030; (503) 667-9212.

The Vegetarian Restaurant, 270 W 8 St, Eugene 97401; (503) 342-4335.

PENNSYLVANIA

Cornucopia, 327 Atwood St, Pittsburgh 15213; (412) 682-7953.

George's Restaurant, 8142 Germantown Ave, Chestnut Hill; (215) 247-5090. International selection of vegetarian entrees, including macrobiotic cuisine.

Nature's Garden, Reading Mall, Reading 19606; (215) 779-3000. Lunch counter and take-out that's part of a health food store.

The Sproutery, 34 North Cherry Lane, York 17403; (717) 854-6885. Raw foods restaurant. Sprouts grown on premises.

The Vegetarian Shop, 1437 Lombard St, Philadelphia 19146; (215) 545-9655. Tiny full-service lunch counter and restaurant.

RHODE ISLAND

Amaras, 321 Wickenden St, Providence 02903; (401) 621-8919. Vegetarian, but not exclusively.

The Merciful Lion, Waites Corner, Kingston 02881; (401) 789-1971.

SOUTH CAROLINA

Basil Pot, 2721 Rosewood Dr, Columbia 29205; (803) 771-9648. Kosher kitchen.

Farmer's Hall Tearoom and Restaurant, On the Square, Pendleton 29670; (803) 646-7024. Request vegetarian food from helpful staff, and enjoy the setting in this 150-year-old antebellum courthouse.

TENNESSEE

Country Life, 2752 Ringgold Rd, Chattanooga 37404; (615) 622-2451.

Country Life Vegetarian Buffet, 1917 Division St, Nashville 37203; (615) 327-3695. Most Country Life restaurants limit what they serve to plant foods.

Laughing Man, 1500 North Gallatin Rd, Madison 37115; (615) 868-2128.

Whole Foods and Cafe Natural, 1779 Kirby Parkway, Memphis 38138; (901) 755-3700.

TEXAS

Family Farm, 911 Boudreaux, Tomball 77375; (713) 370-4054. Health food store and country kitchen.

Hobbit Hole, 1715 South Shepherd, Houston 77019; (713) 528-3418.

Moss Cliff Natural Food Shop, Rte 2, Box 322, San Marcos 78666; (512) 392-5678.

Mother's Cafe and Garden, 4215 Duval, Hyde Park, Austin 78745; (512) 451-3994.

Pelly's Health Farm, 1616 South Bridge Ave, Weslaco 78596; (512) 968-5343. Only organic vegetarian food.

UTAH

Nature's Way Sandwich Shop, 888 South 9 St East, Salt Lake City 84102; (801) 532-9405.

Whole Earth Natural Foods, 1026 Second Ave, Salt Lake City 84103; (801) 355-7401. Lunch counter located in a health food store.

VERMONT

Common Ground, 25 Elliot St, Brattleboro 05301; (802) 257-0855. Worker-owned cooperative. Catering.

Horn of the Moon, 8 Langdon St, Montpelier 05602; (802) 223-2895. Expensive, strictly vegetarian menu.

Mary's, 11 Main St, Bristol 05443; (802) 453-4532. Continental-style vegetarian.

VIRGINIA

Grace Place, 826 West Grace St, Richmond 23220; (804) 353-3680.

Natural Foods, 231 Virginia Beach Blvd, Virginia Beach 23451; (804) 425-5383.

Sprouts, 6184-A Arlington Blvd, Falls Church 22044; 241-7177. Sandwich and juice bar inside the natural food supermarket.

WASHINGTON

Celebration Cookery, 314 North Commercial, Bellingham 98225; (206) 676-9918.

Mountain Song, Milepost 106, North Cascades Highway (near the North Cascades National Park), Marblemount 98267.

Sunlight Cafe, 6401 Roosevelt Way NE, Seattle; (206) 522-9060.

WISCONSIN

Country Life Vegetarian Restaurant, 2465 Perry St, Madison 53713; (608) 257-3286.

Downtown Tea House and Natural Foods, 412 East Wisconsin Ave, Milwaukee 53202; (414) 277-9599.

Main Course, 306 North Brooks St, Madison 53715; (608) 256-4100.

26

Conferences

The following listing is a sampling of the many conferences that are held each year that may be of interest to vegetarians. Check local vegetarian groups for additional gatherings, and check with the organizations listed below for specific conference dates and locations.

Action for Life Conference Sponsored by a coalition of animal welfare and vegetarian organizations, led by Mobilization for Animals, PO Box 1679, Columbus, OH 43216; (614) 267-6993.

AFAR Conference (Attorneys for Animal Rights) 333 Market St, Ste 2300, San Francisco, CA 94105; (415) 665-5896. Two-day conference designed to offer current information and practical advice on how to handle legal questions relating to animal rights.

American Natural Hygiene Society, Natural Living Conference 698 Brooklawn Ave, Bridgeport, CT 06604; (203) 366-6229. Attn H. Jay Dinshah. This annual natural hygiene conference has met more than 35 times.

Animal Rights—A Humane Symposium. Contact Lifeforce, Box 3117, Main Post Office, Vancouver, British Columbia V6B 3X6 Canada. This symposium addresses all issues of animal abuse.

Annual Cancer Convention. Sponsored by the Cancer Control Society, 2043 North Berendo, Los Angeles, CA 90027; (213) 663-7801. Well-known medical doctors, researchers, nutritionists, authors, and attorneys speak on prevention and control of cancer through nutrition, tests and nontoxic therapies such as laetrile, Gerson, enzymes, herbal, and cellular.

Bear Tribe, PO Box 84, Harriman, NY 10926; (914) 928-7257. Native American medicine wheel gathering, where one can participate and learn the mystic vision of Sun Bear, sacred teacher and medicine man of the Bear tribe. Learn through teaching and join in the ceremonies for the healing of the Earth mother. Late spring, early summer.

Biological Farming Conference. Biological Agriculture, c/o Phil Wheeler, 8401 Bollinger Rd. NE, Vestaburg, MI 48891; (517) 268-5541. Contact for details or to be placed on mailing list. Support, knowledge, companionship for the organic farmer and his or her supporters.

Great Lakes Bioregional Conference. PO Box 24, Old Mission, MI 49673. A forum for concerned individuals to network to create alternatives in agriculture, economy, energy, health, peace, human rights, and more.

Harvest Festival Contact the Federated Organic Clubs of Michigan, 4401 Maple Lane, Rives Junction, MI 49277 for details. An educational seminar on holistic health and organic farming and gardening that has been held annually for over 30 years in Michigan.

Health Freedom Conference. Sponsored by the National Health Federation, 212 West Foothill Blvd, Monrovia, CA 91016; (213) 357-2181. An annual conference featuring well-known speakers and many display booths. The federation advocates health in the best interest of people. Their philosophy is often diametrically opposed to that of the American Medical Association.

Healthy Living Programs. Sponsored by the East–West Foundation, PO Box 850, Brookline, MA 02147. Natural health care the macrobiotic way, meeting in different locations throughout the United States and Canada.

Help Yourself To Health—Concepts And Tools—Conference. Contact Unity Institute for Holistic Living, 17505 Second Blvd, Detroit, MI 48203; (313) 342-5814 or 345-4848. Sponsored by the Unity Institute for Holistic Living and the Michigan Holistic Health Association. One-day conference exploring specialized topics including Food Systems for Health and Women's Health. Exhibitions, speakers, networking, resource lists.

Interface, Box 299, 230 Central St, Newton, MA 02166; (617) 964-0500. The role of love and laughter in the healing process.

International Yoga, Psychotherapy, and Self-Transformation Congress. Himalayan Institute Headquarters, RD 1, Box 88, Honesdale, PA 18431. A unique opportunity to explore and compare a wide array of effective methods of personal growth and self-development. Held in June.

Kushi Institute Summer Intensive. Sponsored by the Kushi Institute of Great Britain, 188 Old St, London EC1, England. Those interested in macrobiotics join leading macrobiotic educators from the United States and Europe in an annual summer intensive.

A NONPROFIT HEALTH RIGHTS CORPORATION

National Health Federation. 212 West Foothill Blvd, Monrovia, CA 91016; PO Box 688, (213) 357-2181 or 359-8334. Health rights organization advocating the absolute freedom of choice in matters of personal health where such choices do not infringe on the liberties of others. Sponsors local and national conventions through out the year.

National Vegetarian Conference. Sponsored by the Vegetarian Association of America, PO Box 68, Maplewood, NJ 07040; (201) 731-4902. Discussion groups on topics such as the different aspects of vegetarianism, holistic health, and the future of the vegetarian movement.

Natural Food Associates Convention. PO Box 210, Atlanta, TX 75551. Advocating organic agriculture for good food and good health for more than 25 years. Regional and national conventions.

Natural Living Expo. Sponsored by Pathways/DC Growth and the Yes Educational Society, 3000 Connecticut Ave NW, Ste 136, Washington, D.C. 20008; (202) 237-9282.

North American Vegetarian Conference. Sponsored by the North American Vegetarian Society, PO Box 72, Dolgeville, NY 13329. Speeches, films, discussion groups, workshops.

Turkey Freedom Day. Sponsored by the Vegetarian Society, Inc., of Santa Monica, California, P.O. Box 5688, Santa Monica, CA 90405; (213) 396-5164. Thanksgiving annually, attendance varies, approximately 500. Alternative dinner featuring vegetable nut roast with cranberries, nuts, dried fruits and vegetable juices, herb teas, tofu dishes and more.

Whole Life Expo. Sponsored by *Whole Life Times*, 18 Shepard St, Brighton, MA 02135; (617) 783-8030. Directed by International Health Alliances. Staged in different cities across the country throughout the year. Discussion groups, films, workshops, displays, merchandise for sale.

World Vegetarian Conference. North American Vegetarian Society, PO Box 72, Dolgeville, NY 13329. The grandddaddy of them all, NAVS was honored to sponsor the 1984 World Vegetarian Conference, which met at the University of Maryland. The congress lasts ten days and attracts outstanding speakers, thinkers, practitioners, advocates and enthusiasts from all over the world. True international spirit and flavor.

DO YOU NEED A PLACE FOR YOUR CONFERENCE?

Another Place Conference Center, Greenville, NH 03048; (603) 878-9883. Rents space and facilities.

The Phoenicia Pathwork Center, PO Box 66, Phoenicia, NY 12464; (914) 688-2211. Offers their facility for conferences and gatherings. A place of beauty and power in a Catskill mountain valley. Ideal for large and small groups of up to 120 people. Variety of menus, meditation sanctuary, Indian sweat lodge, swimming, hiking, more.

BOOKS

America's Meeting Places by Redtree Associates. Facts on File, New York, 1984. Listing of many out-of-the-way meeting places in every state.

27

Vegetarian Networking Through Magazines and Newspapers

Throughout the United States, resource organizations, magazines, and newspapers are enabling people to connect. Usually their claim is that all who subscribe to and use their publication adhere to the single philosophy of "right livelihood"; that is, they allow their instincts to lead them to conclusions about the correct way to live, and then follow them. When you have faith in humanity, the heart can be a good guide. Networking can also be a valuable tool. There is a bounty of information waiting to be harvested, and usually friendly, helpful people, too. When traveling, write ahead, and many of the publications listed here will forward a copy to you for a $2.00 postage and handling fee.

Alaskan Well-Being. PO Box 104552, Anchorage, AK 99501.

Alternative Health. PO Box 6337, Hollywood, FL 33021; (305) 920-0166. Informative, interesting articles and plenty of natural food vegetarian networking. Regional as well as statewide advertisements. Copies (53,000) are distributed free in six regional editions; a one-year subscription is $5.00.

Alternatives. PO Box 171, Pittsfield, MA 01202.

Arizona Networking News. PO Box 15103, Phoenix, AZ 85060; (602) 957-3322. Articles, resources, a calendar of events. Their code asks their advertisers to "acknowledge that they do business in a spirit of unity, cooperation and understanding, and maintain a high level of integrity, responsibility and service." Free locally; $1.00 by mail; $4.00 yearly subscription rate.

Arizona Networking News. Published by the International Holistic Center, 3501 East Indian School Rd, Phoenix, AZ, (602) 957-3322. The center is a filter for networking resources and education, offering classes, lectures, workshops. Mailing address is PO Box 15103, Phoenix, AZ 85060.

Attunement. PO Box 2716, Madison, WI 53701; (608) 251-9480. Published six times per year; the annual subscription rate is $8.00. *Attunement* has no resource directory, but it does feature a local calendar of events, as well as articles.

Catalyst. PO Box H, Farmington, UT 84025; (801) 451-5300. Articles and a calendar of events for the Salt Lake City area and statewide. No resource directory. Published four times per year; subscription is $9.00; single issues are $1.50.

Circle of Light. PO Box 64444, Dallas, TX 75206.

Common Ground. 47-155 Okana Rd, Kaneohe, HI 96744; (808) 239-7190

Common Ground. 111 Racine St, Memphis, TN 38111.

Common Ground. 9 Mono Ave, Fairfax, CA 94930; (415) 459-4900. A directory to resources, offering the reader a wide, useful, interesting list of available organizations, classes, services, restaurants, shops, practitioners, etc. Available free in the Bay Area at local outlets, mainly neighborhood and community gathering places, natural food stores, cafes, bookstores. *Common Ground* is available by mail for $4.00 for a year's subscription (four times per year). A single issue can be had for $1.50.

Common Sense. PO Box 770, Norwich, VT 05055.

Community Spirit. PO Box 4628, Carmel, CA 93921; (408) 625-5508. Progressive health and human potential newspaper serving the central California coast. The *Wellness Resource Directory* lists health care professionals, counselors, bodyworks, and supportive health services.

Connections. 1266 I St, Springfield, OR 97477; (503) 726-0534.

Earth Nation Sunrise. RR3, Box 507, Nashville, IN 47448; (812) 988-4332. Subscription rate is $7.00 for four issues of a newspaper devoted to the positive-energy global commuinity.

Earth Star Press. PO Box L-86, Temple, NH 03084.

Eye of the Raven. 91981 Taylor Rd, McKenzie Bridge, OR 97401; 822-6089. A magazine that seeks to inform its readers about important issues of our times with regard to nutrition, gardening, ecology, greenpeace, and more. How-to's and recipes are included. The subscription rate is $8.00 for 12 issues.

Free Spirit. 34 Prospect Pl, Brooklyn, NY 11217; (212) 625-3872. Published four times yearly, this is a resource directory with a long calendar of events. Subscriptions are $8.00 for the year or

$2.00 per issue. Copies (75,000) are distributed free locally.

Greater Cincinnati Resource Directory. 3514 Burch St, Cincinnati, OH 45208.

Heartland Journal. 7000 North Glenwood, Chicago, IL 60626.

Holistic Learning Quarterly. 619 Wood St, Pittsburgh, PA 15221; (412) 731-5533. Subscription rate is $7.00 for four issues.

Holistic Living News. PO Box 16346, San Diego, CA 92116; (619) 280-0317. Good key-in to the San Diego area. Plenty of sources for the vegetarian, holistic, health and fitness minded. Advertising, services, schools, calendar, accessories, businesses, more. Sixty cents.

Horizons. Rising Sun, PO Box 570296, Houston, TX 77257; Houston, (713) 975-1600; Dallas, (214) 824-0545; Fort Worth, (817) 921-3765. The expressed aims of *Horizons* are expansion and connection. They are members of the National Resource Network and the Association of Community Resource Publications.

Inner Quest, 3514 Birch St, Cincinnati, OH 45208.

L.A. Resources. 4026 Beverly Blvd, Los Angeles, CA 90004; (213) 739-0190. Quarterly; free in the Los Angeles area; $2.00 by mail,, $7.00 per year. Access to local natural foods and tools. Includes community news, growth, child raising, women's organizations, services, health care, etc.

Many Hands. 150 Main St, Northhampton, MA 01060.

Montana Common Ground. 470 Strand Ave, Missoula, MT 59801.

The National Resource Network. Box 878, Fairfax, CA 94930; (415) 485-1132 (call between 10 A.M. and 12 Pacific Time). Represents resource directory publishers to advertisers nationwide. They ask three things: (1) The service or product advertised contributes to the greater good and meets the test of reader satisfaction. (2) The organization advertising does business in the spirit of Right Livelihood. (3) The listing itself respects the consciousness of the reader. The network now includes:

East: *Free Spirit* (New York City)
New Frontier Resource Directory (Philadelphia)
Holistic Learning Quarterly (Pittsburgh)
D.C. Growth (Washington, D.C.)

Midwest: *Attunement* (Madison, Wisconsin)
Heartland (Chicago)
Greater Cincinnati Resource Directory

South: *Alternative Health* (Florida)
Horizons (Dallas, Houston, Fort Worth)

Mountain: *Nexus* (Colorado)
Catalyst (Salt Lake City)
Arizona Networking News

West: *Common Ground* (Vancouver)
Common Ground (San Francisco)
Spectrum (Santa Cruz)

Natural Living Resources. 7201 Fifth Ave NE, Seattle, WA 98115; (206) 632-9096. The subscription rate for four issues is $5.00. Calendar of events.

New Chicago. 2930 North Lincoln, Chicago, IL 60657; (312) 235-0312. Six times a year; subscription is $9.00. Single-issue rate is $2.00. Resource guide, events calendar, classified, personal connections.

New Frontier Resource Directory. 129 North 13 St, Philadelphia, PA 19107; (215) 235-0312. A monthly publication; subscription rate is $10.00 for the year. Resources and a calendar of events.

New Life News. 133 Romero St, Sante Fe, NM 87501.

New Texas. Box 12165, Austin, TX 78711; (512) 453-0515. Printed bi-monthly; annual subscription rate is $4.50. Resources, calendar, articles.

New World Fresno. 20511 South Blythe Ave,

Riverdale, CA 93656; (209) 867-3361. Four times a year; subscription is $8.00. Local resource guide.

Nexus. 1495 Canyon Blvd, Ste 205C, Boulder, CO 80302; (303) 442-6662. A quarterly directory giving access to resources in the Boulder/Denver area. Free in the area, subscription rates are $5.00 per year. Single issues are available for $1.50.

Northern Health Communications. 905 Hancock St, Level A, Manitowoc, WI 54220; (414) 684-5859. Advertising and promotion service representing small manufacturers, health food retailers, holistic clinics and others in the health business.

Outpost Coop. 3500 North Holton St, Milwaukee, WI 53212.

Pathways/D.C. Growth. PO Box 4346, Falls Church, VA 22044; (703) 241-1434. The subscription rate for four issues is $3.00. Washington D.C. area. Includes resources and a calendar of events.

phenomeNEWS. 2821 North Woodward, Royal Oak, MI 48072; (313) 435-7727. A Detroit-area forum for the exchange of ideas, news, events, resources, services, products and more. Free locally. Yearly subscription rate by mail, $8.00 ($10.00 in Canada).

Portland Reflection. PO Box 12290, Portland, OR 97212.

Rainbow Visions. 3955 Davie Blvd, Fort Lauderdale, FL 33312; (305) 791-6121. Published four times a year, subscription is $5.00. Resources and calendar.

Resources. 3660 Louisiana St, San Diego, CA 92104. Local resources, published four times per year; subscription rate is $6.00.

Spectrum. 503 Gertrude Ave, Aptos, CA 95003; (408) 662-1971. A quarterly resource directory for the Santa Cruz area. Free in the community, available by mail for $2.00 per issue or $7.00 for the year.

Threshold. PO Box 162108, Sacramento, CA 95816.

Transformation Times. PO Box 227, Beavercreek, OR 97004; (503) 632-7141. An information-sharing, resource-oriented publication, dedicated to expanding awareness of physical, mental and spiritual issues. The subscription rate is $9.00 per year (12 issues). Free locally.

Well-Being Community Calendar. 788 Ferguson Rd, Sebastopol, CA 95472; (707) 823-1489. Published nine times a year; subscription is $6.00.

INTERNATIONAL VEGETARIAN NETWORKING

Common Ground (B.C.), Box 34090, Station D, Vancouver, British Columbia V6J 4M1 Canada; (604) 879-3805 or 261-8324.

Common Ground Toronto, 152 Beech Ave, Toronto, Ontario M4E 3H6 Canada.

Inner Life, 214 Glengarry Ave, Toronto, Ontario M5M 1E4 Canada.

New Alberta, 2127 Broadview Rd NW, Calgary, Alberta T2N 3J1 Canada.

Omkresten, Nowfullsgaten 53, 11345 Stockholm, Sweden.

Transformation/Nucleus Network, 188 Old St, London EC1, England.

The Turning Point, c/o Alison Pritchard, Spring Cottage, 9 New Road, Ironbridge, Shropshire TF8 7AU, England.

Welsh Network of Light, c/o Judith Roe, 21 Bridge St, Llandaf, Cardiff, Wales.

Zirius, PO Box 563, Frankston, Victoria 3199, Australia.

BOOKS

Networking by Jessica Lipnack and Jeffery Stamps. Doubleday, 1982, New York; 416 pp; $24.95. Explains the theory behind networking, then lists various directories to help you get started.

28

Kitchen and Household Tools

CHARTS

Aslan Enterprises, Box 1858, Boulder, CO 80306; (303) 449-1515. Health charts: simple food, protein complementing, herbs, vitamins and minerals, others.

COLANDERS

Simac Appliances, Consumer Information, 14 East 60 St, New York, NY 10022.

CUTTING BOARDS

Crestwood Industries, 2659 Commercial St SE, Salem, OR 97308.

FOOD DEHYDRATORS

Down to Earth Enterprises, 1228 Chestnut Ave, Minneapolis, MN 55403. Round Harvest Maid dehydrator; included in purchase is book, *How to Dry Foods*. Cost is $129.95.

Nutri-Flow, 810 NW Eleventh Ave, Portland, OR 97209; (503) 224-9059. Home food dryer, helps you dry large quantities of food in a short time. Six-tray, $129.00.

NUTRI-FLOW
HOME FOOD DRYER

FOOD STORAGE

Everfresh, PO Box 26090, San Francisco, CA 94126. Vacuum-pack food at home.

FRUIT PRESSES

Happy Valley Ranch, PO Box 9153, Yakima, WA 98909; (509) 248-9338. Cider presses, as low as $49.50, for juice (soft fruit, grapes) or wine.

GARDEN TOOLS

Smith and Hawken Tool Company, 68 Homer, Palo Alto, CA 94301. Traditional tools for gardening and farming. Excellent quality.

GREETING CARDS

Great Northwestern Greeting Seed Company, PO Box 776, Oregon City, OR 97045; (503) 631-3425. A package of seeds incorporated into the design of each card. Elegant and fun.

JUICERS

Champion Juicer, Plastaket Manufacturing, 6220 East Highway 12, Lodi, CA 95240. This juicer retails for $205, but you can usually get it at a discount. It's well worth the money, and will hold up in daily use without problem. Guaranteed for five years.

Mehu-Maija Products, Podunk Road, Trumansburg, NY 14886; (607) 387-6716. Finnish steam processed juice extractor and cooker; $97.50 (stainless).

Phoenix Juicer, PO Box 451, Fresh Meadows, NY 11365; (212) 591-6330. Centrifuge-style juicer with a five-year warranty. Ejects pulp. $109.50.

Ultra Matic MJ 700 Juicer, 3 Elm St, Locust Valley, NY 11560. Pulp-ejecting centrifuge juicer. Literature says it will juice wheat grass. $300.

Vita-Mix Corporation, 8615 Usher Road, Cleveland, OH 44138; (800) 848-2649. Smashes the fruit into a pulp and then water is added to make juice. Also makes flour, kneads dough, makes soup, frozen yogurt, ice cream. Very versatile. $425.00.

KNIVES

The Cherry Company, 820 W 35 St, Davenport, IA 52806.

Sang Kung Kitchen Supplies, 110 Bowery, New York, NY 10013; (212) 925-3059. Excellent knives and cleavers.

MILLS

Kitchenetics Corp, 1450 Dell Ave, Campbell, CA 95008. Flour mills.

S & G Enterprises, 112 West Main St, Cambridge, NY 12816. Household grain mills. Steel, $50; ceramic, $85.

Simple & Good
HOUSEHOLD GRAIN MILL

STAINLESS STEEL POTS AND PANS

Saladmaster, 131 Howell St, Dallas, TX 75207. Manufacturers of stainless steel cookware.

STEAMERS

Rival Manufacturing, 36th and Benington, Kansas City, MO 64129.

VITAMIN DISPENSER

Vita-Bin, 14014 NW Nineteenth Ave, Miami Beach, FL 33054; (305) 769-3030. Vitamin disposer. A flick of the wrist and all the vitamin pills and supplements you take each day come tumbling out. No more opening 28 bottles and jars.

WHEAT-GRASS JUICERS

Beautiful You, 260 Smith St, Providence, RI 02908; (401) 272-6910. Professional quality sprouting systems for home and commercial use. Also wheat-grass juicers, Champion juicers, commercial blenders, Sun Pantry oven food dryers, quite a bit more.

21st Century Products, 401 North Fourth St, PO Box 702, Fairfield, IA 52556. Good selection of juicers, shredders, extractors, and grinders. Affiliated with Viktoras Kulvinskas' Survival Foundation. Sundance Electric Wheat-Grass Juicer is $195.

Sprout House, 210 Riverside Dr, New York, NY 10025; (212) 864-3233. Wheat-grass juicers: electric, $245; convertible (both manual and electric), $265; commercial juicer that juices over 100 ounces per day, $388. Electrify your manual juicer for $196 (conversion motor). Bionaire air purifiers. The Autobionaire 300 for your car, $87. Bionaire 500, lightweight and portable; cleans the air of the average room 3.5 times an hour: $119. Bionaire 1000 cleans 5 times per hour, $269. Bionaire 2001, for office or home, $359. Also, food dehydrators ($114–$157). Champion juicer, $179. Water purifiers and filters.

WOKS

Foods of India Sinha Trading Company, 120 Lexington Ave, New York, NY; (212) 683-4419. Treated wrought-iron Indian wok, called a *kadhai,* available for only $5.99.

Hoan Products, 615 East Crescent Ave, Ramsey, NJ 07446.

YOGURT MAKERS

Bel Natural Yogurt Maker, Finesse Ltd, Box 734, Carmel Valley, CA 93924. Special English yogurt maker, requires no electricity, but uses an insulated container to keep the culture warm; $22.00 plus $2.00 shipping.

MAIL ORDERS

Life Tool Co-op Mail Order Catalog, 401 North Clay St, Green Bay, WI 54301. Prices run 10 to 20 percent below retail. They carry tools that "emphasize environmental awareness, personal responsibility and simplified technology." Catalogue costs $1.00.

Whole Earth Access, 2950 7th St, Berkeley, CA 94710. The catalogue is $5.00, but when they say they will give you access to "everything needed for basic living in the 80s," they're not kidding. Juicers, pasta makers, knives, tools, clothing, cast-iron cookware, how-to books, mills, appliances, utensils, gadgets, everything for gardening and homesteading. Just fantastic! Good prices besides.

AABA Health Hotel Klosters, 54
Action for Life, 4
Action for Life Conference, 169
AGAPE, 12
Agenda , 13
AHIMSA, 12
Airola, Paavo, 2, 23, 33, 67, 76
    Airola Diet, 30, 58, 59
Alaskan Well-Being, 172
ALCYONE, 118
Aletheia, 132
Allergy Research Group, 89
Allergies, 40, 89
    Allergenic Free Vitamins, 89
All Life Sanctuary, 54
Aloe Vera, 108
Alternate Physician
    Referrals, 42-43
Alternative Health, 172, 174
Alternatives, 172
Aluminum, 36, 98
Alzheimer's Disease, 98
American Academy of
    Husband-Coached Childbirth, 66
American Association of Retired
    Persons, 64
American Biologics, 42, 89
American Biologics, Mexico, 48
American Chiropractic
    Association, 42
American College of
    Nutripathy, 132
American College of Nutrition, 132
American Dietetic
    Association, 29-30
American Fund for Alternatives to
    Animal Research
    (AFAAR), 12, 129
American Health: Fitness of Body
    and Mind, 41
American Holistic Medical
    Association, 42
American Holistic Nurses
    Association, 43
American International
    Hospital, 48
American Natural Hygiene
    Society, 15-16
American Natural Hygiene
    Society/Natural Living
    Conference, 169
American Society of Medical
    Preventics, 37
American Statistics Index
    (ASI), 129
American Vegan Society, 12
Animal Rights and Environmental
    Groups, 12-15, 75
Animal Rights Network, 12-13
Animal Rights--A Humane
    Symposium, 169
Animal Welfare Institute, 129
Annual Cancer Convention, 169
Anti-Aging Diet, 64
Antioch University, 132
Apple Cider Vinegar, 36
Argonne Anti-Jet Lag Diet, 33
Arizona Networking News, 172, 174
Aromatherapy Institute, 132
Arrowhead Mills, 81

Arthritis, 33-34
Ashkelon Vegetarian Center, 54
Ashram, 54
Aslan, Dr. Aŋa, 64-65
Association for Creative
    Change, 129
Association for Human
    Resources, 132
Association for Research and
    Enlightenment, 132
Asunaro Institute, 132-133
Athletes, 76-78
Attorneys for Animal Rights
    (AFAR), 13
    AFAR Conference, 169
Attunement, 172, 174
Audubon Naturist Society, 129

Baby Food Cookbook, 72-73
Bach Flower Remedies, 45
Bach, Dr. Edward, Center, 133
Back to Eden, 45
Bear Tribe, 169
Beauty Without Cruelty,
    13, 108, 109-110
Bee Pollen, 103
Bees, 120
Be Healthy Education Company, 138
Best of Health, 133
Better Health and Nutrition
    Center, 138
Biba Hot Springs, 55
Bible, 22
Bible Christian Church, 1
Bioenergy Council, 129
Biological Farming Conference, 169
Birthing, 66-70
Black Health, 37
Book Clubs, 158
Bookstores, state and mail order
    listing, 155-157
Bottled Water, 91
Bragg, Paul, 23, 32
Breaky, Jeff, 21, 38, 83
Breastfeeding, 71
Breatharians, 20-21
Breitenbush Community Center, 55
Brewer's Yeast, 103
Brooks, Wiley, 20
Buckhorn Mineral Wells, 55
Bureau of Nutrition, 129
Burlington College, 133
Burwash, Peter, 76, 77

Calcium Deficiency in the
    Elderly, 62
California Agrarian Action
    Project, 79
California Certified Organic
    Farmers, 80
California College of the Natural
    Healing Arts, 57
California School of Herbal
    Studies, 133
Camp Akiba, 55
Cancer, 35, 38, 47-53
    Directory to Alternative
    Therapies and Testing, 49-53
Cancer Book House, 35-36, 53
Cancer Control Society, 48

Cancer Hospitals and Treatment
    Centers, 48, 59
Cancer Prevention Diet, 30
Catalyst, 172, 174
Catalyst-Activated Water, 91
Cellular Therapy, 52, 65
Center for Community
    Organizations, 129
Center for Environmental
    Education, 129
Center for Medical Consumers, 42
Center for Renewable
    Resources, 130
Center for Science in the Public
    Interest, 3, 81, 130, 157
Charts, 176
Cheese and Milk, 82
Chico-San Products, 81
Children's Garden Associations, 74
Children of the Green Earth, 74
Chlorine, 91
Chlorophyll, 105
Cholesterol, 39, 91
Christopher, Dr. John R.,
    24, 45-46
Circle of Light, 172-173
Citizens Against Chemical
    Contamination, 122
Citizens Energy Project, 130
Clayton University, 133
Clear Water Action Project, 130
Coalition for a Non-Nuclear
    World, 130
Colanders, 176
College of Life Science, 138
College of the Atlantic, 133
Common Ground, 173, 174
Common Sense, 173
Community Spirit, 173
Computer Nutritional Analysis
    Programs, 140
Conference Centers, 171
Congressional Clearing House on
    the Future, 130
Connections 173
Consumer Information Catalog, 131
Consumer Product Safety
    Commission, 129
Convenience Foods, 86-87
Cookbooks, 123-126
Cookies, Cakes, Candies
    (Sugar-free), 86
Cooking Schools, 127-128
Cooperative Childcare
    Network, 66-67
Consumer Health Information
    Center, 42
Cornucopia Project, 114
Corporate Executive Health
    Program, 59
Cosmetics, 108-113
Council on Environmental
    Quality, 130
Council on the Environment,
    New York, 80
Country Life Natural Foods, 81
Crackerbarrel, 81
Creative Audio, 138
Current Nutrition and
    Therapeutics, 41

181